18 78

NIL SATIS NISI OPTIMUM

Everton

THE OFFICIAL GUIDE

2009

Sport Media
A Trinity Mirror Business

HONOURS

DIVISION ONE CHAMPIONS (9)
1890/91, 1914/15, 1927/28, 1931/32, 1938/39, 1962/63, 1969/70, 1984/85, 1986/87

DIVISION ONE RUNNERS-UP (7)
1889/90, 1894/95, 1901/02, 1904/05, 1908/09, 1911/12, 1985/86

DIVISION TWO CHAMPIONS (1)
1930/31

DIVISION TWO RUNNERS-UP (1)
1953/54

FA CUP WINNERS (5)
1906, 1933, 1966, 1984, 1995

FA CUP RUNNERS-UP (7)
1893, 1897, 1907, 1968, 1985, 1986, 1989

LEAGUE CUP RUNNERS-UP (2)
1976/77, 1983/84

FA CHARITY SHIELD WINNERS (8)
(FA COMMUNITY SHIELD)
1928, 1932, 1963, 1970, 1984, 1985, 1987, 1995

FA CHARITY SHIELD SHARED (1)
(FA COMMUNITY SHIELD)
1986

EUROPEAN CUP WINNERS' CUP WINNERS (1)
1984/85

SCREEN SPORT SUPER CUP RUNNERS-UP (1)
1985/86

SIMOD CUP RUNNERS-UP (1)
1988/89

ZENITH DATA SYSTEMS CUP RUNNERS-UP (1)
1990/91

FA YOUTH CUP WINNERS (3)
1964/65, 1983/84, 1997/98

FA YOUTH CUP RUNNERS-UP (4)
1960/61, 1976/77, 1982/83, 2001/02

INTRODUCTION

A warm welcome to the second edition of Everton: The Official Guide, a publication which we are proud to offer you, the supporter, in an effort to replicate all that is good about one of England's most established clubs, both on and off the pitch. Aiming to build on the success on the first edition in 2008, we have retained some of the best elements while reflecting the success of the 2007/08 campaign by way of the most accurate facts, statistics and information, while also utilising our extensive picture sources.

We have again retained the services of Everton expert Gavin Buckland, who has helped generate some of the new content which we hope you will find relevant and informative. The 2007/08 season has proven a rich source of fresh content, with the Blues breaking a full range of long-standing club records, and these are given an airing within these pages.

This year we have changed the structure slightly to organise the wealth of information inside into a more seamless order, while also maintaining key elements. Inside you'll find details about the current first-team squad; the manager; a review of our Reserve, Academy and Ladies' teams; the best moments of 2007/08; and a full record of the UEFA Cup run - and that's just for starters.

Fresh content includes a look back on players who have left since the last publication; player highlights from 2007/08; Everton in Europe facts; Everton players at the Olympic Games - plus, for the first time anywhere, a full record of Everton in the FA Youth Cup and a complete list of all players sent off in our league games.

We produce this publication so it can act as a permanent record, a point of reference which can solve numerous pub quiz questions. We hope you enjoy what is on offer.

Please note that all statistics are correct up until the start of the 2008/09 season.

WRITERS

James Cleary has written, researched and edited key information, with Everton statistician Gavin Buckland providing all the numbers and facts.

Sport Media
A Trinity Mirror Business

Executive Editor: KEN ROGERS Editor: STEVE HANRAHAN
Art Editor: RICK COOKE Production Editor: PAUL DOVE
Sub Editors: JAMES CLEARY, ROY GILFOYLE
Sales and Marketing Manager: ELIZABETH MORGAN
Design Team: BARRY PARKER, COLIN SUMPTER, GLEN HIND, LEE ASHUN, ALISON GILLILAND,
JAMIE DUNMORE, JAMES KENYON, LISA CRITCHLEY
Everton Writers: WILLIAM HUGHES, ALAN JEWELL

ISBN 978 1 9052 66661
Printed and finished by Scotprint, Haddington, Scotland

CLUB TELEPHONE NUMBERS

General Enquiries	0870 442 1878
Feedback	0870 442 1878
Box Office	0870 442 1878
Dial-A-Seat	0870 442 1878
Events and Hospitality	0151 330 2499
Marketing Department	0870 442 1878
Corporate Hospitality	0870 442 1878
Graeme Sharp (Fans Liaison Officer)	0870 442 1878
Communications Department	0870 442 1878
Everton Megastore	0870 005 2300/0870 005 2022
Evertonia	0870 442 1878
Everton in The Community	0870 442 1878/0151 330 2307
Everton Against Racism	0870 442 1878
Everton Former Players' Foundation	0151 520 2362
Everton Disabled Supporters' Association	0151 286 9666/0151 330 2217
Lotteries Department	0151 330 2266
International Department	0151 286 6866
Website Enquiries (General)	0870 442 1878
Everton Academy	0870 442 1878
Everton Mastercard	0870 600 5127
Everton Phonestore	0800 049 6055

SUBSCRIBE TO THE OFFICIAL EFC PROGRAMME, EVERTONIAN OR BLUES MAGAZINE
To take out a subscription please call: 0845 1430001

CLUB WHO'S WHO

Chairman	Bill Kenwright CBE
Deputy Chairman	Jon Woods
Director	Robert Earl
Director and Life President	Sir Philip Carter CBE
Vice-Life President	Keith Tamlin
Team Manager	David Moyes
Acting Chief Executive Officer	Robert Elstone
Head of Finance/Company Secretary	Martin Evans
Head of Football Operations/Club Secretary	David Harrison
Academy Manager	Ray Hall
Head of PR & External Affairs	Ian Ross
Head of Media & Communications	Mark Rowan
Head of Ticketing	Andy Ward
Head of Commercial	Peter Trembling
Head of Stadium Operations	Alan Bowen
Head of Marketing	Tom Shelston

CONTENTS

Including the definitive list of Everton managers, David Moyes' full record as boss, Moyes v the rest of the club's men in charge, and lists including the most prolific appearance makers, goalscorers and the men who have captained the club under his guidance.

The definitive guide to Everton's first-team squad for 2008/09, plus Reserve, Academy and Ladies news, fixtures and statistics.

A full review of the campaign month-by-month, including results, landmarks, quotes and the main action photos. Player highlights and obituaries are also featured.

A look back on a memorable campaign both home and abroad, with our top 10 highlighted with the best-possible photos.

An in-depth look at each of the club's UEFA Cup games during 2007/08, together with Everton's full record in European competition, European records and 'Did You Know'.

A full range of facts and statistics relating to the Blues in the Football League and Premier League, including records, finishes, biggest wins and biggest defeats.

Including the definitive record of top appearance holders and scorers for the club, youngest/oldest Everton players, hat-tricks, individual honours – and much more.

The 2007/08 record of Everton's international contingent, along with Everton players from overseas, international caps of the club's home international stars past and present, Everton players at the Olympics, and a look at the other Everton – based in Chile.

The full list of FA Cup results from 1970 onwards, plus the full League Cup record, FA Youth Cup record, cup facts and statistics, and the Blues' record in the other cup competitions.

A look at each of Everton's top-flight opponents during 2008/09.

Everton off-field information - anything from ticket prices, stadium tour details and Evertonia membership to charity initiatives, key addresses and Everton Tigers basketball team.

FOREWORD

The Guide has quickly become the definitive annual publication for all Evertonians as a permanent record of events both on and off the pitch, providing the most complete collection of Everton facts and statistics currently available in print.

Not surprisingly, the 2009 Guide provides extensive coverage of the 2007/08 season, one that witnessed a best-ever Premier League points haul, a dramatic and record-breaking UEFA Cup run and a first domestic cup semi-final in 13 years. The magnificent Everton Ladies' side also lifted much-deserved silverware following a dramatic League Cup final victory over previously unbeatable Arsenal.

All the action is vividly recalled in both a month-by-month review of the season and a look back at our exciting European adventures, while there was no shortage of candidates to occupy the list of the Top 10 moments of the year. Special billing is given to Player of the Season Joleon Lescott and we also explain why Tim Howard and Ayegbeni Yakubu are Goodison record-breakers. With other sections reflecting on the progress of our Reserve and Academy sides, there is no doubt that the 2009 Guide offers a comprehensive assessment of the most exciting campaign experienced by the club in almost 20 years.

As in the first edition, there is also plenty to keep those with a keen eye for facts and figures busy. Not only have all records been revised and updated, but also this year the Guide incorporates some welcome additions including, for the first time ever, a complete review and record of all the games played by Everton in the FA Youth Cup. We also reflect on the sad passing of Goodison legends Wally Fielding and Brian Harris.

But events on the pitch don't tell the full story, and elsewhere the Guide provides a complete overview of one of the country's oldest and biggest football institutions: from our pioneering work with former players and the community to how we keep supporters informed of all that is happening at Goodison, 24 hours a day. This year's Guide celebrates the acquisition from David France of The Everton Collection – described by auctioneer Sotheby's as the most complete gathering of football memorabilia they had ever seen.

With lots more besides, the Guide provides Blues everywhere with everything they need to know about Everton Football Club.

KEY DATES 2008/2009

(Dates are subject to change)

August 2008

16	Barclays Premier League kick-off
20	England v Czech Republic, international friendly (Wembley Stadium, London)
29	UEFA Cup first-round draw

September 2008

1	Transfer window closes
6	Andorra v England, World Cup qualifier (Barcelona)
6	South Africa v Nigeria, World Cup/Africa Cup of Nations qual. (Port Elizabeth)
6	Hungary v Denmark, World Cup qualifier (Budapest)
6	Ecuador v Bolivia, World Cup qualifier (Quito)
10	Croatia v England, World Cup qualifier (Zagreb)
10	Portugal v Denmark, World Cup qualifier (Lisbon)
10	Uruguay v Ecuador, World Cup qualifier (Montevideo)
18	UEFA Cup first round, first leg
22 (w/c)	Carling Cup third round

October 2008

2	UEFA Cup first round, second leg
7	UEFA Cup group stage draw (11am)
11	England v Kazakhstan, World Cup qualifier (Wembley Stadium, London)
11	Nigeria v Sierra Leone, World Cup/African Cup of Nations qualifier (Abuja)
11	Denmark v Malta, World Cup qualifier (Copenhagen)
12	Ecuador v Chile, World Cup qualifier (Quito)
15	Belarus v England, World Cup qualifier (Minsk)
15	Venezuela v Ecuador, World Cup qualifier (Puerto La Cruz)
23	UEFA Cup group stage matchday 1

November 2008

6	UEFA Cup group stage matchday 2
12 (w/c)	Carling Cup fourth round
19	Germany v England, international friendly (Berlin)
27	UEFA Cup group stage matchday 3

December 2008

1 (w/c)	Carling Cup quarter-finals
3/4	UEFA Cup group stage matchday 4
17/18	UEFA Cup group stage matchday 5
19	UEFA Cup round of 32 & round of 16 draw (12pm)
31	Transfer window re-opens

January 2009

3	FA Cup third round
6/7	Carling Cup semi-final, first leg
20/21	Carling Cup semi-final, second leg

KEY DATES 2008/2009
(Dates are subject to change)

January 2009

24	FA Cup fourth round
31	Transfer window closes (5pm)

February 2009

14	FA Cup fifth round
18/19	UEFA Cup round of 32, first leg
26	UEFA Cup round of 32, second leg

March 2009

1	Carling Cup final (Wembley Stadium, London)
7	FA Cup quarter-finals
12	UEFA Cup round of 16, first leg
18/19	UEFA Cup round of 16, second leg
20	UEFA Cup quarter-finals & semi-finals draw (12pm)
28	Malta v Denmark, World Cup qualifier (Valetta)
28	Ecuador v Brazil, World Cup qualifier (TBA)
31	Ecuador v Paraguay, World Cup qualifier (TBA)

April 2009

1	England v Ukraine, World Cup qualifier (Wembley Stadium, London)
1	Denmark v Albania, World Cup qualifier (Copenhagen)
9	UEFA Cup quarter-finals, first leg
16	UEFA Cup quarter-finals, second leg
18/19	FA Cup semi-finals
30	UEFA Cup semi-final, first leg

May 2009

7	UEFA Cup semi-final, second leg
20	UEFA Cup final (Sukru Saracoglu Stadium, Istanbul, Turkey)
24	Barclays Premier League final day
30	FA Cup final (Wembley Stadium, London)

June 2009

6	Kazakhstan v England, World Cup qualifier (Almaty)
6	Sweden v Denmark, World Cup qualifier (TBA)
6	Peru v Ecuador, World Cup qualifier (TBA)
9	Ecuador v Argentina, World Cup qualifier (TBA)
10	England v Andorra, World Cup qualifier (Wembley Stadium, London)

FIXTURE LIST 2008/2009

August 2008

16	Blackburn Rovers	(H)	-	3pm
23	West Bromwich Albion	(A)	-	3pm
30	Portsmouth	(H)	-	3pm

September 2008

14	Stoke City	(A)	-	1.30pm
18	Standard Liege - UEFA Cup	(H)	-	TBC
21	Hull City	(A)	-	3pm
23	Blackburn Rovers - C. Cup	(A)	-	7.45pm
27	Liverpool	(H)	-	12.45pm

October 2008

2	Standard Liege - UEFA Cup	(A)	-	TBC
5	Newcastle United	(H)	-	4pm
18	Arsenal	(A)	-	3pm
23	UEFA Cup group stage matchday 1			
25	Manchester United	(H)	-	TBC
28	Bolton Wanderers	(A)	-	8pm

November 2008

1	Fulham	(H)	-	12.45pm
6	UEFA Cup group stage matchday 2			
8	West Ham United	(A)	-	TBC
12	Carling Cup fourth round			
16	Middlesbrough	(H)	-	1.30pm
24	Wigan Athletic	(A)	-	8pm
27	UEFA Cup group stage matchday 3			
29	Tottenham Hotspur	(A)	-	TBC

December 2008

3	UEFA Cup group stage matchday 4			
3	Carling Cup fifth round			
6	Aston Villa	(H)	-	TBC
13	Manchester City	(A)	-	3pm
17	UEFA Cup group stage matchday 5			
20	Chelsea	(H)	-	3pm
26	Middlesbrough	(A)	-	3pm
28	Sunderland	(H)	-	2pm

January 2009

3	FA Cup third round			
7	Carling Cup semi-final, first leg			
10	Hull City	(H)	-	3pm
17	Liverpool	(A)	-	TBC
21	Carling Cup semi-final, second leg			

FIXTURE LIST 2008/2009

January 2009

24	FA Cup fourth round			
28	Arsenal	(H)	-	8pm
31	Manchester United	(A)	-	3pm

February 2009

7	Bolton Wanderers	(H)	-	3pm
14	FA Cup fifth round			
18/19	UEFA Cup round of 32, first leg			
21	Newcastle United	(A)	-	TBC
26	UEFA Cup round of 32, second leg			
28	West Bromwich Albion	(H)	-	TBC

March 2009

1	CARLING CUP FINAL			
4	Blackburn Rovers	(A)	-	8pm
7	FA Cup sixth round			
12	UEFA Cup round of 16, first leg			
14	Stoke City	(H)	-	TBC
18/19	UEFA Cup round of 16, second leg			
21	Portsmouth	(A)	-	TBC

April 2009

5	Wigan Athletic	(H)	-	3pm
9	UEFA Cup quarter-finals, first leg			
11	Aston Villa	(A)	-	TBC
16	UEFA Cup quarter-finals, second leg			
18	Chelsea	(A)	-	TBC
18	FA Cup semi-finals			
25	Manchester City	(H)	-	3pm
30	UEFA Cup semi-finals, first leg			

May 2009

2	Sunderland	(A)	-	TBC
7	UEFA Cup semi-finals, second leg			
9	Tottenham Hotspur	(H)	-	TBC
16	West Ham United	(H)	-	3pm
20	UEFA CUP FINAL			
24	Fulham	(A)	-	4pm
30	FA CUP FINAL			

GOODISON PARK PAST AND PRESENT

Current Capacity - 40,216

GWLADYS STREET

Like the Bullens Road, this was originally designed by Archibald Leitch in 1938 (at a cost of £50,000). It is also a two-tier structure divided into the Upper and Lower Gwladys Street End. The lower area contains the most vociferous Evertonians, with the home side regularly choosing to kick towards there in the second half. Apart from the lower area being made all-seated in 1991, the only other change in recent times was the construction of a new roof, erected in 1987.

MAIN STAND

Completed in 1971 at a cost of £1m, this structure was the first three-tier development in England when it was constructed, and was the largest in Britain at the time. Consisting of a Family Enclosure, Main Stand and Top Balcony (the latter being reached by escalator), the area also houses corporate boxes. The stand replaced another Archibald Leitch design, built in 1909 at a cost of £28,000, and also incorporates the tunnel onto the pitch leading from the changing rooms. When it was built the floodlight pylons were removed and lamps were put on gantries along the roof.

BULLENS ROAD

Two-tier structure designed by Archibald Leitch in 1926, which still incorporates his trademark criss-cross finishing. The area is divided into three sections – Upper and Lower Bullens, plus the Paddock, while the south end of the stand, nearest the Park End, houses away fans. The old-fashioned original roof was replaced in the early 1970s by a much flatter modern structure and, as on the Main Stand, gantries incorporating floodlights were installed.

PARK END

Single cantilever stand, built in 1994 to replace the previous two-tier structure that housed away fans, the original being built in 1907 at a cost of £13,000.

NOTES ABOUT THE STADIUM

- The ground staged five games during the 1966 World Cup, including a semi-final (it was due to stage England's last-four tie with Portugal before being switched to Wembley).
- It hosted the 1894 FA Cup final between Notts County and Bolton Wanderers and the FA Cup final replay of 1910 between Newcastle United and Barnsley.
- In 1938, with the development of the Gwladys Street End, it became the first ground in Britain to have four double-decker stands.
- Everton have hosted more international matches than any other English club.
- The first covered dugouts in England were constructed at Goodison Park in 1931, following Everton's visit to Pittodrie to play Aberdeen in a friendly, where such dugouts had been constructed by Dons' trainer Donald Coleman.
- Floodlights came to both Everton and Liverpool in October 1957 – being switched on at Goodison Park for a match between the two sides to celebrate the 75th anniversary of Liverpool County FA.
- Undersoil heating was first introduced in 1958.

RECORD GOODISON PARK ATTENDANCES

HIGH		LOW	
Overall: 78,299 v Liverpool, 18/9/1948		**Overall**:	3,000 v Jarrow, 28/1/1899
League: 78,299 v Liverpool, 18/9/1948		**League Post-war:**	10,829 v Fulham, 25/3/1953
FA Cup: 77,920 v Manchester United, 14/2/1953		**FA Cup**:	3,000 v Jarrow, 28/1/1899
Lge Cup: 54,032 v Bolton W, 18/1/1977		**League Cup**:	7,415 v Wrexham, 9/10/1990
Europe: 62,408 v Inter Milan, 18/9/1963		**Europe**:	16,277 v UCD, 2/10/1984

Goodison shots: Views looking towards the Gwladys Street stand,
from 1980 (top) and summer 2008 (below)

FINCH FARM

Everton's new training complex became fully operational in November 2007, the first-team squad having left their previous Bellefield HQ the month before. At a cost of £14m, Finch Farm is situated in south Liverpool and houses the club's first team, academy players and staff - an arrangement the Blues' previous training ground was unsuitable for (the academy had previously been based in Netherton).

Development of the site took nearly three years, and a range of innovative features have been planned into the complex. One of the 10 training pitches is an exact replica of Goodison Park's own surface, while one side of the main building is for senior players, and the other for academy prospects.

Facilities include classrooms, offices, dining room and changing areas, while a viewing deck overlooks several pitches. There is also a physio area, gymnasium, synthetic indoor pitch, swimming pool, hydrotherapy pools, spa, sauna, dining/sitting area, kit and storage area, media centre (including video lounges) plus the office suites for the manager and his staff.

Everton Academy home matches are staged at the complex, with Saturday fixtures usually kicking off at 11am.

The address for the site is:

Finch Lane
Halewood
Knowsley
Liverpool
L26 3UE

The reception area at Everton's Finch Farm training complex

View at Finch Farm: The Media Theatre (top), and swimming pool

EVERTON'S MANAGERS

The 2008/09 campaign marks the beginning of David Moyes' seventh full season in charge at Goodison Park, a period which has seen him become one of the club's longest-serving managers.

Taking charge on March 14th 2002, he successfully led the Blues to safety in the Premier League before stamping his mark on the team, gradually building a team capable of challenging for honours with the relatively modest resources available.

Although still to bring silverware to the club, his achievements are recognised by the continued improvement Everton have made on the pitch, in terms of consistency through successive European qualifications in the last two seasons (for the first time in nearly 30 years) - and in the past three of the last four campaigns.

Moyes is the club's 13th different manager, Everton being one of the last established clubs in the Football League to employ a full-time boss before appointing then secretary Theo Kelly to the top job. Before then, selection was made by different people including committees, senior coaches and even the captain.

DAVID MOYES	**March 2002-Present**
WALTER SMITH	July 1998-March 2002
HOWARD KENDALL	June 1997-June 1998
DAVE WATSON (caretaker)	April 1997-May 1997
JOE ROYLE	November 1994-March 1997
MIKE WALKER	January 1994-November 1994
JIMMY GABRIEL (caretaker)	December 1993-January 1994
HOWARD KENDALL	November 1990-December 1993
JIMMY GABRIEL (caretaker)	November 1990
COLIN HARVEY	June 1987-October 1990
HOWARD KENDALL	May 1981-June 1987
GORDON LEE	January 1977-May 1981
STEVE BURTENSHAW (caretaker)	January 1977
BILLY BINGHAM	May 1973-January 1977
TOM EGGLESTON (caretaker)	April 1973-May 1973
HARRY CATTERICK	April 1961-April 1973
JOHNNY CAREY	October 1958-April 1961
IAN BUCHAN	August 1956-September 1958
CLIFF BRITTON	September 1948-February 1956
THEO KELLY	June 1939-September 1948

DAVID MOYES' RECORD

In August 2008 the Everton boss completed almost six-and-a-half years at Everton, making him, in terms of time spent in continuous charge, the longest-serving manager since Harry Catterick, who was in the post for 12 years following his appointment in April 1961. Only Cliff Britton – seven years and five months from September 1948 onwards, and like Moyes someone who had Preston North End on his managerial CV – lies between the Scot and our hugely successful boss of the 1960s/early 1970s.

In terms of other domestic managers, only Sir Alex Ferguson (1986), Graham Turner (at Hereford United since 1995) and Arsene Wenger (1996) can point to a longer spell with the same club in English league football.

The 2007/08 campaign was also hugely significant on a personal level for the man who has masterminded a revival in Everton's fortunes in so many ways. The opening-day victory over Wigan Athletic was his 200th league match in charge of the club – and the 1-0 UEFA Cup win over eventual winners Zenit St Petersberg in December 2007 marked game number 250 at Goodison Park. The 1-0 home victory over Manchester City in January also marked the 10th anniversary of his first managerial appointment at Preston.

At the end of the 2007/08, the Scot's full record while at Goodison is:

OVERALL MOYES RECORD							
	Pld	**W**	**D**	**L**	**F**	**A**	**Pts**
LEAGUE	237	96	57	84	297	292	345
FA CUP	13	4	3	6	17	20	-
LEAGUE CUP	18	9	3	6	29	19	-
CHAMPIONS LEAGUE	2	0	0	2	2	4	-
UEFA CUP	12	9	1	2	25	14	-
TOTAL	**282**	**118**	**64**	**100**	**370**	**349**	**-**

(*PENALTY SHOOT-OUTS COUNTED AS DRAWS)

Correct at 15th August 2008

DAVID MOYES' RECORD

MOYES' OPPONENTS

David Moyes has faced 49 clubs as Everton manager, with the best records being against Derby County and Norwich City – both three wins out of three – with other notable successes including six wins and a draw in seven matches against Sunderland.

On the downside, the Blues' boss still awaits a first victory in 18 against Chelsea, but at least the long droughts against Liverpool and Manchester United have been ended under his tenure.

The following table shows the club-by-club record (note that games ending up as penalties are counted as draws):

	P	W	D	L	F	A	Win %
AC Fiorentina	2	1	0	1	2	2	50%
AE Larissa	1	1	0	0	3	1	100%
Arsenal	15	3	2	10	14	33	20%
Aston Villa	12	4	4	4	17	17	33%
AZ Alkmaar	1	1	0	0	3	2	100%
Birmingham City	10	4	5	1	10	8	40%
Blackburn Rovers	14	5	4	5	12	13	36%
Bolton Wanderers	13	7	2	4	18	17	54%
Bristol City	1	0	1	0	2	2	0%
Charlton Athletic	11	4	3	4	11	11	36%
Chelsea	18	0	5	13	11	35	0%
Crystal Palace	2	2	0	0	7	1	100%
Derby County	3	3	0	0	7	3	100%
Dinamo Bucharest	2	1	0	1	2	5	50%
Fulham	15	7	1	7	21	16	47%
Leeds United	4	3	1	0	8	1	75%
Leicester City	3	1	2	0	6	5	33%
Liverpool	12	2	3	7	9	16	17%
Luton Town	2	2	0	0	5	0	100%
Manchester City	12	5	3	4	13	16	42%
Manchester United	13	1	2	10	11	27	8%
Metalist Kharkiv	2	1	1	0	4	3	50%
Middlesbrough	14	6	5	3	13	8	43%
Millwall	2	1	1	0	2	1	50%
Newcastle United	14	5	4	5	25	26	36%
Norwich City	3	3	0	0	7	3	100%
1. FC Nurnberg	1	1	0	0	2	0	100%
Oldham Athletic	1	0	0	1	0	1	0%
Peterborough United	1	1	0	0	2	1	100%
Plymouth Argyle	1	1	0	0	3	1	100%
Portsmouth	10	7	1	2	13	6	70%
Preston North End	1	1	0	0	2	0	100%
Reading	4	2	1	1	4	2	50%
Sheffield United	2	1	1	0	3	1	50%
Sheffield Wednesday	1	1	0	0	3	0	100%
Shrewsbury Town	1	0	0	1	1	2	0%
SK Brann	2	2	0	0	8	1	100%
Southampton	7	3	3	1	9	7	43%
Stockport County	1	1	0	0	3	0	100%
Sunderland	7	6	1	0	17	4	86%
Tottenham Hotspur	12	3	2	7	16	22	25%
Villarreal	2	0	0	2	2	4	0%

DAVID MOYES' RECORD

MOYES' OPPONENTS							
	P	**W**	**D**	**L**	**F**	**A**	**Win %**
Watford	2	2	0	0	5	1	100%
West Bromwich Albion	6	3	1	2	7	9	50%
West Ham United	9	4	3	2	11	7	44%
Wigan Athletic	6	3	2	1	9	6	50%
Wolverhampton Wan.	2	1	0	1	3	2	50%
Wrexham	1	1	0	0	3	0	100%
Zenit St Petersburg	1	1	0	0	1	0	100%
TOTAL	**282**	**118**	**64**	**100**	**370**	**349**	**42%**

PREMIER LEAGUE POINTS: MARCH 2002-MAY 2008

As a measure of the progress made by the club since March 15th 2002, the number of Premier League points accumulated from that date has been exceeded by only four clubs:

Club	Points
Chelsea	514
Manchester United	510
Arsenal	496
Liverpool	429
Everton	345
Blackburn Rovers	333
Tottenham Hotspur	330
Newcastle United	329

David Moyes watches on during the 2-0 win at Derby County in October 2007

DAVID MOYES' RECORD

MOYES' PLAYERS

A total of 66 players have appeared for Everton in a competitive first-team game under David Moyes with (following the departures of Lee Carsley, Alan Stubbs and Thomas Gravesen) only Tony Hibbert now remaining from the squad selected for his opening match in charge, against Fulham in March 2002.

A total of 15 players have made 100 or more appearances for the club in that time, with Nigerian international defender Joseph Yobo leading the way:

Player	Games
Joseph Yobo	203
Lee Carsley	194
Tony Hibbert	185
Alan Stubbs	161
Leon Osman	160
David Weir	140

In terms of goals, Tim Cahill has bagged the most for the Blues since March 2002, the Australian finding the net on 37 occasions. The top six are:

Player	Goals
Tim Cahill	37
Andrew Johnson	22
Leon Osman	22
Ayegbeni Yakubu	21
Tomasz Radzinski	21
Duncan Ferguson	20

MOYES' CAPTAINS

A total of eight players have worn the armband from the start of a game in the 282 competitive matches the Blues have played under David Moyes since March 2002. Phil Neville has been captain on 93 occasions with, at the other end of the scale, Joseph Yobo and Lee Carsley leading the side twice.

The captains' records are as follows:

Captain	P	W	D	L	Win %
Phil Neville	93	43	23	27	46%
Alan Stubbs	72	30	16	26	42%
David Weir	55	18	11	26	33%
Kevin Campbell	42	17	8	17	40%
Duncan Ferguson	12	6	4	2	50%
David Unsworth	4	1	1	2	25%
Lee Carsley	2	1	1	0	50%
Joseph Yobo	2	2	0	0	100%

DAVID MOYES' RECORD

MOYES AND THE REST

The overall record of each Everton manager, in order of longest-serving managers (games managed). Note Howard Kendall's statistics include his three spells in charge:

Manager	Games	W	D	L	F	A
Harry Catterick	594	276	157	161	954	670
Howard Kendall	542	257	131	154	833	592
Cliff Britton	339	125	91	123	497	527
David Moyes	282	118	64	100	370	349
Gordon Lee	234	92	72	70	346	268
Colin Harvey	175	75	52	48	256	181
Billy Bingham	172	64	55	53	229	214
Walter Smith	168	53	50	65	205	216
Johnny Carey	121	50	22	49	222	208
Joe Royle	118	47	36	35	174	140
Theo Kelly	102	38	20	44	137	174
Ian Buchan	99	32	22	45	146	186
Mike Walker	31	6	11	18	35	60

The opening game of the 2007/08 season saw David Moyes become only the fourth manager to take charge of Everton in 200 league matches. Here's how his record compares to other Everton managers in league games (correct at end of 2007/08 campaign) – in order of points per game success.

Manager	Games	W	D	L	PTS	Pts per game
Harry Catterick	500	225	137	138	812	1.62
Howard Kendall	419	186	105	128	663	1.58
Colin Harvey	126	51	37	38	190	1.51
David Moyes	237	96	57	84	345	1.46
Gordon Lee	188	69	63	56	270	1.44
Joe Royle	97	36	31	30	139	1.43
Billy Bingham	146	53	48	45	207	1.42
Johnny Carey	110	44	21	45	153	1.39
Cliff Britton	316	110	90	116	420	1.33
Theo Kelly	93	35	17	41	122	1.31
Ian Buchan	93	29	21	43	108	1.16
Walter Smith	143	41	42	60	165	1.15
Mike Walker	31	6	9	16	27	0.87

Everton

THE SQUAD 2008/09

Tim Howard - Squad number 24

Position	Goalkeeper
Born	North Brunswick, New Jersey, USA
Age (at start of 08/09)	29
Birth date	06/03/79
Height	6ft 3ins
Other clubs	New Jersey Imperials, MetroStars, Man Utd
Honours	2003 FA Comm. Shield, 2004 FA Cup, 2006 League Cup
Everton debut	19/08/06 v Watford
Everton appearances	85 + 0 substitute
Everton goals	0
USA caps	30 (0 goals)
USA honours	2007 Gold Cup

Carlo Nash - Squad number 1

Position	Goalkeeper
Born	Bolton
Age (at start of 08/09)	34
Birth date	13/09/73
Height	6ft 5ins
Other clubs	Rossendale United, Clitheroe, C. Palace, Stockport, Wolves, Man City, M'boro, Preston, Wigan, Stoke
Honours	-
Everton debut	-
Everton appearances	0
Everton goals	0

John Ruddy - Squad number 30

Position	Goalkeeper
Born	St Ives, Cambridgeshire
Age (at start of 08/09)	21
Birth date	24/10/86
Height	6ft 4ins
Other clubs	Cambridge, Walsall, Rushden, Chester, Stockport, Wrexham, Bristol C, Stockport
Honours	-
Everton debut	11/02/06 v Blackburn R
Everton appearances	0 + 1 substitute
Everton goals	0

Iain Turner - Squad number 12

Position	Goalkeeper
Born	Stirling, Scotland
Age (at start of 08/09)	24
Birth date	26/01/84
Height	6ft 4ins
Other clubs	Stirling A, Chester City, Doncaster R, Wycombe W, Crystal Palace, Sheff Wednesday
Honours	2004 Conference
Everton debut	08/02/06 v Chelsea
Everton appearances	5 + 1 substitute
Everton goals	0

Leighton Baines - Squad number 3

Position	Left-back
Born	Liverpool
Age (at start of 08/09)	23
Birth date	11/12/84
Height	5ft 8ins
Other club	Wigan Athletic
Honours	-
Everton debut	25/08/07 v Blackburn Rovers
Everton appearances	17 + 12 substitute
Everton goals	0

Tony Hibbert - Squad number 2

Position	Right-back
Born	Liverpool
Age (at start of 08/09)	27
Birth date	20/02/81
Height	5ft 8ins
Other clubs	-
Honours (Youth)	1998 FA Youth Cup
Everton debut	31/03/01 v West Ham
Everton appearances	181 + 16 substitute
Everton goals	0

Lars Jacobsen - Squad number 15

Position	Right Defence
Born	Odense, Denmark
Age (at start of 08/09)	28
Birth date	20/09/79
Height	5ft 11ins
Other clubs	Odense BK, SV Hamburg, FC Copenhagen, 1. FC Nurnberg
Honours	2004, 2006, 2007 Danish Superliga, 2001 Danish Cup, 1999 Danish First Division
Everton debut	-
Everton appearances	0
Everton goals	0
Denmark caps	16 (0 goals)

Phil Jagielka - Squad number 6

Position	Right/Centre Defence or Midfield
Born	Sale
Age (at start of 08/09)	25
Birth date	17/08/82
Height	5ft 11ins
Other club	Sheffield United
Honours	-
Everton debut	14/08/07 v Tottenham Hotspur
Everton appearances	40 + 9 substitute
Everton goals	2
England caps	1 (0 goals)

Joleon Lescott - Squad number 5

Position	Left/Centre Defence
Born	Birmingham
Age (at start of 08/09)	26
Birth date	16/08/82
Height	6ft 2ins
Other clubs	Wolverhampton W.
Honours	2003 Championship Play-Off Winner
Everton debut	19/08/06 v Watford
Everton appearances	92 + 4 substitute
Everton goals	12
England caps	5 (0 goals)

Phil Neville - Squad number 18

Position	Right/Centre Defence or Midfield
Born	Bury
Age (at start of 08/09)	31
Birth date	21/01/77
Height	5ft 11ins
Other club	Manchester United
Honours	1996, 1997, 1999, 2000, 2001, 2003 League, 1996, 1999, 2004 FA Cup, 1997, 2003 FA Comm. Shield, 1999 Champions League
Everton debut	09/08/05 v Villarreal
Everton appearances	130 + 1 substitute
Everton goals	3
England caps	59 (0 goals)

Nuno Valente - Squad number 19

Position	Left-back
Born	Lisbon, Portugal
Age (at start of 08/09)	33
Birth date	12/09/74
Height	5ft 11ins
Other clubs	Portimonense, S. Lisbon, Maritimo, U. Leiria, FC Porto
Honours	1995 Portuguese Cup, 2003, 2004 Portuguese Lge, 2003 UEFA Cup, 2004 Champions Lge, 2004 World Club C'ship
Everton debut	10/09/05 v Portsmouth
Everton appearances	53 + 5 substitute
Everton goals	0
Portugal caps	33 (1 goal)

Joseph Yobo - Squad number 4

Position	Centre Defence
Born	Kano, Nigeria
Age (at start of 08/09)	27
Birth date	06/09/80
Height	6ft 2ins
Other clubs	Standard Liege, Marseille, Tenerife
Honours	-
Everton debut	28/09/02 v Fulham
Everton appearances	190 + 13 substitute
Everton goals	7
Nigeria caps	59 (5 goals)

Mikel Arteta - Squad number 10

Position	Left/Centre/Right Midfield
Born	San Sebastian, Spain
Age (at start of 08/09)	26
Birth date	26/03/82
Height	5ft 9ins
Other clubs	Barcelona, Paris SG, Rangers, Real Sociedad
Honours	2003 Scottish Lge, 2003 Scottish Cup, 2003 Scot. Lge Cup
Everton debut	06/02/05 v Southampton
Everton appearances	119 + 7 substitute
Everton goals	17

Jose Baxter - Squad number 37

Position	Right Central Midfield/Forward
Born	Bootle
Age (at start of 08/09)	16
Birth date	07/02/92
Height	5ft 7ins
Other clubs	-
Honours	-
Everton debut	-
Everton appearances	0
Everton goals	0

Tim Cahill - Squad number 17

Position	Centre Midfield/Forward
Born	Sydney, Australia
Age (at start of 08/09)	28
Birth date	06/12/79
Height	5ft 10ins
Other clubs	Sydney United, Millwall
Honours	-
Everton debut	30/08/04 v Man Utd
Everton appearances	121 + 5 substitute
Everton goals	37
Australia caps	28 (13 goals)

Segundo Castillo - Squad number 8

Position	Central Midfield
Born	San Lorenzo, Ecuador
Age (at start of 08/09)	26
Birth date	15/05/82
Height	5ft 11ins
Other clubs	Club Deportivo ESPOLI, Club Deportivo El Nacional, Red Star Belgrade
Honours	2005, 2006 Ecuador League, 2007 Serbia League, 2007 Serbia Cup
Everton debut	-
Everton appearances	0
Everton goals	0
Ecuador caps	33 (2 goals)

Marouane Fellaini - Squad number 25

Position	Central Midfield
Born	Etterbeek, Belgium
Age (at start of 08/09)	20
Birth date	22/11/87
Height	6ft 4ins
Other club	Standard Liege
Honours	2008 Belgian League
Everton debut	-
Everton appearances	0
Everton goals	0
Belgium caps	10 (1 goal)

Dan Gosling - Squad number 32

Position	Right/Centre Defence or Midfield
Born	-
Age (at start of 08/09)	18
Birth date	02/02/90
Height	5ft 10ins
Other club	Plymouth Argyle
Honours	-
Everton debut	-
Everton appearances	0
Everton goals	0

John Paul Kissock - Squad number 36

Position	Left/Right Midfield
Born	Liverpool
Age (at start of 08/09)	18
Birth date	02/12/89
Height	5ft 6ins
Other clubs	Gretna
Honours	-
Everton debut	-
Everton appearances	0
Everton goals	0

Leon Osman - Squad number 21

Position	Left/Centre/Right Midfield
Born	Billinge
Age (at start of 08/09)	27
Birth date	17/05/81
Height	5ft 8ins
Other clubs	Carlisle United, Derby County
Honours (Youth)	1998 FA Youth Cup
Everton debut	12/01/03 v Tottenham Hotspur
Everton appearances	135 + 25 substitute
Everton goals	22

Steven Pienaar - Squad number 20

Position	Right/Centre/Left Midfield
Born	Johannesburg, South Africa
Age (at start of 08/09)	26
Birth date	17/03/82
Height	5ft 9ins
Other clubs	Ajax, Borussia Dortmund
Honours	2002 Dutch Cup, 2004 Dutch League
Everton debut	11/08/07 v Wigan
Everton appearances	37 + 3 substitute
Everton goals	2
South Africa caps	28 (2 goals)

Jack Rodwell - Squad number 26

Position	Centre Defence or Midfield
Born	Birkdale
Age (at start of 08/09)	17
Birth date	11/03/91
Height	6ft 2ins
Other clubs	-
Honours	-
Everton debut	20/12/07 v AZ Alkmaar
Everton appearances	0 + 3 as substitute
Everton goals	0

Andy van der Meyde - Squad number 7

Position	Left/Right Midfield
Born	Arnhem, Holland
Age (at start of 08/09)	28
Birth date	30/09/79
Height	5ft 11ins
Other clubs	Ajax, FC Twente, Inter Milan
Honours	1998, 2002 Dutch League, 1998, 1999, 2002 Dutch Cup
Everton debut	26/10/05 v Middlesbrough
Everton appearances	14 + 7 as substitute
Everton goals	0
Holland caps	18 (1 goal)

James Wallace - Squad number 38

Position	Midfield
Born	Liverpool
Age (at start of 08/09)	16
Birth date	19/12/91
Height	5ft 10ins
Other clubs	-
Honours	-
Everton debut	-
Everton appearances	0
Everton goals	0

Kieran Agard - Squad number 35

Position	Centre Forward
Born	London
Age (at start of 08/09)	18
Birth date	10/10/89
Height	5ft 10ins
Other clubs	Arsenal
Honours	-
Everton debut	-
Everton appearances	0
Everton goals	0

Victor Anichebe - Squad number 28

Position	Centre Forward
Born	Lagos, Nigeria
Age (at start of 08/09)	20
Birth date	23/04/88
Height	6ft 1ins
Other clubs	-
Honours	-
Everton debut	28/01/06 v Chelsea
Everton appearances	19 + 48 substitute
Everton goals	10
Nigeria caps	4 (0 goals)
Nigeria honours	2008 Olympics Silver Medal

Lukas Jutkiewicz - Squad number 27

Position	Left/Centre Midfield or Forward
Born	Southampton
Age (at start of 08/09)	19
Birth date	28/03/89
Height	6ft 1ins
Other clubs	Swindon Town, Plymouth Argyle
Honours	-
Everton debut	-
Everton appearances	0
Everton goals	0

Louis Saha - Squad number 9

Position	Centre Forward
Born	Paris, France
Age (at start of 08/09)	30
Birth date	08/08/78
Height	6ft 1ins
Other clubs	Metz, Newcastle U, Fulham, Man Utd
Honours	2001 First Division, 2006 League Cup, 2007, 2008 League, 2008 Champions Lge
Everton debut	-
Everton appearances	0
Everton goals	0
France caps	18 (4 goals)

James Vaughan - Squad number 14

Position	Centre Forward
Born	Birmingham
Age (at start of 08/09)	20
Birth date	14/07/88
Height	5ft 11ins
Other clubs	-
Honours	-
Everton debut	10/04/05 v Crystal Palace
Everton appearances	8 + 23 substitute
Everton goals	7

Ayegbeni Yakubu - Squad number 22

Position	Centre Forward
Born	Benin City, Nigeria
Age (at start of 08/09)	25
Birth date	22/11/82
Height	6ft 0ins
Other clubs	Julius Berger, Hapoel Kfar Saba, Maccabi Haifa, Portsmouth, Middlesbrough
Honours	2001, 2002 Israeli League, 2002 Toto Cup (Israel), 2003 Championship
Everton debut	01/09/07 v Bolton W.
Everton appearances	36 + 4 substitute
Everton goals	21
Nigeria caps	41 (17 goals)

EVERTON FAREWELLS

Profiles of those on the playing staff in 2007/08 who have left Goodison Park:

Anderson Silva de Franca – moved to Barnsley, January 2008

After a protracted transfer, the Brazilian joined Everton in January 2007 and made one first-team outing, against Charlton Athletic in April 2007 as a late substitute. After two loan spells at Barnsley, the move was made permanent on transfer deadline day in January 2008.
Curiously, the midfielder has made two appearances on Merseyside, and on both occasions his side won with virtually the last kick of the game – on his Everton debut, and for Barnsley at Anfield in the FA Cup shortly after moving to Oakwell.

Lee Carsley – moved to Birmingham City, May 2008

Few players have contributed more to the Everton renaissance under David Moyes than the midfielder, who departed from Goodison Park in the early summer with the good wishes of all.
Bought from Coventry City in January 2002, the Eire international played the holding role to perfection, and it is no coincidence that the only season the club has failed to finish in the top six in the past four years was 2005/06, when he was sidelined with injury for most of the campaign.
A great ambassador for the Blues both on and off the pitch – he is a tireless worker for charity – Carsley was also one of the dressing room's great characters. His final two goals at the Gwladys Street End were arguably the highlights of his time with the Toffees: the derby match winner of December 2004 and his stunning last-minute strike to snatch victory from his new club, last term.

Andy Johnson – moved to Fulham, August 2008

Signed for a then club record fee of £8.6m in the summer of 2006, the former Birmingham City and Crystal Palace player moved back to London in a move that could net the Blues upwards of £13m.
After a bright start to his Everton career, which included a memorable derby brace against Liverpool, the forward lost his scoring touch, although he did net a memorable last-minute winner against Arsenal in March 2007. Last season brought a further 10 goals as the arrival of Ayegbeni Yakubu added more competition up front.

James McFadden – moved to Birmingham City, January 2008

The mercurial Scot had a mixed time on Merseyside after arriving from Motherwell in 2003, but the size of his eventual transfer fee - £6m, equating to a generous profit – was good business for Everton as he linked up with his former national boss, Alex McLeish, in the Midlands.
Ironically, it was for his country that the forward had most success when with the Toffees – his tally of international goals at the club has only been exceeded by Dixie Dean – although he did leave fans with the odd gem, such as his BBC Goal of the Month winner against Charlton in April 2007.

Alan Stubbs – moved to Derby County, January 2008

A lifelong Evertonian, the Kirkby-born player enjoyed two separate spells either side of an ill-fated time at Sunderland in the first half of the 2005/06 campaign. The central defender joined the Blues in 2001 having enjoyed a successful period at Celtic, and formed excellent partnerships with David Weir and Joseph Yobo at Goodison, as well as captaining the side for long periods.
The arrival of Joleon Lescott and Phil Jagielka limited his opportunities, and the proud Blue moved to pastures new at Derby County in January. Unfortunately, niggling injuries caught up with Stubbs during his short spell at Pride Park and after picking up a serious injury on the opening day of the Championship season, he announced his retirement in August 2008.

EVERTON FAREWELLS

Bjarni Vidarsson – released, May 2008

Recruited from Iceland when he was 16, the young midfielder made one first-team appearance as a substitute against AZ Alkmaar in December 2007. He was then loaned to FC Twente shortly afterwards - a move that was made permanent in May after he was released by the club.

Stefan Wessels – released, May 2008

The German Under-21 and B international was recruited from FC Cologne on a free transfer before the start of the season, and the good form of Tim Howard meant he was limited to seven games before being released at the end of a one-year contract.

SHORT-LIVED BLUES

The departure of Anderson de Silva and Bjarni Vidarsson brought to an end two of the shortest careers, measured in pure playing time, of any Everton players. Anderson's two-minute cameo against Charlton in 2007 equalled the club record for the shortest career, originally set by Darren Oldroyd at Nottingham Forest in 1985. The briefest Everton careers are:

TIME ON PITCH	PLAYER	VENUE	OPPOSITION	DATE
2 mins	Darren Oldroyd	(a)	Nottingham Forest	11th May 1985
2 mins	Anderson Silva de Franca	(h)	Charlton Athletic	15th April 2007
15 mins	Neill Rimmer	(a)	Luton Town	28th May 1985
20 mins	Ian Bishop	(h)	Manchester United	5th May 1984
22 mins	Bjarni Vidarsson	(a)	AZ67 Alkmaar	20th December 2007
34 mins	Glenn Keeley	(h)	Liverpool	6th November 1982
45 mins	Adam Farley	(a)	Derby County	7th February 1999
62 mins	David Turner	(h)	Chelsea	20th April 1968

* List excludes current players

The now departed trio of James McFadden, Andy Johnson and Anderson Silva de Franca with Leon Osman (far left)

RESERVES

SEASON REVIEW

Andy Holden's side finished eighth in the Barclays Premier Reserve League in 2007/08, collecting four victories from 18 outings.

Steven Morrison with five goals was the top scorer, while defender John Irving was voted player of the season for the second successive year.

Only 13 players appeared in at least half of the side's matches, with the team now used almost primarily to blood players from the club's Academy.

The 2008/09 campaign will be the 10th Premier Reserve League campaign since its establishment, with the teams in the North and South divisions consisting of those in the senior Premier League. The Blues were Northern champions in 2000/01, although the Play-Off Final, in which the Northern champions are pitched against the Southern champions, was not introduced until the 2004/05 season. This term, the leagues will consist of 11 in the North and nine in the South, with the champions of each division meeting in a Play-Off Final on May 20.

Everton's home matches will again be played at Widnes Vikings' 13,350-capacity Stobart Stadium Halton, with matches kicking off at 7pm.

2007/08 STATISTICS

RESERVES APPEARANCES & GOALS 2007/08

	Appearances	Goals
Kieran Agard	17	3
Hope Akpan	2	0
Victor Anichebe	2	1
Leighton Baines	2	0
Moses Barnett	1	0
Jose Baxter	4	0
Patrick Boyle	9	0
Lewis Codling	5	0
Stephen Connor	4	0
Darren Dennehy	11	0
Shaun Densmore	17	0
Aidan Downes	12	1
Anthony Gardner	4	0
Dan Gosling	4	0
Ryan Harpur	15	0
John Irving	16	0
Jamie Jones	6	0
Lukas Jutkiewicz	9	4
John Paul Kissock	9	0
George Krenn	1	0
James McCarten	2	0
Lee Molyneux	5	1
Steven Morrison	17	5
Eunan O'Kane	6	0
Jack Rodwell	12	1
John Ruddy	9	0
Anderson de Silva Franca	1	0
Cory Sinnott	5	0
Iain Turner	3	0
Nuno Valente	2	0
Andy van der Meyde	5	1
James Vaughan	4	3
Bjarni Vidarsson	10	1
Stefan Wessels	2	0

RESERVE LEAGUE RESULTS 2007/08

			Result
30.08.07	Manchester United	A	0-1
04.09.07	Sunderland	H	1-2
18.09.07	Blackburn Rovers	H	3-2
02.10.07	Middlesbrough	A	1-3
09.10.07	Manchester City	H	2-0
24.10.07	Bolton Wanderers	A	1-0
06.11.07	Newcastle United	H	1-1
28.11.07	Wigan Athletic	A	5-1
04.12.07	Liverpool	A	0-3
09.01.08	Manchester United	H	2-2
11.02.08	Middlesbrough	H	0-0
26.02.08	Manchester City	A	2-4
03.03.08	Newcastle United	A	0-3
11.03.08	Wigan Athletic	H	1-2
19.03.08	Sunderland	A	0-0
25.03.08	Bolton Wanderers	H	2-3
01.04.08	Liverpool	H	0-1
15.04.08	Blackburn Rovers	A	0-3

RESERVES LEAGUE NORTH TABLE 2007/08

		Pld	W	D	L	F	A	Pts
1	Liverpool	18	13	4	1	31	8	43
2	Man City	18	8	6	4	34	29	30
3	Man Utd	18	8	5	5	25	19	29
4	Sunderland	18	9	2	7	28	24	29
5	Blackburn R.	18	8	4	6	32	25	28
6	Newcastle U.	18	5	7	6	31	27	22
7	Middlesboro	18	5	7	6	23	26	22
8	**Everton**	**18**	**4**	**4**	**10**	**21**	**31**	**16**
9	Wigan Ath.	18	4	3	11	19	36	15
10	Bolton Wan.	18	3	4	11	13	32	13

FA PREMIER RESERVE LEAGUE NORTHERN SECTION FIXTURES 2008/09

SEPTEMBER

03	Hull City	(A)
16	Manchester City	(H)

OCTOBER

07	Middlesbrough	(H)	
14	Liverpool	(A)	- 7.30pm
21	Bolton Wanderers	(H)	

NOVEMBER

03	Blackburn Rovers	(A)
18	Newcastle United	(H)
25	Wigan Athletic	(A)

DECEMBER

09	Sunderland	(H)
18	Manchester United	(A)

JANUARY

06	Manchester City	(A)
20	Hull City	(H)

FEBRUARY

10	Middlesbrough	(A)
17	Liverpool	(H)
25	Bolton Wanderers	(A)

MARCH

10	Blackburn Rovers	(H)
16	Newcastle United	(A)
24	Wigan Athletic	(H)

APRIL

14	Manchester United	(H)
22	Sunderland	(A)

All fixtures 7pm,unless stated.
Note fixtures are subject to change.

Long-serving reserve-team boss Andy Holden

THE ACADEMY

SEASON REVIEW

The 2007/08 season was an encouraging one for the Under-18s, as they finished runners-up in their extremely competitive FA Premier League Academy section. Only the outstanding form of an excellent Manchester City side stopped the young Blues from lifting the crown, and the 58 points accumulated from 28 matches was almost twice as many as 12 months earlier.

The Academy system is made up of Groups A-D, each consisting of 10 teams. The Blues' youngsters play each team in their group on a home and away basis, with the other 10 regular games made up of inter-group fixtures against teams from the other three groups.

However, there was disappointment in the FA Youth Cup as Everton went down 2-0 to Bristol City at Goodison. Jack Rodwell, now part of the first-team squad, was voted Academy Player of the Year at the club's end-of-season awards.

2007/08 STATISTICS

U18s' LEAGUE & CUP RESULTS 2007/08

			Result
18.08.07	Bristol City	H	4-2
25.08.07	Tottenham Hotspur	A	1-0
01.09.07	Leeds United	H	1-1
08.09.07	Newcastle United	A	4-2
15.09.07	Sheffield United	A	2-1
22.09.07	Sunderland	H	2-1
29.09.07	Wolves	A	1-0
06.10.07	Manchester City	H	0-1
13.10.07	Crewe Alexandra	A	5-0
19.10.07	Blackburn Rovers	H	1-0
27.10.07	Stoke City	A	2-0
03.11.07	Liverpool	A	1-1
10.11.07	West Bromwich Albion	H	2-1
17.11.07	Manchester United	H	2-0
01.12.07	Bolton Wanderers	H	0-0
11.12.07	Bristol City (FAYC)	H	0-2
15.12.07	Stoke City	H	2-1
05.01.08	West Bromwich Albion	A	1-1
11.01.08	Liverpool	H	3-3
19.01.08	Bolton Wanderers	H	0-0
26.01.08	Manchester United	A	3-3
07.02.08	Liverpool (LSC)	H	0-1
09.02.08	Wolves	H	0-0
23.02.08	Bolton Wanderers	A	1-2
01.03.08	Crewe Alexandra	H	0-1
08.03.08	Blackburn Rovers	A	2-0
15.03.08	Derby County	H	6-0
29.03.08	Nottingham Forest	A	1-2
05.04.08	Middlesbrough	A	2-0
12.04.08	Barnsley	H	6-1
19.04.08	Manchester City	A	1-0

U18s' APPEARANCES & GOALS 2007/08

	Appearances	Goals
Kieran Agard	25	10
Hope Akpan	20	2
Moses Barnett	26	1
Jose Baxter	23	6
Moses Barnett	1	0
Lewis Codling	28	12
Gerard Kinsella	1	0
George Krenn	17	1
Conor McAlany	1	0
Lee McArdle	10	0
James McCarten	26	6
Tom McCready	21	2
Michael McEntegart	18	0
Lee Molyneux	2	1
Eunan O'Kane	25	0
Luke Powell	16	4
Danny Redmond	23	1
Jack Rodwell	12	3
Karl Sheppard	11	0
Cory Sinnott	23	1
Scott Spencer	2	1
Michael Stewart	19	0
Lars Stubhaug	10	0
James Wallace	2	0

FA PREMIER ACADEMY 2007/08 GROUP C

	Pld	W	D	L	F	A	Pts
1 Man City	28	21	4	3	75	22	67
2 Everton	28	17	7	4	56	24	58
3 Man Utd	28	14	6	8	47	44	48
4 Crewe Alex.	28	14	6	8	50	51	48
5 Liverpool	28	11	10	7	49	34	43
6 Blackburn R.	28	10	5	13	36	40	35
7 West Brom	28	8	7	13	44	66	31
8 Wolves	28	7	8	13	29	37	29
9 Bolton Wan.	28	6	9	13	42	47	27
10 Stoke City	28	6	7	15	28	42	25

THE ACADEMY

EVERTON IN THE LIVERPOOL SENIOR CUP 2007/08

Round 3   7th February 2008
Everton 0-1 Liverpool   (Stobart Stadium Halton, Widnes)

Everton: Ruddy, Densmore, Barnett, Sinnott, Dennehy, Gosling, Morrison, Rodwell (O'Kane 53), Agard (Codling 68), Downes (Baxter 68), Connor.

EVERTON IN THE FA YOUTH CUP 2007/08

Round 3   11th December 2007
Everton 0-2 Bristol City   (Goodison Park)

Everton: Stubhaug, Stewart, Barnett, Sinnott, McCarten, Akpan (Codling 56), O'Kane, Redmond (McCready 86), Kissock, Baxter, Agard.

FA PREMIER ACADEMY LEAGUE FIXTURES 2008/09 FIXTURES

AUGUST
23   Arsenal   (A)
30   MK Dons   (H)

SEPTEMBER
06   Derby County   (A)
13   Barnsley   (H)
20   Sunderland   (H)
27   Manchester City   (A)

OCTOBER
04   Blackburn Rovers   (H)
11   Stoke City   (A)
18   West Brom.   (H)

NOVEMBER
01   Crewe Alexandra   (A)
08   Manchester United (H)
15   Liverpool   (A)
22   Bolton Wanderers   (H)

DECEMBER
06   Wolverhampton W. (A)
13   West Brom.   (A)

FA YOUTH CUP DATES
RND 3   To be played by December 13
RND 4   To be played by January 17
RND 5   To be played by January 31
Q-F   To be played by February 14

JANUARY
17   Crewe Alexandra   (H)
24   Manchester United (A)
31   Liverpool   (H)

FEBRUARY
07   Bolton Wanderers   (A)
14   Wolverhampton W. (H)
21   Manchester City   (H)

MARCH
07   Blackburn Rovers   (A)
14   Stoke City   (H)
21   Newcastle United   (A)
28   Leeds United   (A)

APRIL
18   Nottingham Forest (H)
25   Middlesbrough   (A)

MAY
02   Sheffield Wed.   (H)

All league fixtures 11am, subject to change.

FA YOUTH CUP DATES
S-F L. 1   To be played by March 7
S-F L. 2   To be played by March 21
F L. 1   To be confirmed
F L. 2   To be confirmed

ALL THE YOUNG BLUES

EVERTON IN THE FA YOUTH CUP 1952 – 2008

Holly Park, then home of South Liverpool, on an early autumn evening in 1952 was the unlikely venue of Everton's first game in the fledgling FA Youth Cup. The competition was created by the Football Association to provide an opportunity for those players who had just left school, but were considered too young for the senior ranks. Up until the 1970s, the early rounds were played on a regional basis.

The Blues romped to a 7-0 victory that night, and it took a goal by the great Duncan Edwards at Old Trafford in the fourth round to halt the Toffees' run in the competition. In the 50 or so years since, Everton have won the trophy on three occasions, as well as being runners-up a further four times. Although future first-team legends such as Colin Harvey, Jimmy Husband, Joe Royle and Kevin Ratcliffe have all featured for the club, it is the contributions of lesser lights such as Tony McLoughlin and Robbie Wakenshaw that ultimately brought the cup to Goodison.

Everton had to wait nine years for a first final appearance, but ended up disappointed as a capable Chelsea team – including Ron Harris and Terry Venables – ran out 5-3 victors on aggregate in the two-legged final of 1960/61, claiming a second successive final win. Somewhat typically, only five of the Everton side – Keith Webber, George Sharples, Alan Tyrer, Roy Parnell and Mick Gannon – played for the first team, and even then only to a limited degree.

Four years later, Jimmy Husband and John Hurst played a key role in the finest side to represent the Toffees at youth level. Rampaging through the earlier rounds with a remarkable goal record of 18-0 – including a 5-0 aggregate semi-final win over a Brian Clough-coached Sunderland – the Goodison youngsters were pushed hard by Arsenal in the final, and it needed an extra-time goal by Aiden Maher in front of a 30,000 crowd at Goodison to clinch the trophy. Three years later, a further assault on the cup was ended at the semi-final stage by a Dave Thomas-inspired Burnley team.

During the first half of the 1970s, the youngsters' fortunes matched those of their senior colleagues, until 1976/77 when, with Colin Harvey now in charge of the youth side, Everton reached a third final. Future club captain Mark Higgins led the team over two tight games against Crystal Palace, a battle settled by the only goal of the tie from future England international Terry Fenwick, a minute from the end of normal time in the second leg at Selhurst Park.

Everton met our closest rivals in each of the next three campaigns, losing at Anfield in 1977/78 but emerging victorious at Goodison Park the following season, and then again at Anfield in December 1979 in the most recent meeting between the clubs in the Youth Cup. Gary Stevens scored the first goal that night, but a strike in the 2-0 win by a young midfielder called Robbie Ash – following a run from the visitors' half – remains one of the best scored by an Everton player on the ground. Twelve months later, the Blues' ambitions were thwarted at Goodison in the fifth round by a Manchester United side featuring Mark Hughes and Norman Whiteside.

The 1982/83 campaign saw a powerful attacking trident of Robbie Wakenshaw, Stuart Rimmer (who had already played for the first team) and Mark Farrington inspire the side to another final appearance against Norwich City. A 3-2 defeat at Carrow Road (with Farrington scoring twice) was followed by an equally dramatic 3-2 win for Everton in the second leg, when the same player missed an opportunity to both complete a hat-trick on the night and bring the cup to Goodison, failing from the spot during extra-time. A third encounter at Goodison in front of a 20,000 crowd was a much tighter affair, with the Canaries winning 1-0. Farrington later played for the Norfolk side before moving to Feyenoord and Fortuna Sittard in Holland. Rimmer became Chester City's leading all-time scorer, while Wakenshaw played several first-team games before moving to the lower divisions. But others in the side who enjoyed lengthy careers were Ian Bishop, Ian Marshall and Johnny Morrissey Jnr.

ALL THE YOUNG BLUES

EVERTON IN THE FA YOUTH CUP 1952 – 2008

The following season, despite losing most of their powerful line-up, the Toffees returned again to the final and emerged triumphant against a Stoke City side who appeared favourites after a 2-2 draw at Goodison in the first leg. The cup was won for a second time – just nine days before the senior team lifted the FA Cup – with goals by Darren Hughes and Wakenshaw in a 2-0 win.

The next 14 years brought no further success until the trophy was lifted for a third time in 1997/98. On this occasion, the bulk of the team would later become Everton regulars, and indeed two of them, Leon Osman and Tony Hibbert, are still first-team stalwarts 10 years on. The Goodison youngsters enjoyed relatively untroubled progress to the final, where they comfortably disposed of Blackburn Rovers 5-3 on aggregate, with a 3-1 win at Ewood Park in the first leg proving the foundation. Francis Jeffers and Phil Jevons formed a deadly strike partnership, with strong support from Danny Cadamarteri. At the back, Richard Dunne proved formidable. Twelve months later, a brave defence of the trophy was ended by an impressive West Ham United side featuring both Joe Cole and Michael Carrick – the Hammers would defeat Coventry City 9-0 on aggregate in the final.

Three years later, a Wayne Rooney-inspired Everton also reached the final, but lost out 4-2 on aggregate to an excellent Aston Villa outfit, who recovered from a goal down to run out easy 4-1 victors at Goodison in the first leg. Since then progress has been mixed, but overall the Toffees' three final wins have been exceeded only by Manchester United and Arsenal.

To view Everton's complete FA Youth Cup results, see pages 166-171

YOUTH CUP RECORDS

Biggest Win: 12-1 v Wigan Athletic (h), 14th January 1964
Biggest Defeat: 0-6 v Newcastle United (a), 10th December 1984
Record Home Attendance: 29,908, Everton v Arsenal, 3rd May 1965

MOST APPEARANCES				MOST GOALS		
PLAYER	**PERIOD**	**GAMES**		**PLAYER**	**PERIOD**	**GOALS**
Robbie Wakenshaw	1982-84	19		Keith Webber	1960-61	13
Billy Kenny (Snr)	1967-72	19		Mark Farrington	1982-83	11
Ian Macowat	1982-84	18		Robbie Wakenshaw	1982-84	10
Ian Marshall	1982-84	18		Francis Jeffers	1997-99	9
Dean Delaney	1997-99	17		Bert Llewellyn	1955-57	9
Tony Hibbert	1997-99	16		Tony McLoughlin	1964-65	9
Darren Hughes	1982-84	16				
George Morton	1959-60	16				

FA YOUTH CUP TRIVIA

* The following fathers and sons have played for Everton in the FA Youth Cup: Billy Brindle (1966-68) and Graham Brindle (1984), Billy Kenny (Snr) (1967-72) and Billy Kenny (Jnr) (1990-92), Steve Seargeant (1967-69) and Christian Seargeant (2003-05).
* The first Everton player dismissed in the competition was Alan Whittle in the 3-2 defeat at Burnley at the semi-final stage in 1968.
* The 6-5 win over Blackpool in 1995 remains possibly the greatest comeback at Goodison. Trailing 4-0 and then 5-2, the young Blues hit back to record a stunning win.
* Everton forward Terry Jones made a remarkable contribution at both ends in the defeat to Preston North End in December 1992. After scoring both goals to put the Blues 2-1 ahead Jones then had to don the goalkeeping gloves following the dismissal of keeper Stephen Reeves. Jones then conceded two late goals as the Toffees went down 3-2.
* Everton's defence of the trophy in 1965/66 ended in unfortunate circumstances. Leading 1-0 at Wrexham in their opening match, the game was abandoned owing to a waterlogged pitch, and in the replayed fixture the Welsh side triumphed 1-0.

EVERTON LADIES

SEASON REVIEW

The Ladies' team enjoyed a highly successful season in 2007/08 under the continued stewardship of manager Mo Marley, and it was quite clear that they were rapidly closing the gap on the all-conquering Arsenal Ladies' team. If proof were needed, then it was duly delivered on a memorable evening in February when Mo Marley's outfit overcame the Gunners in the Premier League Cup final, with Amy Kane's seventh-minute goal proving decisive. It was the club's first major trophy in a decade.

In the Premier League itself, the Ladies finished runners-up for a third successive campaign. The team ended the season with a flourish, with 23 goals scored in the final four matches as second place was secured by some distance, with the gap to Arsenal halved from the 14 points in 2006/07. This achievement was also enhanced after the Blues managed to earn a 0-0 draw at Arsenal in April - ending the Gunners' run of 51 successive league wins.

Elsewhere, their first-ever UEFA Cup journey ended in somewhat unfortunate circumstances at the second group stage, courtesy of two last-minute defeats to Wezemaal and Frankfurt.

The FA Cup witnessed another unlucky loss – this time to Leeds United (now Leeds Carnegie) on penalties at the semi-final stage, following a goalless draw at Marine FC's Arriva Stadium.

However, the season was rounded off in style with Liverpool being defeated in the final of the Liverpool Senior Cup at Goodison Park.

Everton Ladies duo Jill Scott and Fern Whelan scooped accolades at the FA Women's Awards – the former was named Players' Player of the Year, the latter Young Player of the Year.

Everton Ladies celebrate their Premier League Cup success in 2008 (above and opposite)

EVERTON LADIES

2008/09 SQUAD				
PLAYER	**POSITION**	**D.O.B.**	**PREVIOUS CLUB**	**INT. HONOURS**
Rachel Brown	Goalkeeper	02/07/80	Liverpool	England, 51 caps
Lindsay Johnson	Centre-half	08/05/80	Birmingham City	England, 25 caps
Becky Easton	Full-back	16/04/74	Doncaster Belles	England, 70+ caps
Fern Whelan	Defence	05/12/88	Liverpool	England U19
Rachel Unitt	Full-back	05/06/82	NJ Wildcats	England, 64 caps
Fara Williams	Midfield	25/01/84	Charlton Athletic	England, 61 caps
Leanne Duffy	Midfield	20/06/79	-	-
Amy Kane	Midfield	10/09/86	-	England U23
Emily Westwood	Midfield	05/04/84	Wolves	England, 17 caps
Michelle Evans	Left Midfield	18/07/87	Tranmere Rovers	England U19
Jill Scott	Midfield	02/02/87	Sunderland	England, 16 caps
Michelle Hinnigan	Midfield	12/06/90	-	England U19
Josanne Potter	Midfield/Forward	13/11/84	Charlton Athletic	England, 13 caps
Jody Handley	Midfield/Forward	12/03/79	Doncaster Belles	England, 32 caps
Karen Boyle	Forward	03/08/87	-	England U19
Natasha Dowie	Forward	30/06/88	Charlton Athletic	England U23
Toni Duggan	Forward	25/07/91	-	England U19

EVERTON LADIES

ABOUT THE CLUB/MAJOR HONOURS

Former Names:	Hoylake WFC (1983-1988), Leasowe (1988-1994), Leasowe Pacific (1994-1995)
Manager:	Mo Marley
Assistant:	Andy Spence
Home Ground:	The Arriva Stadium, Marine (capacity 2,800)
FA Premier League winners:	1997/98
FA Premier League runners-up:	2005/06, 2006/07, 2007/08
FA Cup winners:	1988/89
FA Cup runners-up:	1987/88, 2004/05
FA Premier League Cup winners:	2007/08
FA Premier League Cup runners-up:	1996/97, 1998/99
FA Community Shield runners-up:	2006/07, 2007/08

2007/08 STATISTICS

WOMEN'S LEAGUE & CUP RESULTS 2007/08

Date	Opponent		Result*
09.08.07	Gintra (UEFA)	N	4-0
11.08.07	Glentoran (UEFA)	N	11-0
14.08.07	Zuchwil (UEFA)	N	5-0
30.09.07	Barnet (PLC)	H	6-0
04.10.07	Liverpool	H	2-1
07.10.07	Birmingham City	A	1-1
11.10.07	R. Wezemaal (UEFA)	N	1-2
13.10.07	FFC Frankfurt (UEFA)	N	1-2
16.10.07	Valur Reykjavik (UEFA)	N	3-1
21.10.07	West Ham Utd (PLC)	A	4-1
31.10.07	Doncaster R. Belles	A	2-1
04.11.07	Sunderland	H	3-0
11.11.07	Watford	H	3-0
15.11.07	Leeds United	A	2-1
18.11.07	Chelsea	A	2-1
02.12.07	Arsenal	H	0-2
12.12.07	Doncaster R. Belles	H	3-1
16.12.07	Watford (PLC)	A	2-1
06.01.08	Barnet (FAC)	A	9-0
27.01.08	Leicester City (FAC)	A	3-0
03.02.08	Bristol Academy	A	3-1
24.02.08	Newcastle Utd (FAC)	A	3-1
28.02.08	Arsenal (PLC)	N	1-0
02.03.08	Cardiff City	A	4-0
16.03.08	Leeds United (FAC)	H	0-0*
26.03.08	Blackburn Rovers	H	5-1
30.03.08	Chelsea	H	3-0
03.04.08	Liverpool	A	5-1
06.04.08	Bristol Academy	H	3-0
09.04.08	Leeds United	H	4-0
13.04.08	Arsenal	A	0-0
17.04.08	Blackburn Rovers	A	2-0
20.04.08	Birmingham City	H	2-2
27.04.08	Charlton	A	6-0
03.05.08	Watford	A	4-1
04.05.08	Cardiff City	H	6-0
11.05.08	Charlton	H	7-0
18.05.08	Liverpool (LCFAC)	H	5-0

*Lost 5-4 on penalties

FA WOMEN'S PREMIER LEAGUE 2007/08

	P	W	D	L	F	A	Pts
1 Arsenal	22	20	2	0	85	15	62
2 Everton	22	18	3	1	69	14	57
3 Leeds Utd	22	12	4	6	45	33	40
4 Bristol Ac.	22	10	4	8	45	35	34
5 Chelsea	22	9	5	8	40	35	32
6 Doncaster	22	8	5	9	44	42	29
7 Watford	21	9	2	11	53	52	29
8 Blackburn	22	8	4	10	50	45	28
9 Birmingham	22	7	4	11	34	39	25
10 Liverpool	22	6	4	12	31	51	22
11 Cardiff	22	3	3	16	19	69	12
12 Charlton	22	0	4	18	6	91	4

Boss Mo Marley with her victorious players

WOMEN'S LEAGUE AND CUP
FIXTURES 2008/09

AUGUST

07	Arsenal (C. Shield)		
	(Macclesfield Town FC)		
17	Doncaster R.B.	(H)	- 1.30pm
24	Fulham	(A)	
26	Liverpool	(A)	- 7.45pm
31	Watford	(H)	

SEPTEMBER

07	Nottingham Forest	(H)	
14	B'gham (FAPLC1)	(H)	
17	Birmingham City	(A)	- 7.45pm
21	Blackburn Rovers	(A)	
28	Leeds Carnegie	(H)	

OCTOBER

05	FA PREMIER LEAGUE CUP RND 2		
12	Bristol Academy	(A)	
19	Chelsea	(A)	
22	Liverpool	(H)	- 7.45pm
26	Arsenal	(H)	

NOVEMBER

02	FA PREMIER LEAGUE CUP RND 3		
05	Birmingham City	(H)	- 7.45pm
09	Arsenal	(A)	
16	Chelsea	(H)	

NOVEMBER

| 23 | Leeds Carnegie | (A) |
| 30 | Doncaster R.B. | (A) |

DECEMBER

07	Blackburn Rovers	(H)
07	FA PREMIER LEAGUE CUP S-FINAL	
14	Nottingham Forest	(A)
21	Bristol Academy	(H)

JANUARY

04	FA CUP ROUND 4	
11	Fulham	(H)
18	Watford	(A)
25	FA CUP ROUND 5	

FEBRUARY

| 22 | FA CUP ROUND 6 |

MARCH

| 22 | FA CUP SEMI-FINAL |

MAY

| 04 | FA CUP FINAL |

All fixtures 2pm, unless stated.
Note fixtures are subject to change.

2008 Premier League Cup matchwinner Amy Kane celebrates with skipper Jody Handley

Everton

THAT WAS THE SEASON - 2007/08

It only seems like yesterday that the season began with a nervy victory over Wigan Athletic. Here is our account of the goings on in what was another eventful campaign for the Blues during 2007/08.

August

Tim Cahill aggravates a foot injury on his comeback during the pre-season friendly draw with Werder Bremen. James Beattie completes his move to Sheffield United, for an initial £4m.
Everton begin the campaign with a 2-1 win over Wigan courtesy of goals from Leon Osman and Victor Anichebe. Indeed, the Blues are top after two games following an eye-catching 3-1 win at much-fancied Tottenham Hotspur (the first time they have won their first two league matches since 1993/94), with Osman again amongst the goalscorers.
One-time Blues full-back/midfielder Neil McDonald becomes the first managerial casualty of the season, being sacked by Carlisle United after just one match of the new League One campaign.
Phil Neville and Andy Johnson are included in the initial England squad to face Germany, while Everton smash their transfer record to sign Middlesbrough striker Ayegbeni Yakubu, the Nigeria striker costing a reported £11.25 million.
The club come out in support of the family of Rhys Jones, the 11-year-old Everton fan who was killed by a bullet fired at him in a pub car park in Croxteth.
An official club ballot results in 59.27% of fans voting in favour of a potential new stadium in Kirkby, with 40.73% against – the turnout was 70.27%.
Leighton Baines makes his first-team debut in the 1-1 draw with Blackburn Rovers, with James McFadden dedicating his equaliser to Rhys Jones and his family. Manuel Fernandes' proposed move to Everton breaks down, the player eventually joining Valencia. Z-Cars is played at Anfield ahead of Liverpool's Champions League qualifier against Toulouse, a tribute to Rhys.
There are three Everton players in the Nigeria squad to face Lesotho next month in an African Cup of Nations qualifier – Yobo, Yakubu and Anichebe - while there are three in the England squad, Joleon Lescott earning a first call-up as a late replacement, along with Neville and Johnson.
Thomas Gravesen returns to the Blues on a season-long loan deal from Celtic, while Everton are drawn to face Ukrainian side Metalist Kharkiv in the UEFA Cup.

Landmark:

David Moyes' 200th league game in charge saw the Blues record an opening day 2-1 victory over Wigan Athletic.

Incoming:

Leighton Baines (Wigan Athletic), Stefan Wessels (FC Cologne),
Ayegbeni Yakubu (Middlesbrough), Thomas Gravesen (Celtic, loan).

Outgoing:

Stephen Connor (Partick Thistle, loan), James Beattie (Sheffield United),
Anderson Silva de Franca (Barnsley, loan).

Quotes of the month:

"Mikel (Arteta) has become such an extraordinary member of this football club and that is the reason why the first month of the close season was making sure he was a long-term Evertonian. He is a delightful footballer and person during all the times we were negotiating."

Bill Kenwright salutes Everton's Spanish star

"I want to play for a club that plays in Europe, and I think they have the ambition to move forward and they want to finish in the first four and the Champions League and UEFA Cup, and for me that is my dream. It is a massive club and it is a great feeling. There are great players and you want to play for a big club. I need to score more than 20 goals."

Ayegbeni Yakubu, excited by Blues move

AUGUST

THE GAMES

11	Wigan Athletic	H	2-1	Osman, Anichebe
14	Tottenham H.	A	3-1	Lescott, Osman, Stubbs
18	Reading	A	0-1	
25	Blackburn R.	H	1-1	McFadden

WHERE THEY STOOD

2	Manchester City
3	Wigan Athletic
4	Liverpool
5	**Everton**
6	Arsenal
7	Newcastle United
8	Portsmouth

MOYES REVEALS TARGET

'We are going to start the Premier League season by saying we can break into the top four again.'

THAT WAS THE SEASON - 2007/08

September

Yakubu makes a scoring debut as Joleon Lescott's last-minute header gives Everton a 2-1 win at Bolton. The Nigeria striker, who opened the scoring on 10 minutes, makes his full debut along with Steven Pienaar and Phil Jagielka, while Thomas Gravesen, whose corner set up Lescott's winner, makes his bow from the bench.

James McFadden enjoys a fruitful few days for Scotland, scoring a superb third goal in their 3-1 Euro 2008 qualifier against Lithuania before hitting a long-range winner to stun France in Paris. Andy Johnson and Phil Neville come on as subs in England's 3-0 win over Israel, the latter also coming on in the 3-0 win over Russia. Tim Howard dislocates a finger in the USA's defeat to Brazil.

Everton Tigers basketball team are officially launched, the club having teamed up with Toxteth Tigers. They will play in the British Basketball League during the 2007/08 season. Stefan Wessels makes his Everton debut in the 1-0 home defeat to Manchester United.

Ticketing problems mean the UEFA Cup first round, first-leg tie with Metalist Kharkiv kicks off half an hour later than scheduled. The Goodison leg proves unhappy for the Blues, who are held to a 1-1 draw by the Ukrainians, who finish the game with nine men. Andy Johnson also misses two penalties on a frustrating night.

England Ladies, including Everton's Rachel Brown and Jill Scott, are knocked out of the World Cup at the quarter-final stage, going down 3-0. An Everton side made up of legends, celebrities and fans are beaten 3-0 by Manchester City in the Premier League All Stars charity tournament. The legends were Neville Southall, Dave Watson and Adrian Heath.

Everton keep their first clean sheet of the season in the 3-0 win at Sheffield Wednesday in the League Cup – Luton Town are next up for the Blues.

Mikel Arteta is short-listed for the North West Premiership Player of the Year award, while the Everton Collection Charitable Trust confirms that the David France Collection of football memorabilia has been acquired, courtesy of a Heritage Lottery Fund grant.

Ladies Day at Goodison sees the Blues overcome Middlesbrough 2-0, Steven Pienaar's first goal for the club sealing the win which moves the Blues up to fifth in the table. Joleon Lescott's opener proved to be the only first-half goal scored by an Everton player at the Gwladys Street End in 07/08.

Outgoing:

Anderson Silva de Franca (Barnsley, loan extended).

Quotes of the month:

"You're normally sat at home in the winter on a Tuesday night watching Manchester United against whoever, and you actually want to be there playing yourself. It's the second time for the boys in Europe and they want to do a lot better."

Andy Johnson, aiming for a busy life

"There is a sense around the ground that the fans want us to win trophies. In the seven years I have been here, this is the strongest squad we have had by quite a lot. If we can build on what we have done last season then it will be a fantastic achievement."

Alan Stubbs, impressed by the club's strength in depth

"Instead of looking for faults...why not give a little congratulations to McFadden for the way he struck the ball. It was a marvellous strike, one of the best I have seen."

Raymond Domenech, the France coach, salutes James McFadden's Scotland winner

"A guy who said I was playing for the wrong team was typical. He wasn't the only Liverpool fan to say something nice so I take that as the ultimate compliment. I do feel I belong (in Liverpool)."

Mikel Arteta, settled on Merseyside

SEPTEMBER

THE GAMES

1	Bolton W.	A	2-1	Yakubu, Lescott
15	Manchester Utd	H	0-1	
20	Metalist Kharkiv	H	1-1	Lescott
23	Aston Villa	A	0-2	
26	Sheffield Wed.	A	3-0	McFadden 2, Yakubu
30	Middlesbrough	H	2-0	Lescott, Pienaar

WHERE THEY STOOD

2	Manchester United
3	Manchester City
4	Liverpool
5	**Everton**
6	Portsmouth
7	Blackburn Rovers
8	Chelsea

MOYES ON BORO WIN

'I think there was just a little change today and I started to smell that things were improving.'

THAT WAS THE SEASON - 2007/08

October

Youngster Cory Sinnott signs his first professional contract, the defender penning a two-year deal, while Tim Howard is runner-up behind Landon Donovan for the US Player of the Year award. Everton qualify for the UEFA Cup group stages after a topsy-turvy 3-2 victory over Metalist Kharkiv in Ukraine. Former Blues assistant-boss Willie Donachie is dismissed as manager of League One side Millwall, while Joe Royle is appointed as Patron of the Everton Collection Charitable Trust. Everton draw AZ Alkmaar, Zenit St Petersburg, 1. FC Nurnberg and AE Larissa in the UEFA Cup Group Stage. James McFadden unveils a giant image of his winning goal for Scotland against France at the Scottish Football Museum at Hampden Park ("I'm sure I will appreciate it when I am older," he says) and is on scoring form again as he nets the third goal in Scotland's 3-1 victory over Ukraine. The first-team enjoy their last training session at Bellefield, their home since 1946, as the new state-of-the-art complex at Finch Farm in Halewood is completed.

Joleon Lescott makes his England debut as a half-time substitute in England's 3-0 stroll over Estonia, Everton team-mate Phil Neville also making an appearance off the bench to win his 59th international cap. There is disappointment for Lee Carsley, though, as his Republic of Ireland side are held at home by Germany, all but ending their Euro 2008 qualification hopes.

The midweek internationals bring disappointment for England and Scotland, Lescott making his first start in the 2-1 defeat in Russia while McFadden wins his 35th cap in the 2-0 defeat in Georgia. Everton go down 2-1 in the 206th Merseyside derby, a Sami Hyypia own goal having put the Blues ahead. Two Dirk Kuyt penalties, the second in the last minute, deny the nine men, with referee Mark Clattenburg at the centre of a series of incidents that appeared to go against the home side. Anderson de Silva Franca returns to the club after enjoying a two-month loan spell at Barnsley. Everton sell-out their ticket allocation for the UEFA Cup tie against Nurnberg in Germany, with an estimated 6,000 Evertonians thought to be making the journey next month.

Tim Cahill scores the opener on his first start of the season as the Blues get their UEFA Cup group campaign off to a flyer, courtesy of a 3-1 victory over AE Larissa.

Everton reach the last eight of the League Cup for the first time since 1988 following a 1-0 win at Luton, sub Tim Cahill netting the winner in extra time. The game also sees James Vaughan appear off the bench, his first involvement of the season following injury.

Landmarks:

Mikel Arteta and Tim Cahill mark their 100th appearances for the club, against AE Larissa and Derby County respectively.

Joseph Yobo captains the Blues for the first time against AE Larissa - only the second overseas player to skipper the club following Slaven Bilic.

Quotes of the month:

"It's up there (with the best nights). Sometimes you can regroup at half-time and show more spirit. That's what we did and the spirit was phenomenal."

James McFadden reflects on a big night in Ukraine

"Progressing in Europe will give the club a little bit of identity back because we have been a little bit down for the last 10 or 15 years. I felt tonight was make or break for us. We have failed at too many first hurdles, and this was a massive game for the club because of that."

Phil Neville, on a similar theme

"It is a really sad day. This place has graced some unbelievable players. I am not in that category."

Alan Stubbs, on leaving Bellefield

"I remember coming here with Blackburn but I didn't play, I was on the bench. It is a different atmosphere here. Blackburn seems to be more passive and here it is more fired up."

Georgios Donis, AE Larissa coach and one-time Blackburn Rovers winger

OCTOBER

THE GAMES

4	Metalist Kharkiv	A	3-2	Lescott, McFadden, Anichebe
7	Newcastle Utd	A	2-3	Johnson, Given o.g.
20	Liverpool	H	1-2	Hyypia o.g.
25	AE Larissa	H	3-1	Cahill, Osman, Anichebe
28	Derby County	A	2-0	Arteta, Yakubu
31	Luton Town	A	1-0 aet	Cahill

WHERE THEY STOOD

6	Liverpool
7	Portsmouth
8	Newcastle United
9	**Everton**
10	Aston Villa
11	West Ham United
12	Reading

MOYES ON IMAGE CHANGE

'I had a touch of man-flu so I decided to keep the suit on rather than the tracksuit.'

THAT WAS THE SEASON - 2007/08

November

Stoppage-time goals from Birmingham-born duo Lee Carsley and sub James Vaughan give the Blues a dramatic 3-1 victory over Birmingham City. Andy Johnson agrees a new five-year deal, tying him to the club until 2012, while Austrian youngster George Krenn signs a pro contract.

Late goals by Mikel Arteta (pen) and sub Victor Anichebe earn David Moyes' men a 2-0 victory in Nurnberg, which all but secures the Blues' progress into the last 32 of the UEFA Cup. It is also Everton's fifth successive win in all competitions, and eighth success in 10 games.

Tim Cahill's spectacular last-minute overhead kick earns the Blues an unlikely point at Chelsea.

Mikel Arteta is named as the inaugural winner of the Premier League's Player of the Year prize at the North West Football Awards, an honour voted for by supporters. The Spanish midfielder beat off competition from Cristiano Ronaldo, Wayne Rooney and Steven Gerrard.

James McFadden's Scotland miss out on a place in Euro 2008 after suffering a 2-1 defeat to Italy.

Everton assistant-manager Alan Irvine accepts the opportunity to take charge of Championship side Preston North End, having been David Moyes' No. 2 for five-and-a-half years.

Joleon Lescott plays as England fail to reach Euro 2008, going down 3-2 at home to Croatia whilst Russia beat Andorra 1-0 to claim second place in the group.

Everton demolish Sunderland 7-1 at Goodison, although the result is slightly overshadowed by the news that club legend Dave Hickson suffers a heart attack ahead of the fixture.

David Moyes laughs off a suggestion he could be in the running to be the next England boss, although he is also hit with an FA charge related to comments made about referee Mark Clattenberg following the Merseyside derby last month.

Mikel Arteta reiterates his desire to play for Spain, while Alan Stubbs takes charge of the reserves for the first time in the 5-1 defeat of Wigan Athletic.

Landmarks:

The win over Birmingham City was the club's fourth on the spin in all competitions, the first time the Blues have achieved this feat (not including drawn matches won on penalties) since August 1993 (last game of 92/93, and first three games of 93/94).

Both Tim Howard and Joleon Lescott make their 50th appearance for the club in the same match – Howard starting all 50 of his games (in all competitions), while Lescott's 50th is league games only. Lescott is also the first player to be involved in the first 50 games played by the club immediately after joining since Peter Beardsley.

Howard is the first Everton keeper to have conceded an average of less than a goal a game in his first 50 matches (48 goals).

The 1-1 result at Chelsea sees Everton become the first side to achieve 1,000 top-flight draws.

Everton's 7-1 defeat of Sunderland is the club's biggest win for 11 years. It is also the first time five different players have appeared on the scoresheet since February 1995 (April 1978 in the league).

Outgoing:

Anderson Silva de Franca (Barnsley, loan), Scott Spencer (Yeovil Town, trial).

Quotes of the month:

"Hearing Chelsea talk about fiscal responsibility is a little like me asking my three-year-old to look after the fireworks."

Keith Wyness, then Everton chief executive, unimpressed by the Roman Abramovich regime

"Everton are a proper football club...they have a lot of history and good, passionate fans who follow their club home and away."

Sunderland boss Roy Keane impressed with the Blues - and that was before the match!

NOVEMBER

THE GAMES

3	Birmingham C.	H	3-1	Yakubu, Carsley, Vaughan
8	1. FC Nurnberg	A	2-0	Arteta (pen), Anichebe
11	Chelsea	A	1-1	Cahill
24	Sunderland	H	7-1	Yakubu 2, Cahill 2, Pienaar, Johnson, Osman

WHERE THEY STOOD

5	Liverpool
6	Aston Villa
7	Portsmouth
8	**Everton**
9	Blackburn Rovers
10	West Ham United
11	Newcastle United

MOYES ON BEING THE BOSS

'It's always been good, not just because we've won five games (on the run). But it makes the job easier!'

THAT WAS THE SEASON - 2007/08

December

Everton secure a hard-fought 0-0 draw at Portsmouth to extend their unbeaten run to eight in all competitions. The FA Cup third-round draw sees the Blues earn a home tie with League One side Oldham Athletic. Victor Anichebe insists his international future lies with Nigeria, although he is left out of the preliminary squad for the African Cup of Nations.

At the club AGM, Robert Earl is appointed onto the Board of Directors.

Everton secure their last-32 place in the UEFA Cup after edging Russian champions Zenit St. Petersburg 1-0 at Goodison. It will be the first time since 1984/85 that the club will be in European action after Christmas. David Moyes requests a personal hearing with the FA after being charged with improper conduct following post-match derby comments back in October.

Yakubu's hat-trick secures a 3-0 victory over Fulham – the Blues' eighth win in 10 games. The success continues as the Blues come from behind (for the first time in any cup match against top-flight opposition since 1984) to defeat West Ham 2-1 courtesy of a late Yakubu winner to secure a place in the League Cup semi-final.

Yakubu takes his season's tally to 11 as the Blues end a successful few days at West Ham with a 2-0 win, sub Andy Johnson hitting the second late on. It is only the seventh post-war occasion Everton have beaten the same opposition in successive games - make it eight against SK Brann. The Blues make it four wins from four in their UEFA Cup group, a 3-2 win at AZ Alkmaar seeing the Blues knock Louis van Gaal's men out of the competition.

Unfortunate defeats to Manchester United and Arsenal – with a win over Bolton sandwiched in between – sees the Blues end 2007 in sixth, after a run of 12 wins in 16 fixtures.

Landmarks:

Ayegbeni Yakubu's hat-trick against Fulham is the first time an Everton player has achieved the feat since Steve Watson in 2003 - and the first second-half treble at the Gwladys Street End since Andy Gray's against Fortuna Sittard in March 1985.

It will be the club's first League Cup semi-final since 1988 – and first in any competition for nearly 13 years.

The victory over AZ Alkmaar is the first time the Dutch outfit have lost on home soil in Europe, and equals a club record set in 1907 of eight successive wins in cup matches.

Jack Rodwell breaks Jimmy Husband's 42-year record by becoming the youngest player to represent Everton in Europe.

The victory over Bolton Wanderers is the Blues' sixth successive home win - last achieved in 1995.

Quotes of the month:

"I would love to tell people in Europe that Everton were champions and but for the Heysel disaster they may have had a long run in Europe. People forget that and don't understand what happened. Everton were unlucky. But not as unlucky as the people involved in the tragedy, of course. I am sure it (the ban) has had an effect, it affected the draw in the Champions League two years ago."

David Moyes reveals his European aims

"I know Tim (Cahill) very well. Maybe I'll try and poison him!"

West Ham's Lucas Neill thinks of a new way to stop his Australia team-mate

"If he gets three chances in a match, we'd be disappointed if he didn't score two. He is as good a striker as I have ever played with. I also know what it is like to play against him and he is an absolute pain in the backside."

Phil Jagielka, on Ayegbeni Yakubu

"He is my friend but this is football. It just happened...the one thing I am sure about is that he put his elbow in my face and that is a red card."

Cesc Fabregas reacts to Mikel Arteta's sending off for an apparent elbow v Arsenal

DECEMBER

THE GAMES

1	Portsmouth	A	0-0	
5	Zenit S.P.	H	1-0	Cahill
8	Fulham	H	3-0	Yakubu 3
12	West Ham	A	2-1	Osman, Yakubu
15	West Ham	A	2-0	Yakubu, Johnson
20	AZ Alkmaar	A	3-2	Johnson, Jagielka, Vaughan
23	Man Utd	A	1-2	Cahill
26	Bolton W.	H	2-0	Neville, Cahill
29	Arsenal	H	1-4	Cahill

WHERE THEY STOOD

3	Chelsea
4	Liverpool
5	Manchester City
6	**Everton**
7	Aston Villa
8	Portsmouth
9	Blackburn Rovers

MOYES ON CARLING CUP WIN

'The first half was probably the best in my management career. If that had been Arsenal we would all have been talking about them.'

THAT WAS THE SEASON - 2007/08

January

The Blues begin the New Year in fine style, earning a 2-0 win at Middlesbrough – the Toffees' 11th away from home in all competitions this term. Everton and Tesco submit a planning application to Knowsley Borough Council for a new 50,000-seat stadium and a massive regeneration of Kirkby.

A Premier League survey reveals that Evertonians are the fifth noisiest fans in the league, and that they sing the most – an average of one song every three minutes.

The Blues are stunned by Oldham in the FA Cup third round, a much-changed side going down 1-0. Andy Johnson reveals the 'A-symbol' celebration being used by several players relates to a charity established by Wigan's Fitz Hall to give kids a chance in life, and positive role models.

A late Joleon Lescott own goal denies Everton a draw in the first leg of the Carling Cup semi-final, the Blues going down 2-1 to 10-man Chelsea after Yakubu had levelled Shaun Wright-Phillips' goal.

David Moyes celebrates 10 years in management with a 1-0 win over Manchester City. Manuel Fernandes completes his loan move, his second spell after a successful stint this time last year. David Moyes reveals that he is unlikely to appoint a new No. 2 before the end of the campaign, while the club reveal a new three-year sponsorship deal with Chang, worth £8m.

James McFadden joins Birmingham City for a fee which could rise to £6m, while former player Wally Fielding passes away at the age of 88. Everton go fourth after winning 2-1 at Wigan Athletic. Tony Hibbert and Leon Osman agree new deals with the club until 2012.

Manuel Fernandes makes his second debut for the Blues in the 1-0 defeat by Chelsea in the Carling Cup semi-final, second leg, the Londoners taking it 3-1 on aggregate.

Ayegbeni Yakubu is on the scoresheet as Nigeria scrape into the last eight of the African Cup of Nations in Ghana. David Moyes believes the Premier League should shut down during the bi-annual tournament, with 35 English-based players currently away with their countries.

Joleon Lescott is included in Fabio Capello's first England squad, while James Vaughan is handed an U21 call-up. Steven Pienaar is an unused sub as South Africa bow out in Ghana. Alan Stubbs and Anderson de Silva Franca are deadline-day departures, with Anthony Gardner coming in.

Incoming:

Dan Gosling (Plymouth Argyle), Manuel Fernandes (Valencia, loan), Anthony Gardner (Spurs, loan).

Outgoing:

Lukas Jutkiewicz (Plymouth Argyle, loan), Scott Spencer (Yeovil Town, loan), James McFadden (Birmingham City), Patrick Boyle (Crewe Alexandra, loan), John Paul Kissock (Gretna, loan), Bjarni Vidarsson (FC Twente, loan), Alan Stubbs (Derby), Anderson Silva de Franca (Barnsley).

Quotes of the month:

"I didn't even know that (that the club were to sign the player on loan). Have I? Not that I know of!"
David Moyes on links with Manuel Fernandes - January 4

"He'll have something to prove. He's a terrific talent. We would have (made it permanent) but because of the third-party agreement it was impossible, which is something I agree with. He's now back and we'll see how he does. Whether we would be able to afford him is another question!"
David Moyes on Manuel Fernandes' loan signing - January 11

"Liverpool is the same kind of support but Everton is a bit more aggressive because Everton is up at the moment. Over the last one or two years, especially, it has been one of the noisiest grounds and has a great atmosphere. Liverpool is the same but now a little bit more genteel."
Arsene Wenger - Impressed with the Everton atmosphere

JANUARY

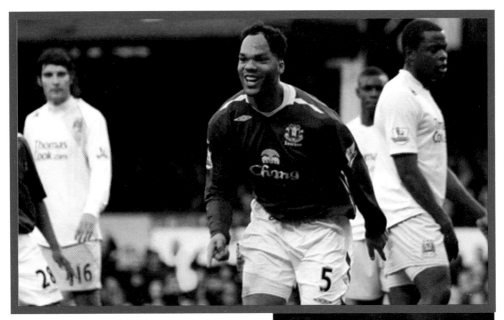

THE GAMES

1	Middlesbrough	A	2-0	Johnson, McFadden
5	Oldham Athletic	H	0-1	
8	Chelsea	A	1-2	Yakubu
12	Manchester City	H	1-0	Lescott
20	Wigan Athletic	A	2-1	Johnson, Lescott
23	Chelsea	H	0-1	
30	Tottenham H.	H	0-0	

WHERE THEY STOOD

2	Arsenal
3	Chelsea
4	**Everton**
5	Aston Villa
6	Manchester City
7	Liverpool
8	Blackburn Rovers

MOYES ON 2008 HOPES

'My aim is try and win things and do as well as we can. I always want my teams to play well.'

THAT WAS THE SEASON - 2007/08

February

The FA drop their charges against David Moyes related to his post-derby comments back in October. The Blues boss is left fuming after Andy Johnson's late 'goal' is disallowed in the 0-0 draw at Blackburn Rovers, the assistant referee deeming the effort offside. Despite Ayegbeni Yakubu's goal, Nigeria bow out of the African Cup of Nations in the quarter-finals, beaten 2-1 by Ghana. Mikel Arteta is named the *Liverpool Echo* Sports Personality of the Year, becoming the 11th Everton name to secure the accolade in its 36-year history - and the first overseas footballer. Tim Cahill is on target for Australia in their 3-0 win over Qatar - the Socceroos' first 2010 World Cup qualifier. Lee Carsley plays for the Republic of Ireland in their 1-0 defeat to Brazil, while Tim Howard is in fine form during the USA's 2-2 draw with Mexico.

Everton join the other 19 Premier League clubs in agreeing to further examine a proposal to create an extra round of fixtures to be played around the world over one weekend in January, beginning in the 2010/11 season. The Premier League also approve a rule allowing clubs to name seven substitutes in a match, beginning next season. Yakubu is left out of the Everton squad to face Reading owing to his late return to the club following African Cup of Nations duty in Ghana. Chairman Bill Kenwright insists he will give David Moyes big money to spend should the Blues qualify for the Champions League.

Brian Harris, a league and FA Cup winner with the club in the 1960s, passes away at the age of 72. The Blues reach the last 16 of the UEFA Cup following their record European win, 6-1 over SK Brann at Goodison – 8-1 on aggregate.

David Moyes outlines his intention to make Steven Pienaar's loan move to Everton permanent in the summer. The 2-0 win at Manchester City leaves the club in fourth – and reveals Joleon Lescott as a lucky omen, the Blues never having lost when the defender has been on the scoresheet. Everton confirm their application for the Intertoto Cup while the club's Ladies side upset the odds to defeat their Arsenal counterparts 1-0 in the League Cup final.

Outgoing:

Patrick Boyle (Crewe Alexandra, loan extended), John Ruddy (Stockport County, loan).

Landmarks:

Everton's 2-0 win at SK Brann is the Blues' sixth successive win in European club competition – a club record.

Yakubu's hat-trick is only the third by an Everton player in Europe – and he is now the first Blues player to hit a treble twice in a season since 1993/94. It is also the first time six or more goals have been scored in two matches in the same season since 1985/86.

Everton's 21 goals in Europe this season is a club record.

The win at Manchester City was the Blues' 14th on the road this season, a total that has only been beaten once – in 1984/85. It also means the club have gone through the first two months of a calendar year unbeaten in the league for the first time in 22 years.

Quotes of the month:

"I feel like a part of a family here with everyone working together. I came back late and I have apologised. It happened for personal reasons but I promise it won't happen again. I think the players were glad to see me back. It is good to be in a team where you know the players want you."

Ayegbeni Yakubu, glad to be back

"I look at Lee Carsley as somebody who holds the team together – he is the glue. I always take a bet on how many minutes into the game he has a pop at somebody – including me!"

Tim Howard, happy to take Lee Carsley's verbals

FEBRUARY

THE GAMES

2	Blackburn R.	A	0-0	
9	Reading	H	1-0	Jagielka
13	SK Brann	A	2-0	Osman, Anichebe
21	SK Brann	H	6-1	Yakubu 3, Johnson 2, Arteta
25	Manchester City	A	2-0	Yakubu, Lescott

WHERE THEY STOOD

1	Arsenal
2	Manchester United
3	Chelsea
4	**Everton**
5	Liverpool
6	Aston Villa
7	Portsmouth

MOYES ON PENALTY MYSTERY

'We have not had a penalty in the league all season. For a side who have scored as many as we have...that is amazing.'

THAT WAS THE SEASON - 2007/08

March

Boss David Moyes backs Joleon Lescott to develop into a future captain. The win over Portsmouth sees the Blues regain fourth spot - Yakubu's brace sees him reach 18 for the season. The club give their backing to Tim Cahill when his Pompey goal celebration - in salute of his jailed older brother - is criticised in the wider media. Everton suffer a big setback at Fiorentina, going down 2-0. David Moyes is named the Barclays Manager of the Month for February, the first time he has won the award for more than two years - and the fourth time in all.

Youngster Jack Rodwell makes his Premier League debut as a late sub in the 1-0 win at Sunderland. Joleon Lescott agrees a new deal with the club, keeping him at Everton until the summer of 2012. The Blues bow out of the UEFA Cup, going down 4-2 on penalties having pulled the aggregate scores level with a 2-0 win at Goodison on a memorable night – Andy Johnson and Mikel Arteta struck in either half, before 30 minutes' extra time failed to separate the sides.

A 1-0 defeat at Fulham is the club's ninth consecutive away defeat to the Cottagers – and the Blues' first league defeat of 2008. Jack Rodwell signs a two-year professional contract.

Joleon Lescott wins his fifth England cap as a half-time sub in the 1-0 defeat in France. Victor Anichebe nets on his Nigeria U23 debut as he helps his country qualify for the Olympics thanks to a 3-0 defeat of South Africa. Tim Howard plays in the USA's 3-0 win in Poland. Tim Cahill is ruled out for the season with a broken foot while the Blues go down 1-0 in the Anfield derby.

Outgoing:

Scott Spencer (Macclesfield Town, loan), Patrick Boyle (Crewe Alexandra, loan extended), John Ruddy (Stockport County, loan extended), Aidan Downes (Yeovil Town, loan).

Landmarks:

Ayegbeni Yakubu's opener against Portsmouth, timed at 47 seconds, was actually scored after just eight seconds of open play, following a stoppage for a foul.

The 1-0 win at Sunderland is the Blues' 15th away win of the season in all competitions – the second best in the club's history.

Tim Cahill makes his 100th Premier League appearance in the 1-0 win at Sunderland.

Quotes of the month:

"I wondered if I could cut it. Then David Moyes had a word with me. He was very reassuring. When I stayed in the team after Joe (Yobo) came back (from the African Cup of Nations) the manager didn't say anything. But it was like a big silent pat on the back. He's very clever with his mannerisms."

Phil Jagielka, backing the boss

"He and I simply have not had a moment to sit down and finalise his contract, although we have both acknowledged to each other that we must – and we will. This is one of the most exciting periods in our club's recent history, and any mischievous reports are not welcome."

Bill Kenwright, on contract talks with David Moyes

"This is one of the best teams that I have ever played in. I believe whenever I have it, I can score. When I signed I thought I would be under pressure, but I'm not under pressure. I know that if I don't score then there are people in the team that can score."

Ayegbeni Yakubu, has belief in current side

"This is a real team who will make us suffer. We'll be against one of the best in Europe."

Cesare Prandelli, AC Fiorentina coach shows concern

"It's been a privilege and an honour to play for a club like this. It's a great place to play. I couldn't be at a better club. When I first came here I didn't realise what it was to come to Everton and wear the badge...and then Duncan Ferguson took me under his wing and Alan Stubbs did as well. They showed me the way. Work hard and train hard and believe in the badge, and you'll always do well."

Tim Cahill, delighted to reach 100 Everton appearances

MARCH

THE GAMES

2	Portsmouth	H	3-1	Yakubu 2, Cahill
6	AC Fiorentina	A	0-2	
9	Sunderland	A	1-0	Johnson
12	AC Fiorentina	H	2-0*aet	Johnson, Arteta
				* Everton lost 4-2 on penalties
16	Fulham	A	0-1	
22	West Ham	H	1-1	Yakubu
30	Liverpool	A	0-1	

WHERE THEY STOOD

3	Arsenal
4	Liverpool
5	**Everton**
6	Portsmouth
7	Blackburn Rovers
8	Aston Villa
9	Manchester City

MOYES ON FUTURE SPENDING

'If we are going to compete we are going to have to find the cash...you have to spend more just to keep ahead...'

THAT WAS THE SEASON - 2007/08

April

Leon Osman reveals his personal pride after donning the skipper's armband in the final 20 minutes of the derby. The 1-0 win over Derby moves the Blues to within three points of Liverpool in fourth.

John Ruddy earns the League Two player of the month award for March courtesy of his outstanding performances at Stockport.

The Blues lose further ground in the race for fourth after being held at Birmingham City. Phil Jagielka admits that a fourth-place finish is now unlikely following the 1-0 home defeat to Chelsea.

Dan Gosling could feature for the first team before the end of the season, according to the Blues' boss.

Steven Pienaar reveals his relief after his loan deal becomes permanent, the South African midfielder penning a three-year contract.

Tim Cahill will undergo the "ultimate procedure" in a bid to solve his recurring foot problems, according to physio Mick Rathbone.

Everton's Nigerian trio Anichebe, Yakubu and Yobo are called up for 2010 World Cup qualifying matches in June.

David Moyes reveals his wish to retain the services of Lee Carsley, the midfielder having been linked with a return to Derby County.

The Blues twice lose a lead as Aston Villa draw 2-2 at Goodison, keeping alive the race for fifth.

Incoming:
Steven Pienaar (Borussia Dortmund).

Landmarks:
The 1-0 defeat of Derby is the club's 20th clean sheet of the season in all competitions.

Joleon Lescott is the highest scoring defender in the Premier League in 2007/08.

Quotes of the month:

"It's a good yardstick for aspiring managers in the Premier League to try and get close to what David Moyes has done. He's been very diligent and shrewd, and there have been stepping stones."
Alex McLeish looks to Goodison for inspiration

"I had a great time at Everton. My whole time there was fantastic. There is a great atmosphere about the club and I had no complaints, apart from not being in the team on a Saturday. I looked forward to training every day, and I settled in quite quickly and was really comfortable there. It was a bit of a wrench to leave but I had to do it and I think I've made the right decision."
James McFadden, reflecting on his time at Everton

"He's (Radhi Jaidi) in my line of sight. He's in an offside position, and he's interfering with me. You try and see the ball as early as you can from the different angles. He got away with it. The guy who robs a bank, if you don't catch him then he keeps the money."
Tim Howard, unhappy with Birmingham's free-kick tactics before their equaliser

"It would be like Everton sacking David Moyes in the morning because they didn't qualify for the Champions League!"
Noel Gallagher, on Sven-Goran Eriksson's predicament at Manchester City

APRIL

THE GAMES

6	Derby County	H	1-0	Osman
12	Birmingham	A	1-1	Lescott
17	Chelsea	H	0-1	
27	Aston Villa	H	2-2	Neville, Yobo

WHERE THEY STOOD

2	Chelsea
3	Arsenal
4	Liverpool
5	**Everton**
6	Aston Villa
7	Portsmouth
8	Blackburn Rovers

MOYES ON YAKUBU

'Yak needs a bit of loving every now and then and a bit of attention, but he has scored a lot of goals for us.'

THAT WAS THE SEASON - 2007/08

May

Everton are rated 21st in Forbes Magazine's list of the richest football clubs in the world. Goodison Park's floodlights are switched on to mark the first anniversary of Madeleine McCann's disappearance. The Blues will need a point from their last game of the season to secure fifth after going down 1-0 at Arsenal, making it 13 visits without a victory at the Gunners. One million fans see Everton during the season, from Bremen in July onwards. The figure takes into account people who purchased a ticket for home and away games. Everton secure fifth spot and a UEFA Cup spot after seeing off Newcastle United 3-1 on the final day of the season.

Phil Jagielka earns his first call-up to the England squad, for friendlies against the USA and Trinidad & Tobago (winning his first cap in the latter as a half-time substitute). Joleon Lescott scoops the Everton Disabled Supporters Association's player of the year award, having already picked up both main awards at the official end-of-season awards night earlier in the month.

Nuno Valente extends his stay with the club for another year, while Everton also finish fifth in the Premier League's fair play table.

Victor Anichebe is called up to the Nigeria squad for the Olympic Games in August.

Everton Ladies secure the Liverpool County FA Cup, beating their Liverpool counterparts 5-0 at Goodison Park.

Lee Carsley will leave the club in order to move back to the Midlands – Birmingham City securing his services. Tim Howard is called up by the USA for forthcoming matches, including a friendly against England at Wembley Stadium.

Wayne Rooney's success with Manchester United nets the Blues £1.5m as a result of clauses as part of the original deal that took the striker to Old Trafford in 2004.

Tim Howard plays for the first half in the USA's 2-0 defeat to England at Wembley, while Victor Anichebe makes his Nigeria debut alongside Everton team-mates Joseph Yobo and Ayegbeni Yakubu in the 1-1 draw in Austria.

The Blues confirm pre-season matches against Cambridge United, Nottingham Forest, Chicago Fire and Colorado Rapids.

Outgoing:

Thomas Gravesen (Celtic, loan completed), Stefan Wessels, Anthony Gardner (Tottenham Hotspur, loan completed), Bjarni Vidarsson, Patrick Boyle, Jamie Jones, Shaun Densmore, Steven Morrison, James Hall, Ryan Harpur, Aidan Downes (Yeovil Town), Stephen Connor, Lee Carsley (Birmingham).

Landmarks:

The Premier League points total of 65 is the club's highest ever.

Ayegbeni Yakubu ends the season with 21 goals, the first Everton player to reach the landmark since 1991/92.

Joleon Lescott reaches 10 goals for the season, the first Everton defender to reach that mark since Derek Mountfield in 1984/85.

The final-day triumph over Newcastle meant for only the seventh time in history the club had recorded 30 wins in a single season - the first time since 1986/87. Michael Owen's goal for the Magpies sees him become the first player since Sir Tom Finney (1955-59) to score against Everton in four consecutive Goodison appearances.

Quotes of the month:

"I definitely see my long-term future at the club. I look at the players we are linked with now and they are big names. Players looking in want to be a part of Everton and why wouldn't they?"

Joleon Lescott, enjoying Everton life

"When I checked my phone there was a stack of messages waiting. The first one I read was from Ossie (Leon Osman) saying: 'Congratulations, you're in the England squad.' Normally when you get something like that from him it means he's winding you up."

Phil Jagielka, on receiving his England call-up

MAY

THE GAMES

| 4 | Arsenal | A | 0-1 | |
| 11 | Newcastle Utd | H | 3-1 | Yakubu 2 (1 pen), Lescott |

WHERE THEY FINISHED

2	Chelsea
3	Arsenal
4	Liverpool
5	**Everton**
6	Aston Villa
7	Blackburn Rovers
8	Portsmouth

MOYES ON FUTURE AIMS

'We need to increase in numbers. Quality will always be first priority, but quantity is also required. I want us to be strong and progress.'

Date	Opposition		Res	Att	Pts	Pos	Line-up					
August												
Sat 11	**Wigan**	H	2-1	39,220	3	6	Howard	Hibbert	Yobo	Stubbs	Lescott	Arteta
Tues 14	Tottenham	A	3-1	35,716	6	1	Howard	Hibbert	Yobo	**Stubbs**	**Lescott**	Arteta
Sat 18	Reading	A	0-1	22,813	6	4	Howard	Hibbert ■	Lescott	Stubbs	Valente	Arteta
Sat 25	**Blackburn**	H	1-1	33,850	7	5	Howard	Hibbert ■	Yobo	Stubbs ■	Baines	Arteta
September												
Sat 1	Bolton	A	2-1	22,064	10	3	Howard	Jagielka	Yobo	**Lescott**	Baines	Arteta
Sat 15	**Man Utd**	H	0-1	39,364	10	7	Wessels	Hibbert	Yobo	Lescott	Baines	Arteta
Thurs 20	Metalist Kharkiv (UEFA 1, 1st leg)	H	1-1	37,120	-	-	Wessels	Hibbert	Yobo	**Lescott**	Baines	Osman
Sun 23	Aston Villa	A	0-2	38,235	10	9	Wessels	Hibbert	Yobo	Lescott	Baines	Osman
Wed 26	Sheffield Wednesday (CC 3rd)	A	3-0	16,463	-	-	Wessels	Hibbert	Stubbs	Lescott	Valente ■	Osman
Sun 30	**Middlesbrough**	H	2-0	31,885	13	5	Howard	Hibbert	Stubbs	**Lescott**	Baines	Arteta ■
October												
Thurs 4	Metalist Kharkiv (UEFA 1, 2nd leg)	A	3-2	27,500	-	-	Howard	Neville	Yobo	Stubbs	**Lescott**	Arteta
Sun 7	Newcastle	A	2-3	50,152	13	10	Howard	Hibbert	Yobo	Lescott	Baines	Arteta
Sat 20	**Liverpool**	H	1-2 +	40,049	13	11	Howard	Hibbert ■	Yobo	Stubbs	Lescott	Arteta
Thurs 25	AE Larissa (UEFA GSI)	H	3-1	33,777	-	-	Howard	Hibbert	Yobo	Lescott	Baines	Arteta
Sun 28	Derby	A	2-0	33,048	16	9	Howard	Jagielka	Yobo	Lescott	Baines	**Arteta**
Wed 31	Luton Town (CC 4th)	A	1-0 ·	8,944	-	-	Wessels	Jagielka	Stubbs	Lescott	Valente	Neville
November												
Sat 3	**Birmingham**	H	3-1	35,155	19	8	Howard	Neville	Yobo	Stubbs	Lescott	Arteta
Thurs 8	1.FC Nurnberg (UEFA GS2)	A	2-0	43,000	-	-	Howard	Neville	Yobo	Lescott	Valente	**Arteta**
Sun 11	Chelsea	A	1-1	41,683	20	9	Howard	Hibbert	Yobo	Lescott	Valente	Osman
Sat 24	**Sunderland**	H	7-1	38,594	23	8	Howard	Neville	Yobo ■	Lescott	Valente	Arteta
December												
Sat 1	Portsmouth	A	0-0	20,102	24	9	Howard	Neville	Yobo	Lescott	Valente	Arteta
Wed 5	Zenit St. Petersburg (UEFA GS3)	H	1-0	38,407	-	-	Howard	Neville	Jagielka	Lescott	Baines	Arteta
Sat 8	**Fulham**	H	3-0	32,743	27	7	Howard	Neville	Yobo	Lescott	Baines	Arteta
Wed 12	West Ham (CC 5th)	A	2-1	28,777	-	-	Howard	Neville	Yobo	Jagielka	Lescott	Arteta
Sat 15	West Ham	A	2-0	34,430	30	6	Howard	Neville	Yobo	Jagielka	Lescott	Arteta
Thurs 20	AZ Alkmaar (UEFA GS4)	A	3-2	16,578	-	-	Wessels	Hibbert	**Jagielka**	Lescott	Valente	Gravesen ■
Sun 23	Man Utd	A	1-2	75,749	30	6	Howard	Hibbert	Yobo	Jagielka	Lescott	Neville
Wed 26	**Bolton**	H	2-0	38,918	33	6	Howard	**Neville**	Yobo	Jagielka	Lescott	Neville
Sat 29	**Arsenal**	H	1-4	39,443	33	6	Howard	Hibbert ■	Yobo	Jagielka	Lescott	Arteta ■
January												
Tues 1	Middlesbrough	A	2-0	27,028	36	5	Howard	Hibbert	Jagielka	Lescott	Valente	**McFadden**
Sat 05	Oldham (FA Cup 3rd)	H	0-1	33,086	-	-	Wessels	Hibbert	Stubbs	Jagielka	Baines ■	Pienaar
Tues 08	Chelsea (CC SF, 1st leg)	A	1-2	41,178	-	-	Howard	Hibbert	Yobo	Jagielka	Lescott	Cahill
Sat 12	**Man City**	H	1-0	38,474	39	5	Howard	Hibbert	**Lescott**	Jagielka	Valente	Arteta
Sun 20	Wigan	A	2-1	18,820	42	4	Howard	Hibbert	**Lescott**	Jagielka	Valente	Arteta
Wed 23	Chelsea (CC SF, 2nd leg)	H	0-1	37,086	-	-	Howard	Neville	Lescott	Jagielka	Valente	Arteta
Wed 30	**Tottenham**	H	0-0	35,840	43	4	Howard	Neville	Lescott	Jagielka	Valente	Arteta
February												
Sat 2	Blackburn	A	0-0	27,946	44	4	Howard	Neville	Lescott	Jagielka	Baines	Arteta
Sat 9	**Reading**	H	1-0	36,582	47	4	Howard	Neville	Yobo	**Jagielka**	Lescott	Arteta
Wed 13	SK Brann (UEFA last 32, 1st leg)	A	2-0	16,207	-	-	Howard	Neville	Yobo	Jagielka	Lescott	**Osman**
Thurs 21	SK Brann (UEFA last 32, 2nd leg)	H	6-1	32,834	-	-	Howard	Neville	Jagielka	Lescott	Valente	**Arteta**
Mon 25	Man City	A	2-0	41,728	50	4	Howard	Hibbert	Yobo	Jagielka	**Lescott**	Osman
March												
Sun 2	**Portsmouth**	H	3-1	33,938	53	4	Howard	Hibbert ■	Yobo	Jagielka	Lescott	Osman
Thurs 6	Fiorentina (UEFA last 16, 1st leg)	A	0-2	32,934	-	-	Howard	Hibbert ■	Yobo	Jagielka	Lescott	Osman
Sun 8	Sunderland	A	1-0	42,595	56	5	Howard	Neville	Yobo	Jagielka	Lescott	Arteta
Wed 12	Fiorentina (UEFA last 16, 2nd leg)	H	2-0 ·	38,026	-	-	Howard	Neville	Yobo	Jagielka	Lescott	**Arteta**
Sun 16	Fulham	A	0-1	25,262	56	5	Howard	Neville	Yobo	Jagielka	Lescott	Arteta
Sat 22	**West Ham**	H	1-1	37,430	57	5	Howard	Neville	Jagielka	Lescott	Baines	Arteta
Sun 30	Liverpool	A	0-1	44,295	57	5	Howard	Hibbert	Yobo	Jagielka	Lescott	Arteta
April												
Sun 6	**Derby**	H	1-0	36,017	60	5	Howard	Neville	Yobo	Lescott	Baines	Arteta ■
Sat 12	Birmingham	A	1-1	25,923	61	5	Howard	Neville	**Lescott**	Jagielka	Baines	Pienaar
Thurs 17	Chelsea	H	0-1	37,112	61	5	Howard	Neville	Yobo	Jagielka	Lescott	Pienaar ■
Sun 27	**Aston Villa**	H	2-2	37,936	62	5	Howard	**Neville**	**Yobo**	Jagielka	Lescott	Pienaar
May												
Sun 4	Arsenal	A	0-1	60,123	62	5	Howard	Hibbert	Yobo	Jagielka	Lescott	Pienaar
Sun 11	**Newcastle**	H	3-1	39,592	65	5	Howard	Neville	Yobo	Jagielka	**Lescott**	Fernandes

+ Own goal   · After extra time   · Everton lost 4-2 on penalties

Substitutes

rsley	**Osman**	**Anichebe**	Johnson	Valente	Pienaar	Jagielka	Van der Meyde	Ruddy		
rsley	**Osman**	Anichebe	Johnson	Valente	Pienaar	Jagielka	McFadden	Ruddy		
rsley	Osman	Anichebe	Johnson	Baines	Pienaar	Jagielka	McFadden	Ruddy		
rsley	Osman	**McFadden**	Johnson	Lescott	Pienaar	Jagielka	Anichebe	Wessels		
sley	Pienaar	**Yakubu**	Johnson	Gravesen	Osman	McFadden	Anichebe	Wessels		
gielka	Osman	Yakubu	Johnson	Carsley	Pienaar	McFadden	Anichebe	Turner		
sley	McFadden	Yakubu	Johnson	Valente	Stubbs	Jagielka	Anichebe	Jutkiewicz	Vidarsson	Ruddy
gielka	Pienaar	Anichebe	Johnson	Valente	Carsley	McFadden	Yakubu	Ruddy		
gielka	Pienaar	**McFadden 2**	**Yakubu**	Baines	Neville	Johnson	Anichebe	Ruddy		
gielka	**Pienaar**	McFadden	Yakubu	Yobo	Carsley	Van der Meyde	Anichebe	Wessels		
gielka	Pienaar	**McFadden**	Yakubu	Hibbert	Baines	Valente	Carsley	**Anichebe**	Jutkiewicz	Wessels
sley	Pienaar	McFadden	Anichebe	Jagielka	Osman	**Johnson**	Yakubu	Wessels		
gielka	Osman	Anichebe	Yakubu	Baines	Pienaar	Carsley	McFadden	Wessels		
man	Pienaar	**Cahill**	McFadden	Valente	Stubbs	Jagielka	Gravesen	Yakubu	**Anichebe**	Wessels
man	Pienaar	Cahill	**Yakubu**	Stubbs	Gravesen	McFadden	Anichebe	Wessels		
man	Pienaar	McFadden	Anichebe	Graveson	**Cahill**	Vaughan	Yakubu	Howard		
man	Pienaar	Cahill	**Yakubu**	Jagielka	Gravesen	McFadden	**Vaughan**	Wessels		
man	Pienaar	Cahill	Yakubu	Hibbert	Jagielka	Gravesen	McFadden	**Anichebe**	Vidarsson	Wessels
ville	Pienaar	**Cahill**	Yakubu	Jagielka	Gravesen	McFadden	Anichebe	Wessels		
sley	**Pienaar**	**Cahill 2**	**Yakubu 2**	Jagielka	Gravesen	**Johnson**	Anichebe	Wessels		
sley	Pienaar	Cahill	Yakubu	Hibbert	Jagielka	Johnson	Anichebe	Wessels		
sley	Pienaar	Johnson	McFadden	Boyle	Gravesen	Osman	Anichebe	Yakubu	Vaughan	Wessels
sley	Pienaar	Cahill	**Yakubu 3**	Jagielka	Johnson	McFadden	Anichebe	Wessels		
sley	Pienaar	Cahill	**Yakubu**	Hibbert	Gravesen	**Johnson**	Anichebe	McFadden		
naar	McFadden	**Johnson**	Anichebe	Boyle	Irving	Rodwell	Vidarsson	Jutkiewicz	**Vaughan**	Ruddy
sley	Pienaar	Johnson	Yakubu	Gravesen	Anichebe	Valente	McFadden	Wessels		
sley	Pienaar	**Cahill**	Yakubu	Johnson	Hibbert	Vaughan	Valente	Wessels		
sley	Pienaar	**Cahill**	Yakubu	Johnson	Anichebe	Vaughan	Valente	Wessels		
sley	Pienaar	**Johnson**	Yakubu	Baines	Vaughan	Anichebe	Stubbs	Wessels		
sley	McFadden	Vaughan	Johnson	Lescott	Silva de Franca	Anichebe	Yakubu	Ruddy		
sley	McFadden	Johnson	**Yakubu**	Valente	Gravesen	Anichebe	Vaughan	Wessels		
ille	McFadden	Cahill	Anichebe	Baines	Stubbs	Gravesen	Vaughan	Ruddy		
ille	Osman	Cahill	**Johnson**	Stubbs	Fernandes	Anichebe	Vaughan	Wessels		
nandes	Osman	Cahill	Johnson	Hibbert	Stubbs	Anichebe	Vaughan	Wessels		
nandes	Baines	Anichebe	Johnson	Stubbs	Van der Meyde	de Franca	Vaughan	Wessels		
nandes	Osman	Cahill	Johnson	Hibbert	Valente	Vaughan	Anichebe	Wessels		
nandes	Osman	Cahill	Johnson	Hibbert	Valente	Van der Meyde	Vaughan	Wessels		
ill	Fernandes	Yakubu	Johnson	Hibbert	Baines	Rodwell	Van der Meyde	**Anichebe**	Vaughan	Wessels
ill	Pienaar	**Yakubu 3**	**Johnson 2**	Hibbert	Baines	Osman	Fernandes	Anichebe	Vaughan	Wessels
ille	Pienaar	Cahill	**Yakubu**	Valente	Fernandes	Johnson	Anichebe	Wessels		
ille	Pienaar	**Cahill**	**Yakubu 2**	Baines	Johnson	Anichebe	Vaughan	Wessels		
ille	Pienaar	Cahill	Yakubu	Baines	Arteta	Gravesen	Johnson	Anichebe	Gosling	Wessels
ill	Pienaar	**Johnson**	Yakubu	Baines	Rodwell	Gravesen	Anichebe	Turner		
han	Pienaar	**Johnson**	Yakubu	Baines	Valente	Hibbert	Rodwell	Gravesen	Anichebe	Wessels
han	Pienaar	Johnson	Yakubu	Baines	Valente	Hibbert	Rodwell	Wessels		
ill	Osman	Anichebe	**Yakubu**	Hibbert	Valente	Fernandes	Gravesen	Wessels		
ille	Pienaar	Osman	Yakubu	Baines	Valente	Fernandes	Gravesen	Wessels		
nandes	**Osman**	Johnson	Yakubu	Valente	Jagielka	Gravesen	Anichebe	Wessels		
ille	Fernandes	Johnson	Yakubu	Yobo	Valente	Gravesen	Anichebe	Wessels		
ille	Fernandes	Johnson	Yakubu	Baines	Rodwell	Gravesen	Anichebe	Wessels		
han	Fernandes	Johnson	Yakubu	Arteta	Anichebe	Baines	Hibbert	Wessels		
ille	Osman	Fernandes	Johnson	Yakubu	Anichebe	Baines	Rodwell	Wessels		
han	Pienaar	Anichebe	**Yakubu 2**	Baines	Gravesen	Rodwell	Gosling	Wessels		

2007/2008 STATISTICS

TOTAL APPEARANCES

	LEAGUE			FA CUP			LGE CUP			UEFA CUP			TOTAL		
	ST	SB	TO	ST	SB	TO	ST	SB	TO	ST	SB	TO	ST	SB	TO
ANICHEBE VICTOR	10	17	**27**	0	1	**1**	1	3	**4**	1	8	**9**	12	29	**41**
ARTETA MIKEL	27	1	**28**	0	0	**0**	2	0	**2**	6	1	**7**	35	2	**37**
BAINES LEIGHTON	13	9	**22**	1	0	**1**	0	1	**1**	3	2	**5**	17	12	**29**
CAHILL TIM	18	0	**18**	0	0	**0**	3	1	**4**	6	0	**6**	27	1	**28**
CARSLEY LEE	33	1	**34**	1	0	**1**	5	0	**5**	9	0	**9**	48	1	**49**
FERNANDES MANUEL	9	3	**12**	0	0	**0**	1	0	**1**	1	1	**2**	11	4	**15**
GRAVESEN THOMAS	1	7	**8**	1	0	**1**	0	1	**1**	1	2	**3**	3	10	**13**
HIBBERT TONY	22	2	**24**	1	0	**1**	2	0	**2**	4	4	**8**	29	6	**35**
HOWARD TIM	36	0	**36**	0	0	**0**	3	0	**3**	8	0	**8**	47	0	**47**
JAGIELKA PHIL	27	7	**34**	1	0	**1**	5	0	**5**	7	2	**9**	40	9	**49**
JOHNSON ANDREW	20	9	**29**	1	0	**1**	2	0	**2**	6	1	**7**	29	10	**39**
LESCOTT JOLEON	37	1	**38**	0	1	**1**	5	0	**5**	10	0	**10**	52	2	**54**
McFADDEN JAMES	5	7	**12**	1	0	**1**	3	0	**3**	5	0	**5**	14	7	**21**
NEVILLE PHIL	37	0	**37**	0	0	**0**	4	1	**5**	8	0	**8**	49	1	**50**
OSMAN LEON	26	2	**28**	0	0	**0**	4	0	**4**	7	0	**7**	37	2	**39**
PIENAAR STEVEN	25	3	**28**	1	0	**1**	3	0	**3**	8	0	**8**	37	3	**40**
RODWELL JACK	0	2	**2**	0	0	**0**	0	0	**0**	0	1	**1**	0	3	**3**
STUBBS ALAN	7	1	**8**	1	0	**1**	2	0	**2**	1	1	**2**	11	2	**13**
VALENTE NUNO	8	1	**9**	0	0	**0**	3	0	**3**	3	0	**3**	14	1	**15**
VAUGHAN JAMES	0	8	**8**	1	0	**1**	0	2	**2**	0	2	**2**	1	12	**13**
VIDARSSON BJARNI	0	0	**0**	0	0	**0**	0	0	**0**	0	1	**1**	0	1	**1**
WESSELS STEFAN	2	0	**2**	1	0	**1**	2	0	**2**	2	0	**2**	7	0	**7**
YAKUBU AYEGBENI	26	3	**29**	0	1	**1**	3	0	**3**	7	0	**7**	36	4	**40**
YOBO JOSEPH	29	1	**30**	0	0	**0**	2	0	**2**	7	0	**7**	38	1	**39**

* ST - Starts, SB - Substitute Appearances, TO - Total Appearances

MINUTES ON THE PITCH: PREMIER LEAGUE 2007/08

PLAYER	MINS	PLAYER	MINS
JOLEON LESCOTT	3,374	TIM CAHILL	1,514
TIM HOWARD	3,269	LEIGHTON BAINES	1,146
PHIL NEVILLE	3,266	VICTOR ANICHEBE	1,086
LEE CARSLEY	2,689	MANUEL FERNANDES	853
PHIL JAGIELKA	2,677	NUNO VALENTE	728
JOSEPH YOBO	2,631	ALAN STUBBS	562
MIKEL ARTETA	2,471	JAMES MCFADDEN	471
LEON OSMAN	2,336	STEFAN WESSELS	182
AYEGBENI YAKUBU	2,171	THOMAS GRAVESEN	173
STEVEN PIENAAR	2,104	JAMES VAUGHAN	147
TONY HIBBERT	1,942	JACK RODWELL	4
ANDREW JOHNSON	1,864		

2007/2008 STATISTICS

PLAYER GOALS

	LEAGUE	FA CUP	LEAGUE CUP	UEFA CUP	TOTAL
YAKUBU	15	0	3	3	21
LESCOTT	8	0	0	2	10
JOHNSON	6	0	0	4	10
CAHILL	7	0	1	2	10
OSMAN	4	0	1	2	7
McFADDEN	2	0	2	1	5
ANICHEBE	1	0	0	4	5
ARTETA	1	0	0	3	4
NEVILLE	2	0	0	0	2
OWN GOAL	2	0	0	0	2
PIENAAR	2	0	0	0	2
JAGIELKA	1	0	0	1	2
VAUGHAN	1	0	0	1	2
CARSLEY	1	0	0	0	1
STUBBS	1	0	0	0	1
YOBO	1	0	0	0	1
TOTAL	**55**	**0**	**7**	**23**	**85**

FINAL TABLE

BARCLAYS PREMIERSHIP STANDINGS

			HOME				AWAY						
Team	PLD	W	D	L	F	A	W	D	L	F	A	PTS	GD
1 MAN UTD	38	17	1	1	47	7	10	5	4	33	15	87	+58
2 CHELSEA	38	12	7	0	36	13	13	3	3	29	13	85	+39
3 ARSENAL	38	14	5	0	37	11	10	6	3	37	20	83	+43
4 LIVERPOOL	38	12	6	1	43	13	9	7	3	24	15	76	+39
5 EVERTON	**38**	**11**	**4**	**4**	**34**	**17**	**8**	**4**	**7**	**21**	**16**	**65**	**+22**
6 ASTON VILLA	38	10	3	6	34	22	6	9	4	37	29	60	+20
7 BLACKBURN	38	8	7	4	26	19	7	6	6	24	29	58	+2
8 PORTSMOUTH	38	7	8	4	24	14	9	1	9	24	26	57	+8
9 MAN CITY	38	11	4	4	28	20	4	6	9	17	33	55	-8
10 WEST HAM	38	7	7	5	24	24	6	3	10	18	26	49	-8
11 TOTTENHAM	38	8	5	6	46	34	3	8	8	20	27	46	+5
12 NEWCASTLE	38	8	5	6	25	26	3	5	11	20	39	43	-20
13 M'BORO	38	7	5	7	27	23	3	7	9	16	30	42	-10
14 WIGAN	38	8	5	6	21	17	2	5	12	13	34	40	-17
15 SUNDERLAND	38	9	3	7	23	21	2	3	14	13	38	39	-23
16 BOLTON	38	7	5	7	23	18	2	5	12	13	36	37	-18
17 FULHAM	38	5	5	9	22	31	3	7	9	16	29	36	-22
18 READING	38	8	2	9	19	25	2	4	13	22	41	36	-25
19 BIRMINGHAM	38	6	8	5	30	23	2	3	14	16	39	35	-16
20 DERBY	38	1	5	13	12	43	0	3	16	8	46	11	-69

APPEARANCES & GOALS FOR EVERTON

includes substitute appearances

CURRENT PLAYING STAFF AND THOSE WHO LEFT THE CLUB DURING 2007/08

	LEAGUE		FA CUP		LGE CUP		EUROPE		EFC CAREER	
	GMS	GLS	GMS	GLS	GMS	GLS	GMS	GLS	GMS	GLS
ANICHEBE	48	5	3	0	7	1	9	4	67	10
ARTETA	104	12	6	1	6	0	10	4	126	17
BAINES	22	0	1	0	1	0	5	0	29	0
CAHILL	101	29	5	2	10	3	10	3	126	37
CARSLEY	166	12	9	0	14	1	9	0	198	13
SILVA DE FRANCA	1	0	0	0	0	0	0	0	1	0
FERNANDES	21	2	0	0	1	0	2	0	24	2
GRAVESEN	149	11	9	0	7	1	3	0	168	12
HIBBERT	164	0	10	0	11	0	12	0	197	0
HOWARD	72	0	1	0	4	0	8	0	85	0
JAGIELKA	34	1	1	0	5	0	9	1	49	2
JOHNSON	61	17	2	1	4	0	7	4	74	22
LESCOTT	76	10	2	0	8	0	10	2	96	12
MCFADDEN	109	11	9	3	12	3	9	1	139	18
NEVILLE	106	3	5	0	8	0	12	0	131	3
OSMAN	132	17	8	2	11	1	9	2	160	22
PIENAAR	28	2	1	0	3	0	8	0	40	2
RODWELL	2	0	0	0	0	0	1	0	3	0
RUDDY	1	0	0	0	0	0	0	0	1	0
STUBBS	169	6	12	1	10	0	2	0	193	7
TURNER	4	0	1	0	1	0	0	0	6	0
VALENTE	43	0	5	0	5	0	5	0	58	0
VAN DER MEYDE	18	0	1	0	2	0	0	0	21	0
VAUGHAN	25	6	2	0	2	0	2	1	31	7
VIDARSSON	0	0	0	0	0	0	1	0	1	0
WESSELS	2	0	1	0	2	0	2	0	7	0
YAKUBU	29	15	1	0	3	3	7	3	40	21
YOBO	176	6	5	0	11	0	11	1	203	7

Tony Hibbert - Approaching 200 appearances for the Blues

MAN OF THE SEASON

Joleon Lescott deservedly secured the club's Player of the Year accolade after an outstanding season which saw the defender reach a career-best double-figure goals tally - as well as winning the first of five England caps.
Other awards went to Victor Anichebe, who was named Young Player of the Year, while Leon Osman's strike against AE Larissa secured him the Goal of the Season prize.

Joleon Lescott shows off his Player of the Year trophies at the end-of-season awards

PLAYER HIGHLIGHTS

There were several different player records to recognise following the 2007/08 campaign - here are just a select few to mull over:

JOLEON'S EVER-PRESENT RECORD

Everton played a total of 96 games in the 2006/07 and 2007/08 seasons, and remarkably Joleon Lescott appeared in every one of those matches. In doing so, the England international defender became the first outfielder since Joe Royle (1968/69-1969/70) to feature in every match of two successive seasons, and in 2007 he became the first outfielder since Peter Reid and Derek Mountfield (both 1984) to appear in every single game of a calendar year.
Only Dennis Stevens (1962/63-1963/64) and George Wood (1977/78-1978/79) in the modern era can match Lescott's achievement of being ever-present in their first two seasons with Everton.

MOST SUCCESSIVE APPEARANCES FROM BEGINNING OF EVERTON CAREER

	GAMES	FIRST GAME-LAST SUCCESSIVE GAME
Jack Taylor	135	(September 1896-March 1900)
George Wood	120	(August 1977-November 1979)
Dennis Stevens	112	(March 1962-August 1964)
Joleon Lescott	96	(August 2006-May 2008)*
Albert Dunlop	65	(October 1956-February 1958)
Gary Ablett	61	(January 1992-March 1993)

(* Unfinished run at start of 2008/09 campaign)

PLAYER HIGHLIGHTS

TIM SETS NEW MARK

At the end of the 2007/08 season, Tim Howard had conceded just 74 goals in his first 85 games for the Toffees, an average of 0.87 goals per match – the lowest by any keeper with more than 25 games for the club.

The 3-1 victory over Birmingham City in November 2007 marked the goalkeeper's 50th appearance for the club and the American international reached that landmark having conceded fewer goals – 48 in total - than any other Everton keeper in history.

FEWEST GOALS CONCEDED ON AVERAGE BY EVERTON GOALKEEPERS

	GAMES	GOALS CONCEDED	AVERAGE
Tim Howard	85	74	0.87
Bobby Mimms	37	33	0.89
Gordon West	402	407	1.01
George Wood	126	134	1.06
Jim Arnold	59	64	1.08
Neville Southall	750	841	1.12
George Kitchen	88	103	1.17
Dai Davies	94	116	1.23

Tim Howard - Best Everton average

PLAYER HIGHLIGHTS

YAK JOINS A UNIQUE CLUB

In 2007/08 Ayegbeni Yakubu became only the sixth Everton player – and only the fourth since the start of the 20th century – to record 20 or more goals in the season of their first-team debut. The Nigerian international's 21 goals – the best in a single campaign by any Everton player for 17 years – included just one penalty.

Gary Lineker leads the way in what was an astonishing single season with the club in 1985/86, while Fred Geary and Jack Southworth were ruthless marksmen of the Victorian era.

MOST GOALS IN SEASON OF DEBUT

	GOALS	SEASON
Gary Lineker	40	1985/86
Jack Southworth	27	1893/94
Fred Geary	25	1889/90
Jimmy Harris	21	1955/56
Ayegbeni Yakubu	21	2007/08
Peter Beardsley	20	1991/92

Ayegbeni Yakubu joins a select group after heading his 20th goal of the season

EVERTON OBITUARIES

JIMMY O'NEILL

Born: 13th October 1931 - Died: 15th December 2007
213 games (1949-60)

Born in Dublin, Jimmy O'Neill was Everton's regular keeper in the first half of the 1950s, after signing professionally in 1949. The Irishman's debut in August 1950 was one to forget as a poor Everton side – later to be relegated – went down 4-0 against Middlesbrough. But O'Neill, like the club, bounced back in 1954 as promotion was gained under Cliff Britton. After losing the goalkeeping jersey to Albert Dunlop in October 1956, he played only 19 times in the next four years before moving to Stoke City for £5,000 in the summer of 1960. Three years later O'Neill was an ever-present in a promotion-winning side that featured Stanley Matthews. Further appearances followed for Darlington and Port Vale before this fine goalkeeper retired in 1967.

Jimmy was a regular and popular visitor to Goodison over the years, and lived in Ormskirk in retirement.

JACK KEELEY

Born: 16th October 1936 - Died: December 2007
7 games, 3 goals (1957-58)

After progressing through the youth ranks, local-born Jack Keeley scored on his debut against Bolton on Boxing Day 1957, and the following month netted twice in a home FA Cup win over Sunderland. The forward then went on to Accrington Stanley before ending his career at Southport.

WALLY FIELDING

Born: 26th November 1919 - Died: 18th January 2008
410 games, 54 goals (1945-1959)

Born Alfred Walter Fielding, the London-born midfield player was a club stalwart for almost 15 years in the aftermath of World War II. "Nobby" Fielding was a marvellously skilful ball-player who was unlucky not to win an international cap, his sole post-war honour being an appearance in the unofficial England v Scotland game in Manchester played in aid of the Bolton Disaster fund in 1946.

Although ostensibly a creator of goals, Fielding – who always played with his sleeves down, buttoned at the wrist – still managed to net more than 50 times, and his strike at West Bromwich Albion in October 1958 made him, at 38 years 305 days, the club's oldest goalscorer. Two weeks later, he played his final match in the 10-4 drubbing at Tottenham Hotspur, before ending his career at Southport. Nobby later settled in Cornwall but remained very much an Evertonian at heart, and he was a welcome guest at various club functions over the years.

Everton Former Players' Foundation trustee Reverend Harry Ross paid this tribute:

"Wally was a wonderful man and it was our privilege to help him through the last few years of his life. The Foundation paid for his meals and health care, and I know that he was always extremely grateful for everything we did. Everyone who has ever attended one of our events or contributed in any way should be proud that they helped such a great man and a great Evertonian."

Wally died aged 88 in January 2008, and there was a period of silence in his memory before the Carling Cup semi-final, second-leg tie against Chelsea at Goodison Park.

EVERTON OBITUARIES

ALAN TYRER

Born: 8th December 1942 - Died: January 2008
10 games, 2 goals (1960-1961)

Alan Tyrer made history in January 1960 when making his debut against Fulham aged just 17 years and 40 days, making him at the time the youngest player to appear for Everton. A small, mobile forward, his first-team chances were limited by John Moores' bankrolled spending of the early 1960s. The local-born Tyrer left for Mansfield in 1963 and had subsequent spells at Bury, Arsenal and Workington.

BRIAN HARRIS

Born: 16th March 1935 - Died: 17th February 2008
360 games, 29 goals (1955-1966)

Everton memories of Brian Harris go far beyond his contribution to the 1963 title-winning side and his role in the FA Cup final team three years later. For whether it was trying on a policeman's hat at Wembley in 1966, or playing the role of court jester on an Australian TV show on an end-of-season tour two years earlier, the midfielder brought a sense of fun to even the most tense occasions.

But those tales should not distract from the fact that the Bebington-born player was a fine midfielder who served the Blue half of Merseyside with distinction for more than a decade. After starting out as a right-winger, it was only when he moved to the left-hand side of midfield in 1958 that he became an indispensable part of the team. That remained the case until the arrival of Tony Kay in 1962, but when the former Sheffield Wednesday player exited the game two years later, Harris regained his place and served as a utility player until his Everton departure in October 1966.

After moving to Cardiff City, he enjoyed a more successful and varied career than most after leaving Goodison. He helped the Bluebirds reach the semi-final of the European Cup Winners' Cup in 1968, and became player-coach at Newport County in 1971 until retiring three years later, when Everton provided the opposition in a well-deserved testimonial. After a spell as Newport manager and Cardiff coach, Harris settled in Chepstow, where he passed away after a short illness.

At the specific request of his family, Brian's funeral service took place at St Luke's Church, adjacent to Goodison Park.

Brian (back left) pictured with his 1966 FA Cup-winning team-mates

10

Unhappy Hammers

Two wins in four days at Upton Park: one league, one Cup. Yakubu's late winner in the League Cup secured the Blues a place in the semi-finals of the competition for the first time in 20 years.

9

Yak first

The Nigerian striker's hat-trick in the 3-0 victory over Fulham back in December was the first by an Everton player in over four years.

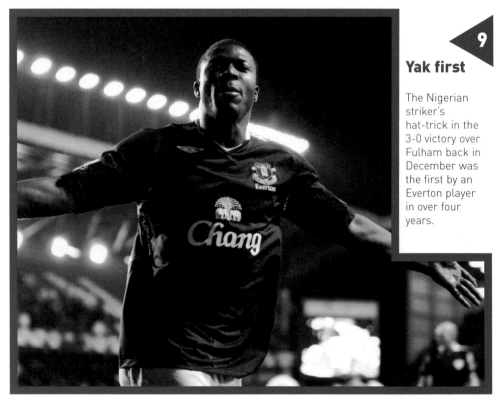

Six of the best

Despite SK Brann proving modest opposition, any 6-1 success should be recognised, and this match is no exception. Another Yakubu hat-trick, this 25-yard Andy Johnson thunderbolt and the fact that it is the club's record European win are reason enough.

Top start

One of the Blues' least-favourite away grounds, the impressive August win at White Hart Lane was the second in a row for David Moyes and his team. This Leon Osman strike was the pick of the goals in a 3-1 success.

Late, late show

Having surrendered a 1-0 lead in the last 10 minutes, a draw with Birmingham looked likely. Enter Lee Carsley and James Vaughan, who memorably intervened in stoppage time to earn a 3-1 win - the first time ever that the Blues have achieved the feat of two goals so late in a game.

Goal of the season

Cahill's pass inside the full-back finds Baines' overlapping run, ball inside to Pienaar, first-time back heel into the path of the onrushing Leon Osman and from over 20 yards out, the sweetest first-time shot curls inside the AE Larissa keeper's right-hand post - a wonderful end to a wonderful move.

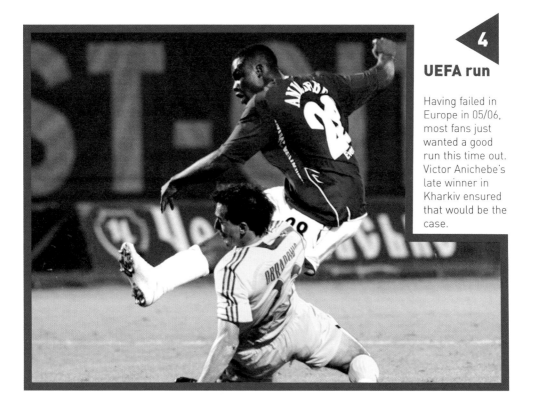

4

UEFA run

Having failed in Europe in 05/06, most fans just wanted a good run this time out. Victor Anichebe's late winner in Kharkiv ensured that would be the case.

3

Penalties... again

The extreme high of the 2-0 win - a dominant display when the team gave their all - was followed by the low of penalty shoot-out disappointment. The AC Fiorentina second leg at Goodison in March will live long in the memory.

2

A warm German welcome

Rarely has an Everton away day anywhere been enjoyed as much as November in Nurnberg. The biggest Evertonian away invasion since Rotterdam in '85, welcoming locals and a 2-0 win made it a memorable occasion for all concerned.

Seventh heaven/Magnificent seven/seven-up...

Yes, whatever 'seven' headline you use, it would not do justice to a unique Goodison occasion against Sunderland. Oozing confidence, the Blues produced some memorable football, quality goals and a 7-1 scoreline - the first time they had achieved the feat in 11 years.

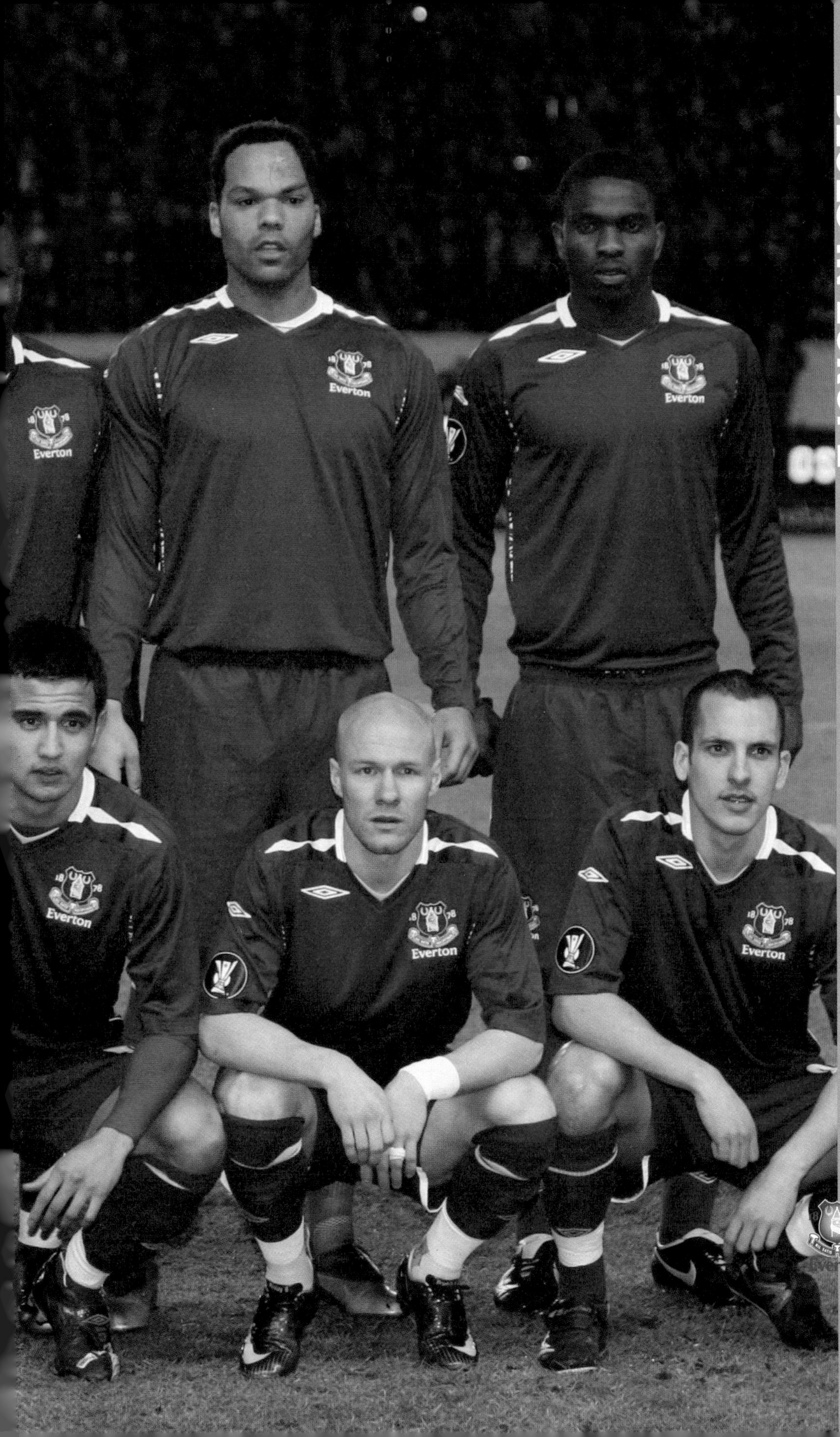

Team line-ups

Everton (4-4-2)

Yakubu Johnson

McFadden Neville Carsley Osman

Baines Lescott Yobo Hibbert

Wessels

Subs: Anichebe (Yakubu) 66, Jagielka (Carsley) 78
Subs not used: Ruddy, Stubbs, Valente, Jutkiewicz, Vidarsson

Metalist Kharkiv (4-4-2):

Rykun Nwoha

Devic Valyayev Slyusar Gueye

Obradovic Gancarczyk Babych Bordiyan

Goryainov

Subs: Antonov (Nwoha) 59, Edmar (Rykun) 67, Mahdoufi (Antonov) 77
Subs not used: Tlumak, Danilau, Zeze, Davydov

EVERTON 1
M. KHARKIV 1

Goodison Park
UEFA Cup,
First round, 1st Leg
Thursday September 20, 2007.
Attendance: 37,120

Goals: Lescott (24), Edmar (78)
Bookings: Anichebe (Everton), Obradovic, Bordiyan (Metalist Kharkiv)
Sendings-off: Gancarczyk, Babych (Metalist Kharkiv)

Referee: Fritz Stuchlik (Austria)

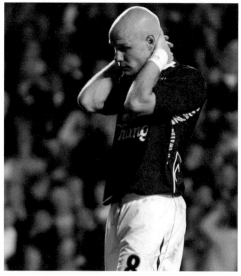

Team line-ups

Metalist Kharkiv (4-4-2):

Rykun Slyusur

Devic Valyayev Edmar Jakobia

Mahdoufi Gueye Mdrakovic Bordiyan

Goryainov

Subs: Danilau (Jakobia) 75, Nwoha (Bordiyan) 85, Zeze (Devic) 89
Subs not used: Tlumak, Davydov, Kostyuk, Svitiychnyi

Everton (4-4-1-1)

Yakubu

McFadden

Pienaar Arteta
Osman
Jagielka

Lescott Neville
Stubbs Yobo

Howard

Subs: Anichebe (Jagielka) 62, Baines (Yakubu) 76, Hibbert (McFadden) 90
Subs not used: Wessels, Valente, Carsley, Jutkiewicz

M. KHARKIV   2
EVERTON   3

Metalist Stadium
UEFA Cup,
First round, 2nd Leg
Thursday October 4, 2007.
Attendance: 27,500

Goals: Edmar (21), Lescott (48), Mahdoufi (52), McFadden (72), Anichebe (88)
Bookings: Danilav (Metalist Kharkiv), Neville, Baines (Everton)
Referee: Jouni Hyytia (Finland)

Team line-ups

Everton (4-1-4-1):

McFadden
Cahill
Pienaar Osman Arteta
Carsley
Baines Lescott Yobo Hibbert
Howard

Subs: Anichebe (McFadden) 65, Gravesen (Cahill) 65, Stubbs (Pienaar) 87
Subs not used: Wessels, Valente, Jagielka, Yakubu

AE Larissa (4-4-1-1):

Bakayoko
Parra
Kiriakidis Sarmiento Fotakis Cleyton
Venetidis Foerster Dabizas Galitsios
Kotsolis

Subs: Kalatzis (Parra) 58, Lampropoulos (Kiriakidis) 75, Venetis (Foerster) 79
Subs not used: Kipouros, Kotsios, Gikas, Katsiaros

EVERTON   3
AE LARISSA   1

Goodison Park
UEFA Cup,
Group stage, matchday 1
Thursday October 25, 2007.
Attendance: 33,777

Goals: Cahill (14), Osman (50), Cleyton (65), Anichebe (85)
Bookings: Lescott, Yobo, Gravesen (Everton), Dabizas (AE Larissa)

Referee: Martin Ingvarsson (Sweden)

Team line-ups

1. FC Nurnberg (4-4-1-1):

Saenko
Mintal
Misimovic, Mnari, Galasek, Kluge
Reinhardt, Wolf, Glauber, Schmidt
Blazek

Subs: Kennedy (Schmidt) 76, Pagenburg (Saenko) 85, Benko (Glauber) 86
Subs not used: Klewer, Beauchamp, Kristiansen, Engelhardt

Everton (4-4-1-1):

Yakubu
Cahill
Pienaar, Osman, Carsley, Arteta
Valente, Lescott, Yobo, Neville
Howard

Subs: Anichebe (Yakubu) 75, Jagielka (Cahill) 90, Hibbert (Pienaar) 90
Subs not used: Wessels, Gravesen, Vidarsson, McFadden

1. FC NURNBERG 0
EVERTON 2

Frankenstadion
UEFA Cup,
Group stage, matchday 2
Thursday November 8, 2007.
Attendance: 43,000

Goals: Arteta (83, pen), Anichebe (88)
Bookings: Glauber, Blazek (1. FC Nurnberg), Valente, Yobo (Everton)

Referee: Alberto Undiano Mallenco (Spain)

Team line-ups

Everton (4-4-2):

McFadden
Johnson

Pienaar
Cahill
Carsley
Arteta

Baines
Lescott
Jagielka
Neville

Howard

Subs: Anichebe (McFadden) 64, Vaughan (Johnson) 81
Subs not used: Wessels, Boyle, Gravesen, Osman, Yakubu

Zenit St. Petersburg (4-3-2-1):

Dominguez

Arshavin
Pogrebnyak

Sirl
Zyrianov
Tymoschuk

Dong Jin
Lombaerts
Skrtel
Anyukov

Malafeev

Subs: Gorshkov (Dominguez) 45, Hagen (Pogrebnyak) 61, Ho (Anyukov) 78
Subs not used: Contofalsky, Radimov, Ionov, Lebedev

EVERTON 1
ZENIT ST. P'BURG 0

Goodison Park
UEFA Cup,
Group stage, matchday 4
Wednesday December 5, 2007.
Attendance: 38,407

Goal: Cahill (85)
Bookings: Johnson (Everton), Pogrebnyak, Sirl (Zenit St. Petersburg)
Sending-off: Lombaerts (Zenit St. Petersburg)

Referee: Kristinn Jakobsson (Iceland)

EVERTON
FOOTBALL CLUB

Team line-ups

AZ Alkmaar (4-4-2):

Pelle — Dembele

da Silva — de Zeeuw — Vormer — Cziommer

Pocognoli — Opdam — Jaliens — Steinsson

Waterman

Subs: Jenner (de Zeeuw) 63, El-Hamdaoui (Cziommer) 64, Agustien (Pocognoli) 77
Subs not used: Klewer, Beauchamp, Kristiansen, Engelhardt

Everton (4-4-2):

Anichebe — Johnson

McFadden — Carsley — Gravesen — Pienaar

Valente — Lescott — Jagielka — Hibbert

Wessels

Subs: Vidarsson (Pienaar) 68, Vaughan (Johnson) 68, Rodwell (Gravesen) 80
Subs not used: Ruddy, Boyle, Irving, Jutkiewicz

AZ ALKMAAR 2
EVERTON 3

DSB Stadion
UEFA Cup,
Group stage, matchday 5
Thursday December 20, 2007.
Attendance: 16,578

Goals: Johnson (2), Pelle (17), Jagielka (44),
Jaliens (66), Vaughan (80)
Bookings: Hibbert, Wessels (Everton)

Referee: Selcuk Dereli (Turkey)

97

Team line-ups

SK Brann (4-4-2):

Helstad Karadas

Moen El-Fakiri Bakke Solli

Hanstveit Sigurdsson Bjarnason Dahl

Opdal

Subs: Demba-Nyren (Karadas) 69, Huseklepp (El-Fakiri) 75, Thwaite (Dahl) 89
Subs not used: Udjus, Guntveit, Misje, Winters

Everton (4-1-3-2):

Yakubu Johnson

Osman Cahill Fernandes

Carsley

Lescott Jagielka Yobo Neville

Howard

Subs: Anichebe (Johnson) 76, Hibbert (Fernandes) 89, Baines (Yakubu) 90
Subs not used: Wessels, Rodwell, van der Meyde, Vaughan

SK BRANN 0
EVERTON 2

Brann Stadion
UEFA Cup,
Round of 32, 1st Leg
Wednesday February 13, 2008.
Attendance: 16,207

Goals: Osman (59), Anichebe (88)
Booking: Fernandes (Everton)

Referee: Anton Genov (Bulgaria)

Team line-ups

Everton (4-4-2):

Yakubu   Johnson

Pienaar   Cahill   Arteta
Carsley

Valente   Neville
Lescott   Jagielka

Howard

Subs: Fernandes (Cahill) 46, Hibbert (Carsley) 46, Anichebe (Yakubu) 73
Subs not used: Wessels, Baines, Osman, Vaughan

SK Brann (4-4-2):

Helstad Demba-Nyren

Moen   El-Fakiri   Bakke   Solli

Hanstveit Sigurdsson Bjarnason   Dahl

Opdal

Subs: Huseklepp (El-Fakiri) 60, Karadas (Bjarnason) 65, Winters (Demba-Nyren) 72
Subs not used: Udjus, Guntveit, Einarsson, Thwaite

EVERTON 6
SK BRANN 1

Goodison Park
UEFA Cup,
Round of 32, 2nd Leg
Thursday February 21, 2008.
Attendance: 32,834

Goals: Yakubu (36, 54, 72), Johnson (41, 90), Moen (60), Arteta (70)
Bookings: Fernandes (Everton), Bakke (SK Brann)

Referee: Nikolay Ivanov (Russia)

Team line-ups

AC Fiorentina (4-3-3):

Jorgensen, Vieri, Osvaldo

Montolivo, Donadel, Kuzmanovic

Pasqual, Dainelli, Gamberini, Ujfalusi

Frey

Subs: Pazzini (Vieri) 67, Santana (Osvaldo) 74, Gobbi (Kuzmanovic) 76
Subs not used: Avramov, Kroldrup, Potenza, Cacia

Everton (4-4-1-1):

Yakubu

Cahill

Pienaar, Neville, Carsley, Osman

Lescott, Jagielka, Yobo, Hibbert

Howard

Subs: Arteta (Osman) 56, Johnson (Hibbert) 73, Hibbert (Pienaar) 90
Subs not used: Wessels, Baines, Gosling, Gravesen, Anichebe

AC FIORENTINA 2
EVERTON 0

Stadio Artemio Franchi
UEFA Cup,
Round of 16, 1st Leg
Thursday March 6, 2008.
Attendance: 32,934

Goals: Kuzmanovic (70), Montolivo (81)
Bookings: Ujfalusi, Gobbi (AC Fiorentina), Yakubu, Pienaar, Howard (Everton)

Referee: Paul Allaerts (Belgium)

Team line-ups

Everton (4-4-2):

Yakubu　Johnson

Pienaar　Osman　•Carsley　Arteta

Lescott　Jagielka　Yobo　Neville

Howard

Subs: Anichebe (Pienaar) 106, Gravesen (Johnson) 119
Subs not used: Wessels, Hibbert, Valente, Baines, Rodwell

AC Fiorentina (4-5-1):

Vieri

Jorgensen　Osvaldo

Montolivo　Donadel　Kuzmanovic

Pasqual　Dainelli　Gamberini　Ujfalusi

Frey

Subs: Pazzini (Vieri) 46, Gobbi (Kuzmanovic) 91, Santana (Jorgensen) 106
Subs not used: Avramov, Kroldrup, Potenza, Cacia

EVERTON　　2
AC FIORENTINA　0
(AC Fiorentina win 4-2 on penalties)

Goodison Park
UEFA Cup,
Round of 16, 2nd leg
Wednesday March 12, 2008.
Attendance: 38,026

Goals: Johnson (15), Arteta (67)
Bookings: Yobo, Yakubu (Everton), Dainelli, Montolivo, Pazzini, Gamberini, Jorgensen
Penalties: Gravesen (1-0), Pazzini (1-1), Yakubu (1-1), Montolivo (1-2), Arteta (2-2), Osvaldo (2-3), Jagielka (2-3), Santana (2-4)

Referee: Eric Braamhaar (Holland)

EVERTON'S RESULTS IN EUROPEAN COMPETITION

Season & Date	Round	Venue	Opponents	Opponent Country	Score	Scorers	Attendance
1962/63	**INTER-CITIES FAIRS CUP (WINNERS - VALENCIA)**						
24th Oct	1 Leg 1	(h)	Dunfermline Ath.	Sco	1-0	Stevens	40,244
31st Oct	1 Leg 2	(a)	Dunfermline Ath.	"	0-2		21,813
1963/64	**EUROPEAN CHAMPIONS CUP (WINNERS - INTER MILAN)**						
18th Sept	1 Leg 1	(h)	Inter Milan	Ita	0-0		62,408
25th Sept	1 Leg 2	(a)	Inter Milan	"	0-1		70,000
1964/65	**INTER-CITIES FAIRS CUP (WINNERS - FERENCVAROS)**						
23rd Sept	1 Leg 1	(a)	Valerengens IF	Nor	5-2	Pickering 2, Harvey, Temple, Scott	17,952
14th Oct	1 Leg 2	(h)	Valerengens IF	"	4-2	Young 2, Hansen (og), Vernon	20,717
11th Nov	2 Leg 1	(a)	Kilmarnock	Sco	2-0	Temple, Morrissey	20,000
23rd Nov	2 Leg 2	(h)	Kilmarnock	"	4-1	Harvey, Pickering 2, Young	30,727
20th Jan	3 Leg 1	(a)	Manchester Utd	Eng	1-1	Pickering	49,075
4th Feb	3 Leg 2	(h)	Manchester Utd	"	1-2	Pickering	54,397
1965/66	**INTER-CITIES FAIRS CUP (WINNERS - BARCELONA)**						
28th Sept	1 Leg 1	(a)	1. FC Nurnberg	W. Ger	1-1	Harris	10,000
12th Oct	1 Leg 2	(h)	1. FC Nurnberg	"	1-0	Gabriel	39,033
3rd Nov	2 Leg 1	(a)	Ujpest Dozsa	Hun	0-3		4,000
16th Nov	2 Leg 2	(h)	Ujpest Dozsa	"	2-1	Harris, Nosko (og)	24,201
1966/67	**EUROPEAN CUP WINNERS' CUP (WINNERS - BAYERN MUNICH)**						
28th Sept	1 Leg 1	(a)	AaB Aalborg	Den	0-0		13,000
11th Oct	1 Leg 2	(h)	AaB Aalborg	"	2-1	Morrissey, Ball	36,628
9th Nov	2 Leg 1	(a)	Real Zaragoza	Spa	0-2		20,000
23rd Nov	2 Leg 2	(h)	Real Zaragoza	"	1-0	Brown	56,077
1970/71	**EUROPEAN CHAMPIONS CUP (WINNERS - AJAX)**						
16th Sept	1 Leg 1	(h)	IBK Keflavik	Ice	6-2	Ball 3, Royle 2, Kendall	28,444
30th Sept	1 Leg 2	(a)	IBK Keflavik	"	3-0	Whittle, Royle 2	9,500
21st Oct	2 Leg 1	(a)	B. Moench'bach	W. Ger	1-1	Kendall	32,000
4th Nov	2 Leg 2	(h)	B. Moench'bach	"	1-1 aet	Morrissey	42,744
			(Everton won 5-4 on penalties)				
9th Mar	3 Leg 1	(h)	Panathinaikos	Gre	1-1	Johnson	46,047
24th Mar	3 Leg 2	(a)	Panathinaikos	"	0-0		25,000
1975/76	**UEFA CUP (WINNERS - LIVERPOOL)**						
17th Sept	1 Leg 1	(h)	AC Milan	Ita	0-0		31,917
1st Oct	1 Leg 2	(a)	AC Milan	"	0-1		60,000
1978/79	**UEFA CUP (WINNERS - BORUSSIA MOENCHENGLADBACH)**						
12th Sept	1 Leg 1	(a)	Finn Harps	Ire	5-0	Thomas, King 2, Latchford, Walsh	5,000
26th Sept	1 Leg 2	(h)	Finn Harps	"	5-0	King, Latchford, Walsh, Ross, Dobson	21,611
18th Oct	2 Leg 1	(h)	Dukla Prague	Cze	2-1	Latchford, King	32,857
1st Nov	2 Leg 2	(a)	Dukla Prague	"	0-1		35,000

EVERTON'S RESULTS IN EUROPEAN COMPETITION

Season & Date	Round	Venue	Opponents	Opponent Country	Score	Scorers	Attendance
1979/80	**UEFA CUP (WINNERS - EINTRACHT FRANKFURT)**						
19th Sept	1 Leg 1	(a)	Feyenoord	Hol	0-1		36,000
3rd Oct	1 Leg 2	(h)	Feyenoord	"	0-1		28,203
1984/85	**EUROPEAN CUP WINNERS' CUP (WINNERS - EVERTON)**						
19th Sept	1 Leg 1	(a)	UC Dublin	Ire	0-0		10,000
2nd Oct	1 Leg 2	(h)	UC Dublin	"	1-0	Sharp	16,277
24th Oct	2 Leg 1	(a)	Slovan Bratislava	Cze	1-0	Bracewell	15,000
7th Nov	2 Leg 2	(h)	Slovan Bratislava	"	3-0	Sharp,Sheedy,Heath	25,007
6th Mar	3 Leg 1	(h)	Fortuna Sittard	Hol	3-0	Gray 3	25,782
20th Mar	3 Leg 2	(a)	Fortuna Sittard	"	2-0	Sharp,Reid	20,000
10th Apr	SF Leg 1	(a)	Bayern Munich	W. Ger	0-0		67,000
24th Apr	SF Leg 2	(h)	Bayern Munich	"	3-1	Sharp,Gray,Steven	49,476
15th May	Final	N	Rapid Vienna	Aus	3-1	Gray,Steven,Sheedy	38,500
1995/96	**EUROPEAN CUP WINNERS' CUP (WINNERS - PARIS SAINT-GERMAIN)**						
14th Sept	1 Leg 1	(a)	KR Reykjavik	Ice	3-2	Ebbrell,Unsworth (pen), Amokachi	6,000
28th Sept	1 Leg 2	(h)	KR Reykjavik	"	3-1	Stuart,Grant,Rideout	18,422
19th Oct	2 Leg 1	(h)	Feyenoord	Hol	0-0		27,526
2nd Nov	2 Leg 2	(a)	Feyenoord	"	0-1		40,000
2005/06	**UEFA CHAMPIONS LEAGUE (WINNERS - BARCELONA)**						
9th Aug	Q.3 Leg 1	(h)	Villarreal	Spa	1-2	Beattie	37,685
24th Aug	Q.3 Leg 2	(a)	Villarreal	"	1-2	Arteta	16,000
2005/06	**UEFA CUP (WINNERS - SEVILLA)**						
15th Sept	1 Leg 1	(a)	D. Bucharest	Rom	1-5	Yobo	11,500
29th Sept	1 Leg 2	(h)	D. Bucharest	"	1-0	Cahill	21,843
2007/08	**UEFA CUP (WINNERS - ZENIT ST PETERSBURG)**						
20th Sept	1 Leg 1	(h)	Metalist Kharkiv	Ukr	1-1	Lescott	37,120
4th Oct	1 Leg 2	(a)	Metalist Kkarkiv	"	3-2	Lescott, McFadden, Anichebe	27,500
25th Oct	Group A: 1	(h)	AE Larissa	Gre	3-1	Cahill, Osman, Anichebe	33,777
8th Nov	Group A: 2	(a)	1. FC Nurnberg	Ger	2-0	Arteta (pen), Anichebe	43,000
5th Dec	Group A: 3	(h)	Z. St Petersburg	Rus	1-0	Cahill	38,407
20th Dec	Group A: 4	(a)	AZ Alkmaar	Hol	3-2	Johnson, Jagielka, Vaughan	16,578
13th Feb	L 32 Leg 1	(a)	SK Brann	Nor	2-0	Osman, Anichebe	16,207
21st Feb	L 32 Leg 2	(h)	SK Brann	"	6-1	Yakubu 3, Johnson 2, Arteta	32,834
6th Mar	L 16 Leg 1	(a)	AC Fiorentina	Ita	0-2		32,934
12th Mar	L 16 Leg 2	(h)	AC Fiorentina (Everton lost 2-4 on penalties)	"	2-0 aet	Johnson, Arteta	38,026

EUROPEAN RECORDS

BIGGEST VICTORIES

Date	Opponents	Venue	Score	Scorers	Attendance
21st Feb 2008	SK Brann	H	6-1	Yakubu 3, Johnson 2, Arteta	32,834
12th Sept 1978	Finn Harps	A	5-0	Thomas, King 2, Latchford, Walsh	5,000
26th Sept 1978	Finn Harps	H	5-0	King, Latchford, Walsh, Ross, Dobson	21,611
16th Sept 1970	Keflavik	H	6-2	Ball 3, Royle 2, Kendall	28,444
23rd Nov 1964	Kilmarnock	H	4-1	Harvey, Pickering 2, Young	30,727

BIGGEST DEFEATS

Date	Opponents	Venue	Score	Scorer	Attendance
29th Sept 2005	D. Bucharest	A	1-5	Yobo	11,500
3rd Nov 1965	Ujpest Dozsa	A	0-3		4,000
31st Oct 1962	Dunfermline	A	0-2		21,813
9th Nov 1966	R. Zaragoza	A	0-2		20,000
6th Mar 2008	AC Fiorentina	A	0-2		32,934

HIGHEST HOME ATTENDANCES

Attendance	Opponents	Competition	Date
62,408	Inter Milan	European Cup	18th Sep 1963
56,077	Real Zaragoza	ECW Cup	23rd Nov 1966
54,397	Manchester Utd	Inter-Cities Fairs Cup	4th Feb 1965
49,476	Bayern Munich	ECW Cup	24th Apr 1985
46,047	Panathinaikos	European Cup	9th Mar 1971

EVERTON SENDINGS-OFF

Date	Name	Competition	Against	Venue	Mins
9th Nov 1966	Johnny Morrissey	ECW Cup	Real Zaragoza	A	45
17th Sept 1975	Mike Bernard	UEFA Cup	AC Milan	H	89
2nd Nov 1995	Craig Short	ECW Cup	Feyenoord	A	90

OPPONENTS' SENDINGS-OFF

Date	Name	Competition	Team	Venue	Mins
11th Oct 1966	Morten Larsen	ECW Cup	AaB Aalborg	H	87
20th Sept 2007	Seweryn Gancarczyk	UEFA Cup	Met. Kharkiv	H	69
20th Sept 2007	Olexandr Babych	UEFA Cup	Met. Kharkiv	H	88
5th Dec 2007	Nicolas Lombaerts	UEFA Cup	Z. St. P'burg	H	30

A new record is set as the Blues secure their best-ever scoreline in European competition against Norwegian champions SK Brann

Zenit St. Petersburg defender Nicolas Lombaerts is harshly dismissed - the fourth man to suffer the fate against the Blues in Europe - at Goodison in December 2007

EVERTON IN EUROPE - DID YOU KNOW?

- Everton's eight victories in the UEFA Cup – from just 10 appearances – during 2007/08 was the highest total by any team in the competition during that campaign – Getafe, Bayer Leverkusen and Hamburg all recorded seven wins.

- Included in that tally were seven successive victories – a club record and only one fewer than the British best set by Tottenham Hotspur 12 months earlier.

- The 23 goals scored in the UEFA Cup were a record for Everton in a single season of European competition – exceeding the 17 netted in 1964/65.

- The 6-1 home victory over SK Brann was statistically our best in Europe, ranking higher than the two 5-0 victories over Finn Harps in 1978 on account of goals scored.

- The hat-trick by Ayegbeni Yakubu against SK Brann was his second in an Everton jersey, the Nigerian becoming the first to record two trebles in a season since Tony Cottee's two in the league in 1993/94. The forward's hat-trick was also the first in a major cup competition at Goodison Park since Graeme Sharp's against Wrexham in the League Cup during 1990.

- Joleon Lescott was the only Everton player to appear in all 10 UEFA Cup games. Against Metalist Kharkiv he became the first defender to score in both legs of a European tie for the club.

- Andy Johnson's opening goal at AZ Alkmaar was timed at 63 seconds, the second fastest by an Everton player in Europe (after Johnny Morrissey's 23-second goal against Borussia Moenchengladbach in 1970). Against Metalist, the striker became the first Everton player to miss two penalties at Goodison in the same game.

Team line-up - plus mascots - before the Everton v SK Brann clash in February 2008

EVERTON IN EUROPE - DID YOU KNOW?

- In the same AZ Alkmaar match of December 2007, Phil Jagielka became the third player to score his first Everton goal in a European game, after Mick Walsh (Finn Harps, 1978) and Tony Grant (Reykyavik, 1995).

- When playing for AE Larissa at Goodison, Ibrahima Bakayoko became the first former Everton player to appear against the Toffees in Europe.

- The attendance of 43,000 at Nurnberg in the group stages was the highest for an away Cup tie involving Everton since a gate of more than 51,000 watched the League Cup semi-final at Highbury against Arsenal in February 1988.

- Against AZ Alkmaar, James Vaughan, at the age of 19 years 159 days, became the club's second-youngest scorer in a European match after David Johnson, who was 19 years 137 days when netting against Panathinaikos in March 1971.

- Victor Anichebe was just five days older than James when he scored against Metalist in October, but in Bergen against SK Brann the Nigerian became only the second Everton player to score in four European matches in the same season, following on from Fred Pickering (1964/65) and Graeme Sharp (1984/85).

- Jack Rodwell became the club's youngest-ever player in European competition at the age of 16 years 284 days when coming on as a late substitute in Alkmaar. The defender broke the previous record set by Jimmy Husband of 18 years 32 days against Ujpest Dozsa in the Inter-Cities Fairs Cup in 1965. Only James Vaughan and Joe Royle had played for the club at a younger age.

Everton first - for Phil Jagielka

LEAGUE BLUES

THE COMPLETE EVERTON LEAGUE RECORD

CLUB BY CLUB

Name	Played	W	D	L	F	A	% Won	% Lost
Accrington	10	5	3	2	21	16	50%	20%
Arsenal	174	54	36	84	214	283	31%	48%
Aston Villa	186	70	46	70	286	286	38%	38%
Barnsley	8	4	3	1	18	12	50%	13%
Birmingham City	114	58	32	24	210	142	51%	21%
Blackburn Rovers	140	55	31	54	229	222	39%	39%
Blackpool	46	20	11	15	66	55	43%	33%
Bolton Wanderers	130	66	30	34	217	173	51%	26%
Bradford City	26	11	9	6	39	30	42%	23%
Bradford PA	8	5	2	1	19	12	63%	13%
Brentford	16	7	2	7	29	22	44%	44%
Brighton & HA	8	4	3	1	15	11	50%	13%
Bristol City	20	12	3	5	34	22	60%	25%
Bristol Rovers	2	1	1	0	4	0	50%	0%
Burnley	98	41	28	29	161	147	42%	30%
Bury	52	21	16	15	87	72	40%	29%
Cardiff City	30	10	8	12	43	35	33%	40%
Carlisle United	2	0	0	2	2	6	0%	100%
Charlton Athletic	48	20	10	18	78	68	42%	38%
Chelsea	138	45	43	50	211	216	33%	36%
Coventry City	70	29	19	22	106	85	41%	31%
Crystal Palace	26	11	7	8	42	26	42%	31%
Darwen	4	2	1	1	17	10	50%	25%
Derby County	126	63	21	42	240	173	50%	33%
Doncaster Rovers	6	2	2	2	15	11	33%	33%
Fulham	40	19	8	13	65	44	48%	33%
Glossop North End	2	1	1	0	5	2	50%	0%
Grimsby Town	22	12	4	6	46	28	55%	27%
Huddersfield Town	56	22	13	21	80	81	39%	38%
Hull City	6	3	0	3	10	5	50%	50%
Ipswich Town	52	20	18	14	69	61	38%	27%
Leeds United	104	28	29	47	132	150	27%	45%
Leicester City	96	36	30	30	179	151	38%	31%
Leyton Orient	2	1	0	1	3	3	50%	50%
Lincoln City	4	1	2	1	5	6	25%	25%
Liverpool	178	56	55	67	213	241	31%	38%
Luton Town	38	16	8	14	56	46	42%	37%
Manchester City	150	54	39	57	206	214	36%	38%
Manchester United	158	52	37	69	229	245	33%	44%
Middlesbrough	110	53	27	30	187	141	48%	27%
Millwall	6	4	1	1	11	6	67%	17%
Newcastle United	148	57	31	60	217	224	39%	41%
Northampton Town	2	2	0	0	7	2	100%	0%
Norwich City	42	16	13	13	61	54	38%	31%
Nottingham Forest	120	52	26	42	198	147	43%	35%
Notts County	66	37	13	16	126	68	56%	24%
Oldham Athletic	28	9	8	11	42	46	32%	39%
Oxford United	6	2	3	1	7	4	33%	17%
Plymouth Argyle	6	4	0	2	22	12	67%	33%

THE COMPLETE EVERTON LEAGUE RECORD

CLUB BY CLUB								
Name	Played	W	D	L	F	A	% Won	% Lost
Port Vale	2	1	0	1	5	4	50%	50%
Portsmouth	54	23	9	22	84	95	43%	41%
Preston North End	88	33	25	30	120	120	38%	34%
QPR	42	18	10	14	69	61	43%	33%
Reading	6	4	1	1	9	4	67%	17%
Rotherham United	6	2	3	1	11	8	33%	17%
Sheffield United	120	48	30	42	184	154	40%	35%
Sheffield Wednesday	128	55	37	36	227	193	43%	28%
Southampton	76	37	17	22	133	86	49%	29%
Stoke City	104	50	27	27	183	112	48%	26%
Sunderland	146	63	22	61	243	242	43%	42%
Swansea City	12	8	4	0	31	12	67%	0%
Swindon Town	2	1	1	0	7	3	50%	0%
Tottenham Hotspur	142	45	44	53	192	221	32%	37%
Watford	16	13	1	2	41	20	81%	13%
West Brom	138	55	32	51	231	230	40%	37%
West Ham United	106	52	22	32	180	122	49%	30%
Wigan Athletic	6	3	2	1	9	6	50%	17%
Wimbledon	28	9	11	8	40	36	32%	29%
Wolverhampton W.	116	55	20	41	198	164	47%	35%
GRAND TOTAL	**4,268**	**1,748**	**1,051**	**1,469**	**6,776**	**6,009**	**41%**	**34%**

Aston Villa v Everton/Everton v Aston Villa, the most-played fixture in English football

EVERTON LEAGUE RECORDS

SEQUENCES

FIGURE	SEQUENCE	FIRST GAME-FINAL GAME (MOST RECENT)
12	Consecutive wins	24th March 1894-13th October 1894
5 (3 occasions)	Consecutive draws	4th May 1977-16th May 1977
6 (8 occasions)	Consecutive defeats	27th August 2005-15th October 2005
20	Unbeaten games	29th April 1978-16th December 1978
7	Clean sheets	1st November 1994-17th December 1994
40	Consecutives games scored in	15th March 1930-7th March 1931
14	Games without a win	6th March 1937-4th September 1937
27	Games without a clean sheet	15th April 1950-23rd December 1950
6 (3 occasions)	Games without scoring	27th August 2005-15th October 2005

ATTENDANCES (HIGHEST)

DATE	HOME/AWAY VENUE	OPPOSITION	ATTENDANCE
18th Sept 1948	Goodison Park	Liverpool	78,299
28th Aug 1954	Goodison Park	Preston North End	76,839
23rd Dec 2007	Old Trafford	Manchester United	75,749
29th Nov 2006	Old Trafford	Manchester United	75,723
27th Dec 1954	Goodison Park	Wolverhampton W.	75,322
27th Dec 1960	Goodison Park	Burnley	74,867
22nd Sept 1962	Goodison Park	Liverpool	72,488
4th Sept 1957	Goodison Park	Manchester United	71,868
16th Sept 1950	Goodison Park	Liverpool	71,150
7th Apr 1950	Goodison Park	Blackpool	71,088
27th Aug 1949	Goodison Park	Liverpool	70,812

ATTENDANCES (LOWEST)

The publication of match attendances for league matches was only a requirement made by the Football League from the 1925/26 season onwards. Prior to that attendances were only usually provided by newspapers, and then only as an estimate.

The club's lowest official attendance at home is 7,802 for the visit of Sheffield Wednesday on 1st May 1935.

Prior to 1925 the lowest attendance was one of 1,000 for the away match at Bolton on 16th April 1894, with the lowest home gate being 2,000 for the game at Goodison against Newcastle on 6th January 1900. Official figures are as follows:

DATE	AWAY VENUE	OPPOSITION	ATTENDANCE
26th Jan 1993	Selhurst Park	Wimbledon	3,039 (*Post WW2 record)
29th Jan 1936	Leeds Road	Huddersfield Town	3,404
10th Mar 1992	Selhurst Park	Wimbledon	3,569
25th Apr 1934	Leeds Road	Huddersfield Town	4,842
3rd Feb 1937	Leeds Road	Huddersfield Town	5,216
3rd Feb 1936	Hillsborough	Sheffield Wednesday	5,938
28th Apr 1934	Roker Park	Sunderland	5,976
1st Oct 1988	Plough Lane	Wimbledon	6,367
24th Nov 1990	Selhurst Park	Wimbledon	6,411
3rd Mar 1990	Selhurst Park	Wimbledon	6,512

EVERTON LEAGUE RECORDS

HIGHEST (SEASON TOTALS)

FIGURE	SUBJECT	SEASON(S)
66	Points total (2 points for a win)	1969/70
90	Points total (3 points for a win)	1984/85
95	If 3 points for a win	1969/70
29	Wins	1969/70
18	Draws	1925/26, 1971/72, 1974/75
22	Defeats	1950/51, 1993/94
121	Goals scored	1930/31
35	Players used in a season	1888/89, 1919/20
51,603	Average home attendance	1962/63

LOWEST (SEASON TOTALS)

FIGURE	SUBJECT	SEASON(S)
32	Points total (42 games, 2 points for a win)	1950/51
40	Points total (38 games, 3 points for a win)	1997/98
9	Wins	1888/89, 1971/72, 1997/98
1	Draws	1890/91
5	Defeats	1969/70
34	Goals scored	2005/06
16	Players used in a season	1969/70
7,189	Average home attendance	1888/89
19,288	Average home attendance (post-war)	1983/84

BIGGEST WINS (ALL HOME)

DATE	OPPOSITION	SCORELINE
3rd Sept 1906	Manchester City	9-1
27th Dec 1930	Plymouth Argyle	9-1
2nd Nov 1889	Stoke City	8-0
20th Nov 1971	Southampton	8-0

BIGGEST AWAY WIN

DATE	OPPOSITION	SCORELINE
7th Feb 1931	Charlton Athletic	7-0

BIGGEST DEFEATS (ALL AWAY)

DATE	OPPOSITION	SCORELINE
26th Dec 1934	Sunderland	0-7
22nd Feb 1939	Wolverhampton Wanderers	0-7
10th Sept 1949	Portsmouth	0-7
11th May 2005	Arsenal	0-7

BIGGEST HOME DEFEAT

DATE	OPPOSITION	SCORELINE
26th Oct 1912	Newcastle United	0-6

PREMIER LEAGUE FACTS & FIGURES

LEAGUE RECORD

Season	P	W	D	L	F	A	Pts	Pos	Av. Att
1992/1993	42	15	8	19	53	55	53	13	20,457
1993/1994	42	12	8	22	42	63	44	18	23,129
1994/1995	42	11	17	14	44	51	50	15	31,035
1995/1996	38	17	10	11	64	44	61	6	35,424
1996/1997	38	10	12	16	44	57	42	15	36,188
1997/1998	38	9	13	16	41	56	40	17	35,355
1998/1999	38	11	10	17	42	47	43	14	35,760
1999/2000	38	12	14	12	59	49	50	13	33,342
2000/2001	38	11	9	18	45	59	42	16	34,131
2001/2002	38	11	10	17	45	57	43	15	33,582
2002/2003	38	17	8	13	48	49	59	7	38,481
2003/2004	38	9	12	17	45	57	39	17	38,837
2004/2005	38	18	7	13	45	46	61	4	36,834
2005/2006	38	14	8	16	34	49	50	11	36,860
2006/2007	38	15	13	10	52	36	58	6	36,739
2007/2008	38	19	8	11	55	33	65	5	36,955

BIGGEST WINS (ALL HOME)

DATE	OPPONENTS	SCORE	EVERTON SCORERS	ATT.
24th Nov 2007	Sunderland	7-1	Yakubu 2, Cahill 2, Pienaar, Johnson, Osman	38,594
16th Nov 1996	Southampton	7-1	Stuart, Kanchelskis 2, Speed 3, Barmby	35,669
8th May 1999	West Ham United	6-0	Campbell 3, Ball (pen), Hutchison, Jeffers	40,049
29th Sept 2001	West Ham United	5-0	Campbell, Hutchison (og), Gravesen, Watson, Radzinski	32,049
26th Dec 1999	Sunderland	5-0	Hutchison 2, Jeffers, Pembridge, Campbell	40,017
17th Feb 1999	Middlesbrough	5-0	Barmby 2, Dacourt, Materazzi, Unsworth	31,606

BIGGEST AWAY WIN

DATE	OPPONENTS	SCORE	EVERTON SCORERS	ATT.
26th Feb 2000	West Ham United	4-0	Barmby 3, Moore	26,025

BIGGEST DEFEATS (ALL AWAY)

DATE	OPPONENTS	SCORE	EVERTON SCORERS	ATT.
11th May 2005	Arsenal	0-7		38,073
9th Dec 2000	Manchester City	0-5		34,516
29th Mar 2002	Newcastle United	2-6	Ferguson, Alexandersson	51,921
15th May 2004	Manchester City	1-5	Campbell	47,284
4th Dec 1999	Manchester Utd	1-5	Jeffers	55,193
2nd Apr 1994	Sheffield Wed.	1-5	Cottee	24,096

BIGGEST HOME DEFEAT

DATE	OPPONENTS	SCORE	EVERTON SCORER	ATT.
25th Sept 1993	Norwich City	1-5	Rideout	20,531

PREMIER LEAGUE CLUB-BY-CLUB RECORD

EVERTON'S PREMIER LEAGUE RECORD

	PLAYED	WON	DREW	LOST	FOR	AGAINST	PTS PER GAME
Arsenal	32	5	7	20	25	63	0.7
Aston Villa	32	7	10	15	29	44	1.0
Barnsley	2	1	1	0	6	4	2.0
Birmingham City	10	4	5	1	10	8	1.7
Blackburn Rovers	28	11	6	11	27	30	1.4
Bolton Wanderers	18	9	5	4	27	22	1.8
Bradford City	4	3	1	0	7	1	2.5
Charlton Athletic	16	7	3	6	21	18	1.5
Chelsea	32	4	12	16	31	51	0.8
Coventry City	18	3	9	6	15	19	1.0
Crystal Palace	8	5	0	3	16	8	1.9
Derby County	14	7	2	5	17	15	1.6
Fulham	14	7	0	7	19	15	1.5
Ipswich Town	10	4	2	4	11	9	1.4
Leeds United	24	7	10	7	29	24	1.3
Leicester City	16	4	11	1	20	18	1.4
Liverpool	32	8	11	13	32	38	1.1
Manchester City	22	10	4	8	28	33	1.5
Manchester United	32	3	4	25	25	67	0.4
Middlesbrough	26	12	7	7	40	26	1.7
Newcastle United	30	10	6	14	36	45	1.2
Norwich City	8	3	2	3	8	13	1.4
Nottingham Forest	10	6	0	4	16	8	1.8
Oldham Athletic	4	2	1	1	5	4	1.8
Portsmouth	10	7	1	2	13	6	2.2
Queens Park Rangers	8	2	1	5	14	21	0.9
Reading	4	2	1	1	4	2	1.8
Sheffield United	6	2	2	2	7	6	1.3
Sheffield Wednesday	16	3	5	8	20	30	0.9
Southampton	26	11	8	7	36	26	1.6
Sunderland	14	7	2	5	24	17	1.6
Swindon Town	2	1	1	0	7	3	2.0
Tottenham Hotspur	32	4	11	17	33	51	0.7
Watford	4	4	0	0	12	4	3.0
West Bromwich Albion	6	3	1	2	7	9	1.7
West Ham United	26	13	7	6	45	21	1.8
Wigan Athletic	6	3	2	1	9	6	1.8
Wimbledon	16	6	6	4	24	21	1.5
Wolverhampton W.	2	1	0	1	3	2	1.5
GRAND TOTAL	**620**	**211**	**167**	**242**	**758**	**808**	**1.3**

(Figures correct at end of 2007/08 season)

LEAGUE DISMISSALS - EVERTON

EVERTON SENDINGS OFF IN LEAGUE MATCHES

The following two pages are a breakdown of every Everton player sent off in a league game - with Football League and Premier League games listed separately.

DATE	PLAYER	OPPONENTS	VENUE	MINUTE	RESULT
7th September 1889	Charlie Parry	Blackburn Rovers	(h)	S/H	3-2
16th September 1889	Dan Doyle	Wolverhampton Wan.	(a)	60	1-2
21st November 1896	Alf Milward	Liverpool	(a)	S/H	0-0
5th January 1907	Jack Taylor	Preston North End	(a)	88	1-1
24th December 1910	James Gourlay	Bristol City	(h)	70	4-3
16th October 1920	George Brewster	Huddersfield Town	(h)	62	0-0
11th March 1922	Hunter Hart	Bradford City	(a)	30	1-3
7th January 1928	Tony Weldon	Middlesbrough	(h)	62	3-1
26th September 1936	Charlie Gee	Huddersfield Town	(h)	85	2-1
26th April 1947	Wally Fielding	Preston North End	(h)	78	2-0
7th September 1949	Jack Hedley	Manchester City	(a)	75	0-0
26th December 1951	John Willie Parker	Doncaster Rovers	(h)	65	1-1
21st February 1953	George Cummins	Swansea Town	(h)	82	0-0
31st October 1953	Dave Hickson	Leicester City	(h)	88	1-2
7th December 1957	Dave Hickson	Manchester City	(a)	68	2-6
18th April 1959	John Bramwell	Chelsea	(a)	50	1-3
29th October 1960	Roy Vernon	Nottingham Forest	(a)	85	2-1
9th November 1963	Tony Kay	Blackburn Rovers	(h)	66	2-4
7th November 1964	Sandy Brown	Leeds United	(h)	4	0-1
16th October 1965	Colin Harvey	Fulham	(a)	80	2-3
28th October 1967	Gordon West	Newcastle United	(a)	88	0-1
23rd March 1968	Alan Ball	Newcastle United	(h)	47	1-0
14th May 1969	Colin Harvey	Leicester City	(a)	80	1-1
21st August 1976	Dave Jones	Queens Park Rangers	(a)	17	4-0
14th May 1977	Bob Latchford	Birmingham City	(a)	82	1-1
30th September 1978	Dave Thomas	Bristol City	(a)	49	2-2
15th September 1979	Andy King	Wolverhampton Wan.	(h)	90	2-3
20th October 1979	Garry Stanley	Liverpool	(a)	70	2-2
7th November 1981	Eamonn O'Keefe	Liverpool	(a)	80	1-3
4th September 1982	John Bailey	Tottenham Hotspur	(h)	88	3-1
6th November 1982	Glenn Keeley	Liverpool	(h)	31	0-5
27th November 1982	Alan Irvine	West Ham United	(a)	89	0-2
29th September 1984	Terry Curran	Watford	(a)	90	5-4
8th December 1984	Pat van den Hauwe	Queens Park Rangers	(a)	35	0-0
12th October 1985	Neville Southall	Chelsea	(a)	59	1-2
21st March 1987	Ian Snodin	Charlton Athletic	(h)	75	2-1
17th October 1987	Adrian Heath	Newcastle United	(a)	74	1-1
20th April 1991	Martin Keown	Crystal Palace	(a)	89	0-0

Off! Pat van den Hauwe in 1984 (left) and Iain Turner (2006)

PREMIER LEAGUE DISMISSALS - EVERTON

EVERTON SENDINGS OFF IN LEAGUE MATCHES

DATE	PLAYER	OPPONENTS	VENUE	MINUTE	RESULT
28th December 1992	Neville Southall	Queens Park Rangers	(a)	19	2-4
28th December 1992	Paul Rideout	Queens Park Rangers	(a)	44	2-4
6th February 1993	Neville Southall	Sheffield Wednesday	(a)	43	1-3
14th January 1995	Duncan Ferguson	Arsenal	(a)	53	1-1
1st February 1995	Earl Barrett	Newcastle United	(a)	61	0-2
1st February 1995	Barry Horne	Newcastle United	(a)	66	0-2
4th March 1995	Vinny Samways	Leicester City	(a)	49	2-2
4th March 1995	Duncan Ferguson	Leicester City	(a)	61	2-2
9th May 1995	Stuart Barlow	Ipswich Town	(a)	87	1-0
9th September 1995	David Unsworth	Manchester United	(h)	80	2-3
14th October 1995	Barry Horne	Bolton Wanderers	(a)	61	1-1
30th December 1995	Dave Watson	Leeds United	(h)	17	2-0
21st September 1996	Duncan Ferguson	Blackburn Rovers	(a)	88	1-1
16th April 1997	David Unsworth	Liverpool	(h)	81	1-1
13th September 1997	Andy Hinchcliffe	Derby County	(a)	67	1-3
24th September 1997	Slaven Bilic	Newcastle United	(a)	62	0-1
26th November 1997	Slaven Bilic	Chelsea	(a)	90	0-2
14th February 1998	Duncan Ferguson	Derby County	(h)	15	1-2
7th March 1998	Slaven Bilic	Southampton	(a)	68	1-2
12th September 1998	Olivier Dacourt	Leeds United	(h)	55	0-0
5th December 1998	Richard Dunne	Chelsea	(h)	75	0-0
18th January 1999	Alec Cleland	Aston Villa	(a)	15	0-3
13th March 1999	Don Hutchison	Arsenal	(h)	18	0-2
11th April 1999	Marco Materazzi	Coventry City	(h)	85	2-0
11th August 1999	John Collins	Aston Villa	(a)	64	0-3
28th August 1999	Richard Dunne	Derby County	(a)	25	0-1
27th September 1999	Francis Jeffers	Liverpool	(a)	75	1-0
30th October 1999	David Weir	Middlesbrough	(a)	76	1-2
8th May 2000	Richard Dunne	Leeds United	(a)	50	1-1
8th May 2000	Don Hutchison	Leeds United	(a)	87	1-1
29th October 2000	Tommy Gravesen	Liverpool	(a)	75	1-3
24th February 2001	Alex Nyarko	Ipswich Town	(a)	71	0-2
8th April 2001	Alessandro Pistone	Manchester City	(h)	88	3-1
21st April 2001	Abel Xavier	Arsenal	(a)	80	1-4
8th December 2001	David Weir	Fulham	(a)	77	0-2
16th March 2002	Thomas Gravesen	Fulham	(h)	29	2-1
1st April 2002	Duncan Ferguson	Bolton Wanderers	(h)	20	3-1
28th August 2002	Alan Stubbs	Birmingham City	(h)	48	1-1
10th October 2002	David Weir	Manchester United	(a)	89	0-3
1st December 2002	Joseph Yobo	Newcastle United	(a)	21	1-2
7th December 2002	David Unsworth	Chelsea	(h)	87	1-3
26th December 2002	Wayne Rooney	Birmingham City	(a)	81	1-1
19th April 2003	David Weir	Liverpool	(h)	81	1-2
19th April 2003	Gary Naysmith	Liverpool	(h)	90	1-2
16th August 2003	Li Tie	Arsenal	(a)	87	1-2
13th September 2003	Gary Naysmith	Newcastle United	(h)	58	2-2
20th March 2004	Duncan Ferguson	Leicester City	(a)	41	1-1
21st August 2004	Gary Naysmith	Crystal Palace	(a)	70	3-1
11th September 2004	Tim Cahill	Manchester City	(a)	60	1-0
28th December 2004	Duncan Ferguson	Charlton Athletic	(a)	83	0-2
12th February 2005	James Beattie	Chelsea	(h)	8	0-1
27th August 2005	Phil Neville	Fulham	(a)	90	0-1
28th December 2005	Phil Neville	Liverpool	(h)	68	1-3
28th December 2005	Mikel Arteta	Liverpool	(h)	90	1-3
31st January 2006	Duncan Ferguson	Wigan Athletic	(a)	80	1-1
11th February 2006	Iain Turner	Blackburn Rovers	(h)	9	1-0
25th March 2006	Andy Van der Meyde	Liverpool	(a)	73	1-3
26th August 2006	Kevin Kilbane	Tottenham Hotspur	(a)	32	2-0
24th September 2006	Tony Hibbert	Newcastle United	(a)	79	1-1
20th October 2007	Tony Hibbert	Liverpool	(h)	53	1 2
20th October 2007	Phil Neville	Liverpool	(h)	90	1-2
29th December 2007	Mikel Arteta	Arsenal	(h)	84	1-4

LEAGUE DISMISSALS - OPPOSITION

OPPOSITION SENDINGS OFF IN LEAGUE MATCHES

The following two pages are a breakdown of every opposition player sent off in a league game against Everton - with Football League and Premier League games listed separately.

DATE	PLAYER	OPPONENTS	VENUE	MINUTE	RESULT
16th September 1889	David Wykes	Wolverhampton Wan.	(a)	60	1-2
12th November 1892	Arthur Evans	Stoke City	(h)	S/H	2-2
2nd December 1899	Sreve Bloomer	Derby County	(h)	S/H	3-0
28th September 1901	Frank Lloyd	Aston Villa	(a)	S/H	1-1
14th November 1903	A Barrie	Sunderland	(h)	S/H	0-1
12th November 1904	Harry Davis	Sheffield Wednesday	(a)	81	5-5
5th January 1907	Tommy Rodway	Preston North End	(a)	89	1-1
24th December 1910	Billy Wedlock	Bristol City	(h)	70	4-3
7th January 1928	James McClelland	Middlesbrough	(h)	62	3-1
26th September 1936	Alf Young	Huddersfield Town	(h)	85	2-1
26th April 1947	William Watson	Preston North End	(h)	78	2-0
20th November 1948	Bert Smith	Aston Villa	(a)	81	1-0
26th December 1951	Syd Bycroft	Doncaster Rovers	(h)	70	1-1
21st February 1953	Dai Thomas	Swansea City	(h)	82	0-0
21st March 1959	Matt Woods	Blackburn Rovers	(a)	88	1-2
14th November 1959	John Watts	Birmingham City	(h)	50	4-0
28th October 1967	Ollie Burton	Newcastle United	(a)	60	0-1
4th October 1969	Derek Dougan	Wolverhampton Wan.	(a)	63	3-2
2nd October 1971	Chris Cattlin	Coventry City	(h)	77	1-2
4th November 1972	Mel Blyth	Crystal Palace	(a)	75	0-1
17th March 1973	Tony Currie	Sheffield United	(h)	53	2-1
19th October 1974	John Dempsey	Chelsea	(h)	90	1-1
20th October 1979	Terry McDermott	Liverpool	(a)	70	2-2
29th November 1980	Frank Worthington	Birmingham City	(h)	70	1-1
24th November 1981	Brian Kilcline	Notts County	(a)	88	2-2
28th December 1981	Steve Jacobs	Coventry City	(h)	55	3-2
20th March 1982	Trevor Francis	Manchester City	(a)	43	1-1
4th September 1982	John Lacy	Tottenham Hotspur	(h)	72	3-1
27th November 1982	Alvin Martin	West Ham United	(a)	89	0-2
27th December 1982	George Berry	Stoke City	(a)	62	0-1
22nd October 1983	Steve Terry	Watford	(h)	62	1-0
26th December 1983	Gordon Chisholm	Sunderland	(h)	61	0-0
7th April 1984	Mal Donaghy	Luton Town	(a)	51	3-0
8th December 1984	Simon Stainrod	Queens Park Rangers	(a)	35	0-0
15th December 1984	Chris Fairclough	Nottingham Forest	(h)	32	5-0
31st August 1985	Ken Armstrong	Birmingham City	(h)	67	4-1
8th November 1986	Kevin McAllister	Chelsea	(h)	68	2-2
21st March 1987	Andy Peake	Charlton Athletic	(h)	75	2-1
20th April 1987	Neil McDonald	Newcastle United	(h)	90	3-0
9th May 1987	Peter Nicholas	Luton Town	(h)	57	3-1
3rd October 1987	Andy Townsend	Southampton	(a)	82	4-0
21st November 1987	Kevin Dillon	Portsmouth	(a)	87	1-0
21st November 1987	Mick Kennedy	Portsmouth	(a)	88	1-0
26th December 1987	Mick Harford	Luton Town	(h)	88	2-0
29th March 1988	Vinnie Jones	Wimbledon	(h)	72	2-2
4th February 1989	Vinnie Jones	Wimbledon	(h)	71	1-1
7th September 1991	Andy Thorn	Crystal Palace	(h)	35	2-2
30th November 1991	Chris Fairclough	Leeds United	(a)	64	0-1
7th December 1991	Tim Breacker	West Ham United	(h)	68	4-0
2nd May 1992	Ken Monkou	Chelsea	(h)	33	2-1

PREMIER LEAGUE DISMISSALS - OPPOSITION

OPPOSITION SENDINGS OFF IN LEAGUE MATCHES					
DATE	**PLAYER**	**OPPONENTS**	**VENUE**	**MINUTE**	**RESULT**
3rd March 1993	Tim Sherwood	Blackburn Rovers	(h)	61	2-1
10th April 1993	Andy Kernaghan	Middlesbrough	(a)	55	2-1
15th January 1994	Andy Mutch	Swindon Town	(h)	48	6-2
5th March 1994	Graeme Sharp	Oldham Athletic	(h)	69	2-1
30th August 1994	Steve Chettle	Nottingham Forest	(h)	85	1-2
15th March 1995	Terry Phelan	Manchester City	(h)	61	1-1
14th April 1995	Robert Lee	Newcastle United	(h)	88	2-0
14th October 1995	Richard Sneekes	Bolton Wanderers	(a)	51	1-1
11th December 1995	Ludek Miklosko	West Ham United	(h)	43	3-0
16th December 1995	John Beresford	Newcastle United	(a)	33	0-1
13th January 1996	Mark Hughes	Chelsea	(h)	62	1-1
10th February 1996	Michael Frontzeck	Manchester City	(h)	86	2-0
30th March 1996	Garry Flitcroft	Blackburn Rovers	(a)	3	3-0
16th April 1997	Robbie Fowler	Liverpool	(h)	81	1-1
11th May 1997	Frode Grodas	Chelsea	(h)	20	1-2
7th March 1998	Ken Monkou	Southampton	(a)	36	1-2
11th April 1998	Lucas Radebe	Leeds United	(h)	17	2-0
25th April 1998	Andy Booth	Sheffield Wednesday	(h)	80	1-3
26th September 1998	Martin Dahlin	Blackburn Rovers	(h)	78	0-0
5th December 1998	Dennis Wise	Chelsea	(h)	36	0-0
13th March 1999	Emmanuel Petit	Arsenal	(h)	60	0-2
27th September 1999	Sander Westerveld	Liverpool	(a)	75	1-0
27th September 1999	Steven Gerrard	Liverpool	(a)	90	1-0
20th November 1999	Frank Lebouef	Chelsea	(h)	56	1-1
18th December 1999	Neil Cox	Watford	(a)	90	3-1
8th May 2000	Michael Duberry	Leeds United	(a)	54	1-1
23rd August 2000	Carl Tiler	Charlton Athletic	(h)	36	3-0
25th November 2000	J.F. Hasselbaink	Chelsea	(h)	71	2-1
31st March 2001	Stuart Pearce	West Ham United	(a)	45	2-0
8th April 2001	Paul Dickov	Manchester City	(h)	88	3-1
16th April 2001	Igor Biscan	Liverpool	(h)	77	2-3
19th May 2001	Don Hutchison	Sunderland	(h)	64	2-2
20th August 2001	Gary Doherty	Tottenham Hotspur	(h)	62	1-1
20th August 2001	Gus Poyet	Tottenham Hotspur	(h)	65	1-1
3rd November 2001	Souleymane Diawara	Bolton Wanderers	(a)	87	2-2
8th December 2001	Luis Boa Morte	Fulham	(a)	77	0-2
3rd March 2002	Dominic Matteo	Leeds United	(h)	38	0-0
1st April 2002	Kostas Konstandinis	Bolton Wanderers	(h)	30	3-1
31st August 2002	Shaun Wright-Phillips	Manchester City	(a)	27	1-3
14th December 2002	Lucas Neill	Blackburn Rovers	(h)	76	2-1
16th August 2003	Sol Campbell	Arsenal	(a)	30	1-2
13th September 2003	Laurent Robert	Newcastle United	(h)	40	2-2
9th April 2004	Stephen Carr	Tottenham Hotspur	(h)	75	3-1
13th November 2004	Muzzy Izzet	Birmingham City	(a)	69	1-0
26th December 2004	Christian Negouai	Manchester City	(h)	83	2-1
20th March 2005	Milan Baros	Liverpool	(a)	77	1-2
20th April 2005	Gary Neville	Manchester United	(h)	71	1-0
20th April 2005	Paul Scholes	Manchester United	(h)	90	1-0
30th April 2005	Papa Bouba Diop	Fulham	(a)	75	0-2
7th May 2005	Shola Ameobi	Newcastle United	(h)	56	2-0
15th May 2005	Bruno N'Gotty	Bolton Wanderers	(a)	45	2-3
3rd December 2005	Andy Todd	Blackburn Rovers	(a)	31	2-0
4th February 2006	Stephen Jordan	Manchester City	(h)	90	1-0
21st January 2006	Cesc Fabregas	Arsenal	(h)	90	1-0
31st January 2006	Jason Roberts	Wigan Athletic	(a)	83	1-1
25th March 2006	Steven Gerrard	Liverpool	(a)	18	1-3
24th September 2006	Titus Bramble	Newcastle United	(a)	78	1-1
21st October 2006	Claude Davis	Sheffield United	(h)	32	2-0
25th February 2008	Martin Petrov	Manchester City	(a)	90	2-0

RECORD APPEARANCES & GOALS

	TOTAL APPEARANCES	
	PLAYER	**APPS**
1	Neville Southall	750
2	Brian Labone	534
3	Dave Watson	528
4	Ted Sagar	497
5	Kevin Ratcliffe	493
6	Mick Lyons	473
7	Jack Taylor	456
8	Peter Farrell	453
9	Graeme Sharp	446
10	Dixie Dean	433
11	Tommy Eglington	428
12	Tommy T.E. Jones	411
13	Wally Fielding	410
14	John Hurst	402
=	Gordon West	402

	TOTAL GOALS		
	PLAYER	**APPS**	**GLS**
1	Dixie Dean	433	383
2	Graeme Sharp	446	159
3	Bob Latchford	289	138
4	Alex "Sandy" Young	314	125
5	Joe Royle	276	119
6	Roy Vernon	203	111
=	Dave Hickson	243	111
8	Edgar Chadwick	300	109
9	Tony Cottee	240	99
10	Alfred Milward	224	97
=	Jimmy Settle	269	97
=	Kevin Sheedy	368	97
13	Adrian Heath	307	94
14	Alex Stevenson	271	90

	LEAGUE APPEARANCES	
	PLAYER	**APPS**
1	Neville Southall	578
2	Ted Sagar	463
3	Brian Labone	451
4	Dave Watson	423
5	Peter Farrell	422
6	Jack Taylor	400
7	Dixie Dean	399
8	Tommy Eglington	394
9	Mick Lyons	390
10	Tommy T.E. Jones	383
11	Wally Fielding	380
12	Kevin Ratcliffe	359

	LEAGUE GOALS		
	PLAYER	**APPS**	**GLS**
1	Dixie Dean	399	349
2	Graeme Sharp	322	111
3	Alex "Sandy" Young	275	110
4	Bob Latchford	236	106
5	Joe Royle	232	102
6	Roy Vernon	176	101
7	Edgar Chadwick	270	97
8	Dave Hickson	225	95
9	Alfred Milward	201	85
10	Jimmy Settle	237	84
11	John Willie Parker	167	82
=	Alex Stevenson	255	82

	PREMIER LEAGUE APPEARANCES	
	PLAYER	**APPS**
1	David Unsworth	302
2	Duncan Ferguson	239
3	David Weir	235
4	Dave Watson	223
5	Neville Southall	207
6	Joseph Yobo	176
7	Alan Stubbs	169
8	Lee Carsley	167
9	Tony Hibbert	164
10	Thomas Gravesen	149
11	Kevin Campbell	145
12	Andy Hinchcliffe	143
13	Graham Stuart	136
14	Gary Naysmith	134
15	Leon Osman	132

	PREMIER LEAGUE GOALS		
	PLAYER	**APPS**	**GLS**
1	Duncan Ferguson	239	60
2	Kevin Campbell	145	45
3	David Unsworth	302	33
4	Tim Cahill	101	29
5	Paul Rideout	111	29
6	Tony Cottee	68	28
7	Tomasz Radzinski	91	25
8	Graham Stuart	136	22
9	Andrei Kanchelskis	52	20
10	Francis Jeffers	67	18
=	Nick Barmby	116	18
12	Andy Johnson	61	17
=	Leon Osman	132	17
14	Gary Speed	58	16

RECORD FA CUP APPEARANCES & GOALS

EUROPEAN APPEARANCES		
	PLAYER	APPS
1	Colin Harvey	19
=	Brian Labone	19
3	Johnny Morrissey	17
=	Tommy Wright	17
5	Derek Temple	16
6	Jimmy Gabriel	15
7	Neville Southall	13
=	Gordon West	13
=	Alex Young	13
10	Brian Harris	12
=	Tony Hibbert	12
=	Phil Neville	12
=	Andy Rankin	12
=	Dennis Stevens	12

EUROPEAN GOALS			
	PLAYER	APPS	GLS
1	Fred Pickering	9	6
2	Andy Gray	3	5
3	Andy King	5	4
=	Joe Royle	6	4
=	Andy Johnson	7	4
=	Graeme Sharp	8	4
=	Victor Anichebe	9	4
=	Mikel Arteta	10	4
=	Alan Ball	10	4

FA CUP APPEARANCES		
	PLAYER	APPS
1	Neville Southall	70
2	Kevin Ratcliffe	57
3	Jack Taylor	56
4	Graeme Sharp	54
5	Harry Makepeace	52
6	Dave Watson	48
7	Brian Labone	45
8	Jack Sharp	42
9	Gordon West	40
10	Alex "Sandy" Young	39
11	Billy Balmer	38
=	Billy Scott	38
=	Kevin Sheedy	38
=	Gary Stevens	38

FA CUP GOALS			
	PLAYER	APPS	GLS
1	Dixie Dean	32	28
2	Graeme Sharp	54	20
3	Dave Hickson	18	16
4	Kevin Sheedy	38	15
=	Alex "Sandy" Young	39	15
6	Jack Taylor	56	14
7	Jimmy Settle	32	13
8	Alfred Milward	23	12
=	Edgar Chadwick	30	12
=	Jack Sharp	42	12
11	Tommy Browell	10	11
12	Bob Latchford	18	10
=	Jimmy Husband	22	10

LEAGUE CUP APPEARANCES		
	PLAYER	APPS
1	Neville Southall	65
2	Graeme Sharp	48
3	Kevin Ratcliffe	46
4	Dave Watson	39
5	Mick Lyons	37
6	Adrian Heath	35
7	Kevin Sheedy	32
8	Andy King	30
=	Gary Stevens	30
10	Bob Latchford	28
11	Trevor Steven	27
12	Alan Harper	25
=	Peter Reid	25

LEAGUE CUP GOALS			
	PLAYER	APPS	GLS
1	Bob Latchford	28	19
2	Graeme Sharp	48	15
3	Tony Cottee	23	11
=	Adrian Heath	35	11
5	Andy King	30	10
6	Kevin Sheedy	32	9
7	Martin Dobson	22	8
8	Frank Wignall	3	7
=	Paul Wilkinson	4	7
=	Paul Rideout	13	7
=	Dave Watson	39	7

HAT-TRICKS

A breakdown of Everton hat-tricks player-by-player. For a detailed historical list of hat-tricks, including goal times, please see the 2008 Guide. Note that all hat-tricks were scored in league games, unless stated.

PLAYER-BY-PLAYER

PLAYER	HAT-TRICKS	OPPONENTS	H/A	DATE	COMP
Alan Ball	3	West Brom - 4 goals	A	16/03/1968	
		West Brom	H	28/09/1968	
		IBK Keflavik	H	16/09/1970	Eur. Cup
Nick Barmby	1	West Ham United	A	26/02/2000	
Peter Beardsley	1	Coventry City	H	21/09/1991	
Stan Bentham	1	Sunderland	H	10/04/1939	
John Bell	3	Southport	A	02/02/1895	FA Cup
		Aston Villa	A	30/09/1895	
		West Brom	H	17/04/1897	
Robert Bell	1	Leeds United	H	22/10/1938	
Hugh Bolton	2	Middlesbrough	H	29/12/1906	
		Oldham Athletic - 4 goals	H	05/02/1908	FA Cup
Alexander Brady	1	Derby County	H	18/01/1890	FA Cup
John Brearley	1	Middlesbrough	H	03/01/1903	
Tom Browell	2	Bury - 4 goals	H	08/02/1912	FA Cup
		Stockport County	H	15/01/1913	FA Cup
John Cameron	1	Burnley	H	28/11/1896	
Kevin Campbell	1	West Ham United	H	08/05/1999	
Harry Catterick	1	Fulham	A	07/10/1950	
Edgar Chadwick	3	Burnley	H	27/12/1890	
		Sunderland	H	30/09/1893	
		Sheffield United	H	05/10/1895	
Wilf Chadwick	3	Middlesbrough	A	17/02/1923	
		Manchester City - 4 goals	H	22/12/1923	
		Tottenham Hotspur	H	19/04/1924	
Sam Chedgzoy	1	Huddersfield Town	H	14/04/1922	
Wayne Clarke	1	Newcastle United	H	20/04/1987	
Joe Clennell	2	Tottenham Hotspur	A	02/09/1914	
		Bradford City	H	08/11/1919	
Jack Cock	1	Middlesbrough	H	28/02/1923	
Tony Cottee	6	Newcastle United	H	27/08/1988	
		Wrexham	A	25/09/1990	Lge Cup
		Sunderland - 4 goals	H	22/01/1991	ZDS Cup
		Tottenham Hotspur	H	05/10/1991	
		Sheffield United	H	21/08/1993	
		Swindon Town	H	15/01/1994	
Jackie Coulter	1	Sunderland	H	30/01/1935	FA Cup
Bobby Collins	2	Newcastle United	H	19/11/1960	
		Cardiff City	H	15/04/1961	
Jimmy Cunliffe	3	Stoke City - 4 goals	H	02/11/1935	
		West Brom - 4 goals	H	11/04/1936	
		Derby County	H	25/12/1936	
Stan Davies	1	Manchester United	H	27/08/1921	
Dixie Dean	37	Burnley	A	17/10/1925	
		Leeds United	H	24/10/1925	
		Newcastle United	A	12/12/1925	

HAT-TRICKS

PLAYER	HAT-TRICKS	OPPONENTS	H/A	DATE	COMP
Dixie Dean	37	Newcastle United	H	24/04/1926	
		Sunderland - 4 goals	H	25/12/1926	
		Manchester Utd - 5 goals	H	08/10/1927	
		Portsmouth	A	29/10/1927	
		Leicester City	H	05/11/1927	
		Aston Villa	A	10/12/1927	
		Liverpool	A	25/02/1928	
		Burnley - 4 goals	A	28/04/1928	
		Arsenal	H	05/05/1928	
		Bolton Wanderers	H	25/08/1928	
		Portsmouth	H	01/09/1928	
		Newcastle United	H	22/12/1928	
		Bolton Wanderers	A	29/12/1928	
		Derby County	H	01/01/1929	
		Portsmouth	A	28/09/1929	
		Stoke City	H	22/11/1930	
		Oldham Athletic - 4 goals	H	06/12/1930	
		Plymouth Argyle - 4 goals	H	27/12/1930	
		Crystal Palace - 4 goals	A	24/01/1931	FA Cup
		Charlton Athletic	A	07/02/1931	
		Southport - 4 goals	H	28/02/1931	FA Cup
		Liverpool	A	19/09/1931	
		Sheffield United	A	10/10/1931	
		Sheffield Wed - 5 goals	H	17/10/1931	
		Chelsea - 5 goals	H	14/11/1931	
		Leicester City - 4 goals	H	28/11/1931	
		Blackburn Rovers	H	26/12/1931	
		Huddersfield Town	H	19/03/1932	
		West Ham United	H	16/04/1932	
		Newcastle United - 4 goals	A	12/10/1932	C. Shield
		Leicester City	H	08/03/1933	
		Tottenham Hotspur	H	29/12/1934	
		Birmingham City	H	25/04/1936	
		West Bromwich Albion	H	07/11/1936	
Martin Dobson	1	Wimbledon	H	29/08/1978	Lge Cup
Jock Dodds	3	Wolverhampton W.	A	21/02/1948	
		Huddersfield Town	A	28/04/1948	
		Preston North End	H	25/09/1948	
Jimmy Dunn	1	Birmingham City	H	29/08/1931	
Tommy Eglington	1	Doncaster Rovers - 5 goals	H	27/09/1952	
Stan Fazackerley	1	Chelsea	H	06/04/1921	
Duncan Ferguson	1	Bolton Wanderers	H	28/12/1997	
Bertie Freeman	6	Sheffield United	A	17/10/1908	
		Sunderland	H	07/11/1908	
		Sheffield United	H	20/02/1909	
		Chelsea	H	20/03/1909	
		Sheffield Wednesday	A	20/09/1909	
		Bolton Wanderers	H	30/10/1909	
Fred Geary	3	Stoke City	H	2/11/1889	
		Derby County	H	18/01/1890	FA Cup

HAT-TRICKS

PLAYER	HAT-TRICKS	OPPONENTS	H/A	DATE	COMP
Fred Geary	3	Derby County	A	5/11/1892	
Albert Geldard	1	Grimsby Town	H	12/01/1935	FA Cup
Andy Gray	1	Fortuna Sittard	H	06/03/1985	ECW Cup
Jimmy Harris	1	Tottenham Hotspur	A	11/10/1958	
Abe Hartley	1	Wolverhampton W.	H	18/09/1897	
Adrian Heath	1	Notts County	H	04/02/1984	
Dave Hickson	2	Brentford	H	07/02/1953	
		Stoke City	A	07/11/1953	
Bobby Irvine	2	Aston Villa	H	21/01/1922	
		Huddersfield Town	H	14/04/1922	
David Johnson	1	Southampton	H	20/11/1971	
Tommy Johnson	1	Blackburn Rovers	H	27/12/1932	
Andrei Kanchelskis	1	Sheffield Wednesday	A	27/04/1996	
Andy King	1	Bristol City	H	10/02/1979	
Bill Lacey	1	Notts County	H	21/01/1911	
Bob Latchford	5	QPR - 4 goals	A	08/10/1977	
		Coventry City	H	26/11/1977	
		Wimbledon - 5 goals	H	29/08/1978	Lge Cup
		Leeds United	H	13/11/1979	
		Crystal Palace	H	20/09/1980	
Alex Latta	6	Notts County	H	07/12/1889	
		West Bromwich Albion	H	07/11/1891	
		Notts County	H	16/04/1892	
		Derby County	A	05/05/1892	
		Manchester United - 4 goals	A	19/10/1892	
		Birmingham City	A	03/11/1894	
Tommy Lawton	3	Middlesbrough	H	05/11/1938	
		Doncaster Rovers - 4 goals	H	21/01/1939	FA Cup
		Middlesbrough - 4 goals	A	11/03/1939	
Gary Lineker	3	Birmingham City	H	31/08/1985	
		Manchester City	H	11/02/1986	
		Southampton	H	03/05/1986	
Thomas McInnes	1	Stoke City	H	14/12/1895	
Alex McKinnon	1	Derby County	H	27/10/1888	
Alfred Milward	2	Derby County	H	18/01/1890	FA Cup
		Birmingham City	A	07/12/1895	
Johnny Morrissey	2	West Bromwich Albion	H	29/09/1962	
		Sunderland	H	16/05/1967	
Frank Oliver	1	Notts County	H	14/10/1905	
Joe Peacock	1	Derby County	H	11/09/1920	
Fred Pickering	2	Nottingham Forest	H	14/03/1964	
		Tottenham Hotspur	H	29/08/1964	
Bobby Parker	7	Manchester United	H	26/12/1913	
		Liverpool	A	03/10/1914	
		Sunderland	H	21/11/1914	
		Sheffield Wed - 4 goals	A	28/11/1914	
		Manchester City	H	12/12/1914	
		Aston Villa	A	10/02/1915	
		Bolton Wanderers	H	22/03/1915	
John Parker	4	Hull City	H	11/04/1952	

HAT-TRICKS

PLAYER	HAT-TRICKS	OPPONENTS	H/A	DATE	COMP
John Parker	4	Oldham Athletic	H	29/08/1953	
		Plymouth Argyle - 4 goals	H	27/02/1954	
		Rotherham United	H	13/03/1954	
Harry Potts	1	Bury	A	13/12/1952	
Paul Rideout	1	Lincoln City	A	21/09/1993	Lge Cup
Joe Royle	3	Leicester City	H	30/11/1968	
		Southampton	H	27/09/1969	
		Southampton - 4 goals	H	20/11/1971	
Jimmy Settle	2	Wolverhampton W.	H	07/09/1901	FA Cup
		Southampton	H	04/03/1905	
Alan Shackleton	1	Birmingham City	H	14/11/1959	
Graeme Sharp	4	Newcastle United	H	03/12/1986	FM Cup
		Southampton - 4 goals	A	03/10/1987	
		Sheffield Wednesday	A	27/01/1988	FA Cup
		Wrexham	H	09/10/1990	Lge Cup
Jack Sharp	1	Sheffield United	H	10/02/1906	
Jack Southworth	4	Sheffield Wed - 4 goals	H	23/12/1893	
		West Brom - 6 goals	H	30/12/1893	
		Birmingham City	H	03/09/1894	
		Nottingham Forest	H	15/09/1894	
Gary Speed	1	Southampton	H	16/11/1996	
Jimmy Stein	1	Plymouth Argyle - 4 goals	H	27/12/1930	
Alex Stevenson	1	Portsmouth	H	30/04/1938	
Jack Taylor	2	West Bromwich Albion	A	16/01/1897	
		Wolverhampton W.	H	07/09/1901	
Derek Temple	1	Ipswich Town	H	16/09/1961	
Edward Thomas	2	Preston North End - 4 goals	H	08/03/1958	
		Nottingham Forest	H	23/01/1960	
Roy Vernon	3	Arsenal	H	29/04/1961	
		Cardiff City	H	28/04/1962	
		Fulham	H	11/05/1963	
Eddie Wainwright	4	Sunderland	H	15/02/1947	
		Blackpool - 4 goals	H	05/03/1949	
		Huddersfield Town	H	03/09/1949	
		Derby County	A	13/02/1954	
Steve Watson	1	Leeds United	H	28/09/2003	
Tommy White	3	Sunderland	H	03/05/1930	
		Portsmouth	A	02/09/1931	
		Blackburn Rovers	H	14/10/1933	
Frank Wignall	1	Tranmere Rovers	A	21/12/1960	Lge Cup
Paul Wilkinson	1	Newport County	A	07/10/1986	Lge Cup
Thomas Wylie	1	Derby County - 4 goals	H	13/12/1890	
Ayegbeni Yakubu	2	Fulham	H	08/12/2007	
		SK Brann	H	21/02/2008	UEFA Cup
Alex "Sandy" Young	5	Liverpool - 4 goals	H	01/04/1904	
		Nottingham Forest - 4 goals	H	05/11/1904	
		Manchester City - 4 goals	H	03/09/1906	
		Manchester City	H	26/09/1908	
		Blackburn Rovers	H	19/11/1910	
Alex Young	1	Sheffield Wednesday	H	31/08/1965	

MOST GOALS FOR EVERTON IN A LEAGUE SEASON

NAME	SEASON	DIVISION	GAMES	GOALS	GOAL AVE.
Dixie Dean	1927/28	1	39	60	1.54
Dixie Dean	1931/32	1	38	45	1.18
Dixie Dean	1930/31	2	37	39	1.05
Bert Freeman	1908/09	1	37	38	1.03
Bobby Parker	1914/15	1	35	36	1.03
Tommy Lawton	1938/39	1	38	34	0.89
Dixie Dean	1925/26	1	38	32	0.84
John Willie Parker	1953/54	2	38	31	0.82
Bob Latchford	1977/78	1	39	30	0.77
Gary Lineker	1985/86	1	41	30	0.73

MOST GOALS FOR EVERTON IN A SEASON - ALL COMPETITIONS

NAME	SEASON	GAMES	GOALS	GOAL AVE.
Dixie Dean	1927/28	41	63	1.54
Dixie Dean	1930/31	42	48	1.14
Dixie Dean	1931/32	39	46	1.18
Gary Lineker	1985/86	57	40	0.70
Bert Freeman	1908/09	38	38	1
Bobby Parker	1914/15	40	38	0.95
Tommy Lawton	1938/39	43	38	0.88
Fred Pickering	1964/65	51	37	0.73
Dixie Dean	1925/26	40	33	0.83
Dixie Dean	1932/33	46	33	0.72
John Willie Parker	1953/54	41	33	0.80
Bob Latchford	1977/78	46	32	0.70
Wilf Chadwick	1923/24	44	30	0.68
Graeme Sharp	1984/85	55	30	0.55

FASTEST EVERTON PREMIER LEAGUE GOALS

SECONDS	SCORER	OPPONENTS	DATE
23	John Ebbrell	Wimbledon	01/01/1996
32	David Unsworth	Fulham	16/03/2002
41	Olivier Dacourt	Liverpool	03/04/1999
42	Nick Barmby	Middlesbrough	17/02/1999
42	Kevin Campbell	Newcastle United	17/04/1999
47	Ayegbeni Yakubu	Portsmouth	02/03/2008

- The fastest Premier League goal scored against Everton was Chris Sutton's 13-second strike for Blackburn Rovers at Goodison Park in April 1995.

- Everton's fastest-ever goal was Peter Farrell's at Anfield on Christmas Eve, 1949 – unofficially timed at 12 seconds.

EVERTON RECORD TRANSFERS

TOP 10 FEES PAID OUT (EXC. ADD-ONS)		
PLAYER	**FEE**	**DATE**
Marouane Fellaini	£15m	September 2008
Ayegbeni Yakubu	£11.25m	August 2007
Andrew Johnson	£8.6m	May 2006
James Beattie	£6m	January 2005
Nick Barmby	£5.75m	October 1996
Leighton Baines	£5m	August 2007
Joleon Lescott	£5m	June 2006
Per Kroldrup	£5m	June 2005
Joseph Yobo	£5m	July 2002
A. Kanchelskis	£5m	August 1995

TOP 10 FEES RECEIVED (EXC. ADD-ONS)		
PLAYER	**FEE**	**DATE**
Wayne Rooney	£20m	August 2004
Andrew Johnson	£10.5m	August 2008
Francis Jeffers	£8m	June 2001
A. Kanchelskis	£8m	January 1997
Duncan Ferguson	£7m	November 1998
Michael Ball	£6.5m	August 2001
Olivier Dacourt	£6.5m	June 1999
Nick Barmby	£6m	July 2000
Gary Speed	£5.5m	February 1998
James McFadden	£5m	January 2008

One of Everton's record buys - and sales - Andrei Kanchelskis

YOUNGEST/OLDEST EVERTON PLAYERS

YOUNGEST PLAYER

PLAYER	OPPOSITION	DATE OF DEBUT	AGE
James Vaughan	Crystal Palace	10th April 2005	16 years & 271 days
Joe Royle	Blackpool	15th January 1966	16 years & 282 days
Jack Rodwell	AZ Alkmaar	20th December 2007	16 years & 284 days
Wayne Rooney	Tottenham Hotspur	17th August 2002	16 years & 297 days
Francis Jeffers	Manchester United	26th December 1997	16 years & 335 days
Alan Tyrer	Fulham	16th January 1960	17 years & 40 days
George Sharples	West Brom.	5th November 1960	17 years & 47 days
Alec Farrall	Lincoln City	22nd April 1953	17 years & 51 days
Roy Parnell	Wolves	21st January 1961	17 years & 105 days
Richard Dunne	Swindon Town	5th January 1997	17 years & 107 days

*Note Jose Baxter played against Blackburn Rovers at Goodison Park in August 2008, aged 16 years & 191 days

PREVIOUS YOUNGEST PLAYER RECORD HOLDERS

PLAYER	OPPOSITION	DATE OF DEBUT	AGE
Edgar Chadwick	Accrington Stanley	8th September 1888	19 years & 55 days
Alfred Milward	Blackburn Rovers	10th November 1888	18 years & 60 days
William Brown	Manchester City	12th December 1914	17 years & 215 days
Tommy Lawton	Wolves	13th February 1937	17 years & 130 days

YOUNGEST PLAYER TO SCORE

PLAYER	OPPOSITION	DATE OF DEBUT	AGE
James Vaughan	Crystal Palace	10th April 2005	16 years & 271 days*
Wayne Rooney	Wrexham	1st October 2002	16 years & 342 days
Tommy Lawton	Wolves	13th February 1937	17 years & 130 days*
Alan Tyrer	Leeds United	23rd April 1960	17 years & 137 days
Bert Llewellyn	Blackpool	22nd August 1956	17 years & 200 days

(* Scored on debut)

PREVIOUS YOUNGEST GOALSCORER RECORD HOLDERS

PLAYER	OPPOSITION	DATE OF DEBUT	AGE
Edgar Chadwick	Accrington Stanley	15th September 1888	19 years & 62 days
Alfred Milward	Stoke City	12th January 1889	18 years & 123 days

OLDEST PLAYER

PLAYER	OPPOSITION	DATE OF FINAL GAME	AGE
Ted Sagar	Plymouth Argyle	15th November 1952	42 years & 281 days
Ted Taylor	Tottenham Hotspur	11th February 1928	40 years & 341 days
Nigel Martyn	Chelsea	28th January 2006	39 years & 170 days
Neville Southall	Tottenham Hotspur	29th November 1997	39 years & 74 days
Richard Gough	Bradford City	28th April 2001	39 years & 23 days
Wally Fielding	Tottenham Hotspur	11th October 1958	38 years & 319 days
Jack Taylor	Barnsley	31st March 1910	38 years & 63 days
Dave Watson	Tottenham Hotspur	15th January 2000	38 years & 56 days
Tom Fern	Sunderland	1st January 1924	37 years & 279 days
George Jackson	Portsmouth	24th April 1948	37 years & 101 days

OLDEST PLAYER TO SCORE

PLAYER	OPPOSITION	DATE OF FINAL GOAL	AGE
Wally Fielding	West Brom.	27th September 1958	38 years & 305 days

PREMIER LEAGUE NUMBERS GAME

SQUAD NUMBERS

Below is a comprehensive list of every Everton player to have represented the club in Premier League games - including what shirt number they wore, and how many appearances made.

NUMBER	PLAYERS (PREMIER LEAGUE APPEARANCES IN BRACKETS)				
1	Southall (207),	Myhre (42),	Gerrard (45),	Wright (60)	
2	Jackson (67),	Barrett (57),	Cleland (27),	S. Watson (126),	Kroldrup (1), Hibbert (37)
3	Hinchcliffe (143), Ball (62),		Pistone (101),	Naysmith (22),	Baines (22)
4	Snodin (32),	Barrett (17),	Unsworth (65),	Williamson (15),	Dacourt (30), Gough (38)
	Stubbs (124),	Yobo (97)			
5	D. Watson (183),	Weir (186),	Lescott (38)		
6	Ablett (71),	Phelan (24),	Unsworth (187), Arteta (104)		
7	Ma. Ward (27),	Samways (19),	Stuart (78),	Madar (17),	Collins (55), Alexandersson (58),
	Bent (54),	Van der Meyde (8)			
8	Stuart (58),	Rideout (34),	Barmby (91),	Nyarko (22),	Radzinski (91), Beattie (43),
	Johnson (61)				
9	Cottee (42),	Ferguson (116),	Campbell (145), Ferguson (27),		Beattie (33)
10	Horne (89),	Speed (58),	Hutchison (75),	S. Hughes (18),	Ferguson (84), Davies (45),
	Gravesen (8)				
11	Beagrie (29),	Amokachi (18),	Limpar (30),	Spencer (9),	Gemmill (14), Pembridge (60),
	Jeffers (18),	McFadden (75)			
12	Holmes (16),	Amokachi (25),	Barmby (25),	Short (53),	Pembridge (31), Ball (29),
	Blomqvist (15),	Tie (34)			
13	Kearton (1),	Gerrard (43),	Simonsen (29),	Turner (4)	
14	Ebbrell (97),	Grant (23),	Weir (35),	Jeffers (12),	Tal (7), Kilbane (102),
	Vaughan (8)				
15	Rideout (53),	Jackson (14),	Thomsen (24),	Beagrie (6),	Materazzi (27), Dunne (34),
	Naysmith (112),	Stubbs (37)			
16	Radosavljevic (23),	Burrows (19),	Samways (4),	Branch (32),	Cadamarteri (17), Gravesen (141),
	Carsley (5),	Lescott (38),	Jagielka (34)		
17	Limpar (36),	Kanchelskis (52), Farrelly (27),		Jeffers (21),	Gemmill (76), Cahill (101)
18	Parkinson (90),	Madar (2),	Weir (14),	Phelan (1),	S. Hughes (11), Gascoigne (31),
	Rooney (67),	Neville (106)			
19	Barlow (36),	Hottiger (17),	Oster (40),	Xavier (20),	J. Moore (37), McBride (8),
	Chadwick (1),	Valente (43)			
20	Warzycha (7),	Durrant (5),	Grant (35),	Thomas (8),	Gemmill (7), Jevons (3),
	Cleland (8),	Yobo (79),	Ferrari (8),	Pienaar (28)	
21	Rowett (4),	Short (46),	Mi. Ward (24),	Cadamarteri (19),	Weifeng (1), Nyarko (11),
	Osman (126)				
22	Angell (20),	McCann (11),	Degn (4),	Linderoth (40),	Hibbert (65), Vaughan (14),
	Yakubu (29)				
23	Branch (28),	Tiler (21),	J. Moore (15),	M. Hughes (9)*,	Rodrigo (4), Pistone (2),
	Fernandes (12)				
24	O'Connor (5),	Grant (2),	Ferguson (12),	Ginola (5),	Xavier (12), McFadden (23),
	Howard (72)				
25	N. Moore (4),	Ball (30),	Baardsen (1),	Martyn (86)	
26	Unsworth (16),	Allen (6),	Bakayoko (23),	Johnson (3),	M. Hughes (9)*, Jevons (4),
	Carsley (89),	Westerveld (2),	Carsley (72)		
27	Dunne (26),	Clarke (8),	Van der Meyde (10)		
28	Cadamarteri (1),	Bilic (28),	Xavier (11),	Hibbert (59),	Anichebe (46)
29	Cadamarteri (56),	McLeod (5),	Vaughan (1)		
30	Jevons (1),	Clarke (1),	Chadwick (13),	Ruddy (1)	
31	Myhre (22),	Osman (6),	Vaughan (2),	M. Hughes (1)	
32	O'Kane (14),	Hibbert (3)			
33	Tal (22),	Wessels (2)			
34	Holmes (1),	Jeffers (16)			
35	Hills (3),	Simonsen (1), Myhre (6),		Gerrard (2)	
36	Milligan (4)				
37	Farley (1),	Fernandes (9), Rodwell (2)			
38	Anichebe (2),	Silva de Franca (1)			

*Please note 'M. Hughes' (No. 23 & 26) was striker Mark Hughes (D.O.B. 1/11/1963);
'M. Hughes' (No. 31) was defender Mark Hughes (D.O.B. 9/12/1986)

INTERNATIONAL BLUES

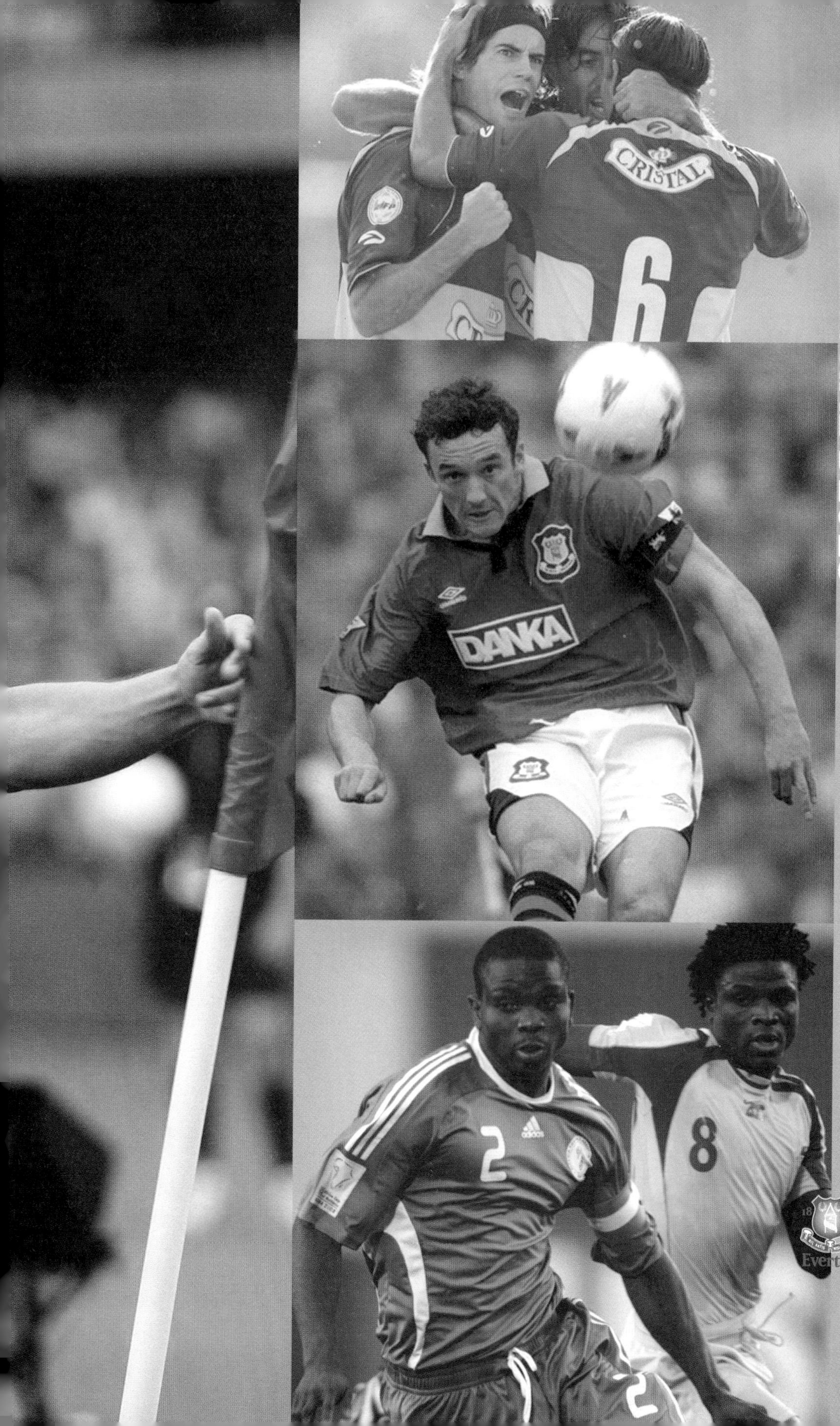

18 78
Everton

EVERTON INTERNATIONALS 2007/08

In keeping with the modern game, the matches featuring Everton players in 2007/08 were spread right across the globe – from Europe to the African continent, and then to Tim Howard's matches in the United States, as well as Tim Cahill's appearance in Australia.

There were several highlights: before departing in January 2008, James McFadden scored one of the most famous international goals of modern times – a strike of some 35 yards in Scotland's memorable 1-0 win over France in Paris in September 2007. When leaving in January, the forward had scored 13 international goals as an Everton player, a total exceeded only by Dixie Dean (18).

There were also well-deserved England debuts for the defensive pairing of Joleon Lescott and Phil Jagielka. The former made his international bow against Estonia in October, and with fellow substitute Phil Neville they became the first pair of Everton players to occupy the full-back berths for England in the same match since Tommy Wright and Ray Wilson 39 years earlier. Phil Jagielka's entrance on the international stage was in the unusual setting of Port of Spain, Trinidad, in June. Andy Johnson also played in the 3-0 win over Israel in September.

Everton continued to be well represented in the Nigerian national team, and for only the second time in the club's history – the first being Sweden in 2002 – the Blues were represented by three players in an overseas country's international side, when Joseph Yobo, Victor Anichebe and Ayegbeni Yakubu played in the friendly against Austria in May 2008. Despite the regular presence of our two forwards, it was the Everton centre-half who was the unlikely match-winner in later matches against Sierra Leone and Equatorial Guinea.

Elsewhere, Tim Howard confirmed his status as the United States' first-choice keeper, while Tim Cahill showed that he is – injury notwithstanding – equally as important to his country as he is to Everton.

Note that in keeping with the agreed principle, only caps won while with Everton on a permanent deal are shown in this section. For example, in 2007/08 Steven Pienaar only signed towards the end of the season, being officially recognised as a Borussia Dortmund player (from whom he was on loan) before then.

INTERNATIONAL APPEARANCES BY EVERTON PLAYERS IN 2007/08

PLAYER	COUNTRY	OPPOSITION	VENUE	SCORE	DATE
Phil Jagielka	England	Trinidad & Tobago	(a)	3-0	01/06/2008
Andrew Johnson	England	Israel	(h)	3-0	08/09/2007
Joleon Lescott	England	Estonia	(h)	3-0	13/10/2007
		Russia	(a)	1-2	17/10/2007
		Austria	(a)	1-0	16/11/2007
		Croatia	(h)	2-3	21/11/2007
		France	(a)	0-1	26/03/2008
Phil Neville	England	Israel	(h)	3-0	08/09/2007
		Russia	(h)	3-0	12/09/2007
		Estonia	(h)	3-0	13/10/2007
James McFadden	Scotland	Lithuania	(h)	3-1 - 1 goal	08/09/2007
		France	(a)	1-0 - 1 goal	12/09/2007
		Ukraine	(h)	3-1 - 1 goal	13/10/2007
		Georgia	(a)	0-2	17/10/2007
		Italy	(h)	1-2	17/11/2007

EVERTON INTERNATIONALS 2007/08

INTERNATIONAL APPEARANCES BY EVERTON PLAYERS IN 2007/08

PLAYER	COUNTRY	OPPOSITION	VENUE	SCORE	DATE
Lee Carsley	Rep. of Ire.	Slovakia	(a)	2-2	08/09/2007
		Czech Republic	(a)	0-1	12/9/2007
		Germany	(h)	0-0	13/10/2007
		Wales	(a)	2-2	17/11/2007
		Brazil	(h)	0-1	06/02/2008
Tim Cahill	Australia	Qatar	(h)	3-0 - 1 goal	06/02/2008
Tim Howard	USA	Sweden	(a)	0-1	22/08/2007
		Brazil	(h)	2-4	09/09/2007
		South Africa	(a)	1-0	17/11/2007
		Mexico	(h)	2-2	06/02/2008
		Poland	(a)	3-0	26/03/2008
		England	(a)	0-2	28/05/2008
		Spain	(a)	0-1	04/06/2008
		Argentina	(h)	0-0	08/06/2008
Steven Pienaar	S. Africa	Nigeria	(a)	0-2	01/06/2008
		Eq. Guinea	(h)	4-1	07/06/2008
		Sierra Leone	(a)	0-1	14/06/2008
		Sierra Leone	(h)	0-0	21/06/2008
Victor Anichebe	Nigeria	Austria	(a)	1-1	27/05/2008
		South Africa	(h)	2-0	01/06/2008
		Eq. Guinea	(a)	1-0	15/06/2008
		Eq. Guinea	(h)	2-0	21/06/2008
Ayegbeni Yakubu	Nigeria	Ivory Coast	N	0-1	21/01/2008
		Mali	N	0-0	25/01/2008
		Benin	N	2-0 - 1 goal	29/01/2008
		Ghana	N	1-2 - 1 goal	03/02/2008
		(Above matches in African Cup of Nations, held in Ghana)			
		Austria	(a)	1-1	27/05/2008
		South Africa	(h)	2-0	01/06/2008
		Sierra Leone	(a)	1-0	07/06/2008
		Eq. Guinea	(a)	1-0	15/06/2008
		Eq. Guinea	(h)	2-0 - 1 goal	21/06/2008
Joseph Yobo	Nigeria	Ivory Coast	N	0-1	21/01/2008
		Mali	N	0-0	25/01/2008
		Benin	N	2-0	29/01/2008
		Ghana	N	1-2	03/02/2008
		(Above matches in African Cup of Nations, held in Ghana)			
		Austria	(a)	1-1	27/05/2008
		South Africa	(h)	2-0	01/06/2008
		Sierra Leone	(a)	1-0 - 1 goal	07/06/2008
		Eq. Guinea	(a)	1-0 - 1 goal	15/06/2008
		Eq. Guinea	(h)	2-0	21/06/2008

ENGLAND

EVERTON PLAYERS CAPPED BY ENGLAND

PLAYER	CAPS WON AT EVERTON	TOTAL CAPS	PLAYER	CAPS WON AT EVERTON	TOTAL CAPS
Alan Ball	39	72	Paul Bracewell	3	3
Ray Wilson	33	63	Charlie Gee	3	3
Brian Labone	26	26	Tommy Johnson	3	5
Gary Stevens	26	46	Fred Pickering	3	3
Trevor Steven	25	36	Jimmy Settle	3	6
Wayne Rooney	17	43	Gordon West	3	3
Dixie Dean	16	16	Tom Booth	2	2
Peter Reid	13	13	Wally Boyes	2	3
Bob Latchford	12	12	Bert Freeman	2	5
Gary Lineker	11	80	Fred Geary	2	2
Tommy Wright	11	11	George Harrison	2	2
Cliff Britton	9	9	Frank Jefferis	2	2
Johnny Holt	9	10	Joe Royle	2	6
Martin Keown	9	43	Jack Sharp	2	2
Sam Chedgzoy	8	8	Walter Abbott	1	1
Tommy Lawton	8	23	Benjamin Baker	1	2
Keith Newton	8	27	Michael Ball	1	1
Edgar Chadwick	7	7	William Balmer	1	1
Phil Neville	**7**	**59**	Warney Cresswell	1	7
Dave Watson	6	12	Jimmy Cunliffe	1	1
Andy Johnson	6	8	Martin Dobson	1	5
Nick Barmby	5	23	Dicky Downs	1	1
Joleon Lescott	**5**	**5**	Colin Harvey	1	1
Joe Mercer	5	5	Bob Howarth	1	5
Tony Cottee	4	7	**Phil Jagielka**	**1**	**1**
Albert Geldard	4	4	Tony Kay	1	1
Harry Hardman	4	4	Derek Temple	1	1
Andy Hinchcliffe	4	7	David Unsworth	1	1
Harry Makepeace	4	4	Tommy White	1	1
Alf Milward	4	4	Sam Wolstenholme	1	3
Ted Sagar	4	4			

(Left to right) Phil Neville, Andy Johnson and Phil Jagielka, on England duty during 2007/08

SCOTLAND

EVERTON PLAYERS CAPPED BY SCOTLAND

PLAYER	CAPS WON AT EVERTON	TOTAL CAPS	PLAYER	CAPS WON AT EVERTON	TOTAL CAPS
David Weir	43	61	Ian Wilson	3	5
James McFadden	32	37	George Wood	3	4
Gary Naysmith	32	40	Jimmy Gabriel	2	2
Scot Gemmill	13	26	Neil McBain	2	3
Graeme Sharp	12	12	Alex Young	2	8
Stuart McCall	11	40	Alex "Sandy" Young	2	2
Don Hutchison	10	26	George Brewster	1	1
Asa Hartford	8	50	John Connolly	1	1
Pat Nevin	8	28	Jimmy Dunn	1	6
Bobby Collins	6	31	Andy Gray	1	20
John Collins	6	58	Alex Parker	1	15
Bruce Rioch	6	24	Jack Robertson	1	16
Torry Gillick	5	5	Jock Thomson	1	1
Alex Scott	5	16	Alec Troup	1	5
Jack Bell	3	10	George Wilson	1	6
Duncan Ferguson	3	7			

WALES

EVERTON PLAYERS CAPPED BY WALES

PLAYER	CAPS WON AT EVERTON	TOTAL CAPS	PLAYER	CAPS WON AT EVERTON	TOTAL CAPS
Neville Southall	92	92	Dave Smallman	4	7
Kevin Ratcliffe	58	59	Smart Arridge	3	8
Barry Horne	23	59	Stanley Davies	3	18
T.G. Jones	17	17	John Oster	3	13
Dai Davies	16	52	Joe Davies	2	11
Mark Pembridge	16	54	Ll. Davies	2	13
Pat van den Hauwe	13	13	Ted Hughes	2	14
Roy Vernon	13	32	Aubrey Powell	2	8
Simon Davies	12	50	Leigh Roose	2	24
Gary Speed	9	85	Phil Griffiths	1	1
Tom Griffiths	8	21	Jack Humphreys	1	1
Charlie Parry	6	13	Rob Jones	1	1
Ben Williams	6	10	Mickey Thomas	1	51

NORTHERN IRELAND

EVERTON PLAYERS CAPPED BY NORTHERN IRELAND

PLAYER	CAPS WON AT EVERTON	TOTAL CAPS	PLAYER	CAPS WON AT EVERTON	TOTAL CAPS
Billy Scott	16	25	Tommy Eglington	6	6
Val Harris	14	20	Tommy Jackson	6	35
Alex Stevenson	14	19	Jackie Coulter	5	11
Billy Bingham	12	56	Jimmy Sheridan	5	6
Dave Clements	12	48	Jimmy Hill	3	7
Billy Cook	12	15	John Houston	3	6
Bryan Hamilton	11	50	Alec McCartney	2	15
Bobby Irvine	11	15	Peter Scott	2	10
Bill Lacey	10	23	Norman Whiteside	2	38
Peter Farrell	7	7			

REPUBLIC OF IRELAND

EVERTON PLAYERS CAPPED BY REP. OF IRELAND

PLAYER	CAPS WON AT EVERTON	TOTAL CAPS	PLAYER	CAPS WON AT EVERTON	TOTAL CAPS
Kevin Sheedy	42	46	Jim McDonagh	4	25
Peter Farrell	26	28	Mick Meagan	4	17
Kevin Kilbane	24	87	Gerry Peyton	4	33
Tommy Eglington	22	24	Mike Walsh (1981-83)	4	4
Lee Carsley	21	39	Tommy Clinton	3	3
Jimmy O'Neill	17	17	Terry Phelan	3	42
Alex Stevenson	6	7	Gareth Farrelly	2	6
Don Donovan	5	5	James Kendrick	1	4
Richard Dunne	5	42	Eamonn O'Keefe	1	5
Peter Corr	4	4	Mick Walsh (1978-79)	1	21

(Left to right) Bryan Hamilton and Kevin Kilbane, Irish Evertonians

OVERSEAS INTERNATIONALS

INTERNATIONAL RECORD OF EVERTON PLAYERS WHO APPEARED DURING 2007/08 SEASON

PLAYER	AT EVERTON		OVERALL	
	CAPS	GOALS	CAPS	GOALS
Victor Anichebe	4	0	4	0
Tim Cahill	24	7	28	13
Lee Carsley *	21	0	39	0
Tim Howard	14	0	30	0
Phil Jagielka	1	0	1	0
Andrew Johnson	6	0	8	0
Joleon Lescott	5	0	5	0
James McFadden *	33	13	37	13
Phil Neville	7	0	59	0
Steven Pienaar	4	0	28	2
Nuno Valente	12	0	33	0
Andy van der Meyde	0	0	18	0
Ayegbeni Yakubu	9	3	41	17
Joseph Yobo	42	5	59	5

* Record on departure from club

INTERNATIONAL RECORD OF PREVIOUS OVERSEAS PLAYERS AT EVERTON

PLAYER	COUNTRY	CAPS	GOALS
Niclas Alexandersson	Sweden	23	2
Daniel Amokachi	Nigeria	6	2
Ibrahima Bakayoko	Ivory Coast	4	0
Slaven Bilic	Croatia	13	2
Jesper Blomqvist	Sweden	1	0
Thomas Gravesen	Denmark	44	5
Marc Hottiger	Switzerland	7	0
Andrei Kanchelskis	Russia	15	2
Anders Limpar	Sweden	10	0
Tobias Linderoth	Sweden	23	0
Joe-Max Moore	USA	22	4
Thomas Myhre	Norway	23	0
Alex Nyarko	Ghana	1	0
Tomasz Radzinski	Canada	9	6
Idan Tal	Israel	11	1
Robert Warzycha	Poland	17	1
Abel Xavier	Portugal	7	0

* Please note international records for Stefan Rehn (Sweden) and Li Tie (China) are not available

EVERTON AND THE OLYMPICS

BEIJING 2008

Not many Premier League footballers can lay claim to winning an Olympic medal, but young Nigerian striker Victor Anichebe joined a select band after his country of birth reached the soccer final at the 2008 Beijing Games.

The youngster played five matches in the Chinese capital – all as a substitute. After taking an opening bow 10 minutes from the end of Nigeria's goalless draw against Holland in their opening match, Anichebe scored Nigeria's second goal in a 2-1 victory over Japan before a third substitute appearance came in the 2-1 win over the United States in the last group match.

The forward sat out the quarter-final win over Ivory Coast before playing the last half-hour of what was a comfortable 4-1 semi-final victory over Belgium - for whom new Everton club-record signing Marouane Fellaini was an unused substitute. The final against Argentina was a repeat of that staged in 1996, but this time it was the South Americans' turn to get their hands on gold following a tight 1-0 win, with the Everton man coming close to an equaliser in yet another cameo. The winners featured Liverpool's Javier Mascherano in their line-up, meaning the two players can uniquely claim to have faced each other in both a derby match and an Olympic final.

THE BLUES' FOOTBALL OLYMPIANS

Fellow squad member Tim Cahill appeared in the 2004 Olympics shortly after joining the Toffees from Millwall. The midfielder scored against Serbia & Montengro before Australia lost out to Iraq at the quarter-final stage. The previous Evertonian in the Olympics had been Daniel Amokachi, who struck gold with Nigeria in 1996 shortly before leaving for Besiktas in Turkey.

Evertonians Harold Hardman and Arthur Berry both won Olympic gold in the early part of the 20th century, although neither was on our books at the time.

Two other players out of the current squad have been involved in the Games, both in Sydney 2000: Ayegbeni Yakubu was part of the Nigerian side who reached the quarter-finals, while goalkeeper Tim Howard was in the USA squad.

OTHER OLYMPIC FOOTBALL LINKS

Edgar Chadwick, who scored 110 goals in 300 appearances between 1888 and 1899, managed Holland in the 1908 (London) and 1912 (Stockholm) Games. Reputedly the first Englishman to coach abroad, he led the Dutch to the bronze medal in both tournaments. They were beaten 4–0 by Great Britain in the semi–finals in London and lost to Denmark at the same stage four years later.

It wasn't until Seoul 1988 that future Everton players appeared in the Olympic Games. Anders Limpar and Stefan Rehn represented Sweden, who eventually lost to Italy in the quarter–finals. Four years later in Barcelona, future quartet Alex Nyarko (Ghana), Claus Thomsen (Denmark), Niclas Alexandersson (Sweden) and Joe Max–Moore (USA) represented their countries - Nyarko clinching bronze when his side defeated Australia.
Alessandro Pistone (Italy) and Olivier Dacourt (France) appeared in the 1996 Games in Atlanta, while one-time loan defender Matteo Ferrari represented Italy in both Sydney 2000 and four years later in Athens - playing every game in Greece to help his country to bronze.

Victor Anichebe in action during the Olympic final (top), while below Daniel Amokachi (second right) celebrates gold at Atlanta, 1996

EVERTON CHILE

ABOUT

Founded on June 24, 1909, 'Everton de Vina del Mar' were named after Everton FC after being founded by visiting Liverpudlian sailors.
Nicknamed "The Ruleteros" (rouletters, so-called because the coastal city of Vina del Mar, where the team play, is a popular gambling resort), the team won their first Chilean championship for 32 years in summer 2008, beating Colo Colo 3-2 on aggregate following a memorable 3-0 second-leg triumph at home. In front of a 15,000 crowd, second-half goals from Argentine forward Ezequiel Miralles (2) and Jaime Riveros ensured the title and qualification for the Copa Libertadores (South American Champions League) in 2009, only the second time Everton have achieved the feat.
The success also denied their more illustrious opponents a fifth successive title - having won the Apertura (January-June tournament) and Clasura (July-December) in 2006 and 2007.

THE RULETEROS SOCIETY

Formed in 2002 through an initiative by Evertonian John Shearon, the society aims to encourage the development of links between Everton and their Chilean namesakes.
Meeting regularly pre-match near Goodison Park, the society also holds an end-of-season gathering in Chile, towards the end of the calendar year.
The group aims to celebrate the Chilean club's centenary in 2009, the hope being that a game can be set up between the two clubs.
The society's motto is:

"Once an Evertonian - Twice an Evertonian."

If you are interested in joining the group, annual membership is £5 adults, £3 seniors and students, and free for juniors. Please write to:

The Secretary
The Ruleteros Society
17 Cecil Road
Dronfield
Sheffield
S18 2GW

EVERTON CHILE

Stadium   Estadio Sausalito   (Capacity: 22,000)
Honours   Primera Division   1950, 1952, 1976, 2008 (Apertura)
                Copa Chile   1984
                Primera B   1974, 2003
                Copa Libertadores   1977 - 1st round
Manager   Nelson Acosta
                Former Uruguayan international who became a nationalised Chilean in 1984. Managed Chile between 1996 and 2001, leading them to the 1998 World Cup, and also coached Bolivia in 2004. Re-appointed coach of Chile a year later, leading them in the 2007 Copa America. He took over Everton in September 2007.

GOALKEEPERS
Gustavo Dalsasso, Sebastian Perez, Paulo Garces
DEFENDERS
Cristian Oviedo, Mauricio Arias, Francisco Sanchez, Leandro Delgado, Benjamin Ruiz, Adrian Rojas

MIDFIELDERS
Juan Luis Gonzalez, Angel Rojas, Jaime Riveros, Cristian Uribe, Roberto Reyes, Raul Gutierrez, Jose Luis Cabion, Fernando Saavedra, Paul Leiva
STRIKERS
Mathias Vidangossy, John Jairo Castillo, Cristian Canio, Ezequiel Miralles

78

Everton

THE FA CUP RESULTS

(*1958-2008 - Full record available in The Official Guide 2008*)

Date	Round	Venue	Opponents	Score	Scorers	Attendance
1957/58	**(WINNERS - BOLTON WANDERERS)**					
4th Jan	3	A	Sunderland	2-2	Hickson 2	34,602
8th Jan	3 Replay	H	Sunderland	3-1	Keeley 2, Hickson	56,952
29th Jan	4	H	Blackburn Rovers	1-2	J. Harris	75,818
1958/59	**(WINNERS - NOTTINGHAM FOREST)**					
10th Jan	3	H	Sunderland	4-0	Hickson 2, J. Harris, Thomas	57,788
24th Jan	4	A	Charlton Athletic	2-2	Thomas, Collins	44,094
28th Jan	4 Replay	H	Charlton Athletic	4-1	Hickson 2, Collins 2	74,782
14th Feb	5	H	Aston Villa	1-4	Hickson	60,225
1959/60	**(WINNERS - WOLVERHAMPTON WANDERERS)**					
9th Jan	3	A	Bradford City	0-3		23,550
1960/61	**(WINNERS - TOTTENHAM HOTSPUR)**					
7th Jan	3	H	Sheffield United	0-1		48,593
1961/62	**(WINNERS - TOTTENHAM HOTSPUR)**					
6th Jan	3	H	King's Lynn	4-0	Collins, Vernon (pen), Bingham, Fell	44,916
27th Jan	4	H	Manchester City	2-0	Vernon, Lill	56,980
17th Feb	5	A	Burnley	1-3	Collins	50,514
1962/63	**(WINNERS - MANCHESTER UNITED)**					
15th Jan	3	A	Barnsley	3-0	B. Harris, Stevens, Vernon	30,011
29th Jan	4	A	Swindon Town	5-1	Vernon 2, Gabriel, Bingham, Morrissey	26,239
16th Mar	5	A	West Ham United	0-1		31,770
1963/64	**(WINNERS - WEST HAM UNITED)**					
4th Jan	3	A	Hull City	1-1	Scott	36,478
7th Jan	3 Replay	H	Hull City	2-1	Scott, B. Harris	56,613
25th Jan	4	A	Leeds United	1-1	Vernon (pen)	48,826
28th Jan	4 Replay	H	Leeds United	2-0	Vernon, Gabriel	66,167
15th Feb	5	A	Sunderland	1-3	B. Harris	62,817
1964/65	**(WINNERS - LIVERPOOL)**					
9th Jan	3	H	Sheffield Wednesday	2-2	Burgin o.g., Pickering	44,732
13th Jan	3 Replay	A	Sheffield Wednesday	3-0	Pickering, Harvey, Temple	50,080
30th Jan	4	A	Leeds United	1-1	Pickering (pen)	50,051
2nd Feb	4 Replay	H	Leeds United	1-2	Pickering	65,940
1965/66	**(WINNERS - EVERTON)**					
22nd Jan	3	H	Sunderland	3-0	Temple, Pickering, Young	47,893
12th Feb	4	A	Bedford Town	3-0	Temple 2, Pickering	18,407
3rd Mar	5	H	Coventry City	3-0	Young, Temple, Pickering	60,350
26th Mar	6	A	Manchester City	0-0		63,034
29th Mar	6 Replay 1	H	Manchester City	0-0		60,349
5th Apr	6 Replay 2	N	Manchester City	2-0	Temple, Pickering	27,948
23rd Apr	SF	N	Manchester United	1-0	Harvey	60,000
14th May	F	N	Sheffield Wednesday	3-2	Trebilcock 2, Temple	100,000

THE FA CUP RESULTS

Date	Round	Venue	Opponents	Score	Scorers	Attendance
1966/67	**(WINNERS - TOTTENHAM HOTSPUR)**					
28th Jan	3	A	Burnley	0-0		42,482
31st Jan	3 Replay	H	Burnley	2-1	Young 2	57,449
18th Feb	4	A	Wolverhampton W.	1-1	Ball (pen)	53,439
21st Feb	4 Replay	H	Wolverhampton W.	3-1	Husband 2, Temple	60,020
11th Mar	5	H	Liverpool	1-0	Ball	64,851
8th Apr	6	A	Nottingham Forest	2-3	Husband 2	47,510
1967/68	**(WINNERS - WEST BROMWICH ALBION)**					
27th Jan	3	A	Southport	1-0	Royle	18,795
17th Feb	4	A	Carlisle United	2-0	Husband, Royle	25,000
9th Mar	5	H	Tranmere Rovers	2-0	Royle, Morrissey	61,982
30th Mar	6	A	Leicester City	3-1	Husband 2, Kendall	43,519
27th Apr	SF	N	Leeds United	1-0	Morrissey (pen)	63,000
18th May	F	N	West Bromwich Alb.	0-1 aet		99,665
1968/69	**(WINNERS - MANCHESTER CITY)**					
4th Jan	3	H	Ipswich Town	2-1	Royle, Hurst	49,047
25th Jan	4	H	Coventry City	2-0	Royle, Hurst	53,289
12th Feb	5	H	Bristol Rovers	1-0	Royle	55,294
1st Mar	6	A	Manchester United	1-0	Royle	63,464
22nd Mar	SF	N	Manchester City	0-1		63,025
1969/70	**(WINNERS - CHELSEA)**					
3rd Jan	3	A	Sheffield United	1-2	Ball (pen)	29,116
1970/71	**(WINNERS - ARSENAL)**					
2nd Jan	3	H	Blackburn Rovers	2-0	Husband 2	40,471
23rd Jan	4	H	Middlesbrough	3-0	H. Newton, Harvey, Royle	54,875
13th Feb	5	H	Derby County	1-0	Johnson	53,490
6th Mar	6	H	Colchester United	5-0	Kendall 2, Royle, Husband, Ball	53,028
27th Mar	SF	N	Liverpool	1-2	Ball	62,144
1971/72	**(WINNERS - LEEDS UNITED)**					
15th Jan	3	A	Crystal Palace	2-2	Whittle, Harvey	32,331
18th Jan	3 Replay	H	Crystal Palace	3-2	Scott, Kenyon, Hurst	45,408
5th Feb	4	H	Walsall	2-1	Johnson, Whittle	45,462
26th Feb	5	H	Tottenham Hotspur	0-2		50,511
1972/73	**(WINNERS - SUNDERLAND)**					
13th Jan	3	H	Aston Villa	3-2	Belfitt, Buckley, Harper	42,222
3rd Feb	4	H	Millwall	0-2		37,277
1973/74	**(WINNERS - LIVERPOOL)**					
5th Jan	3	H	Blackburn Rovers	3-0	Harper, Hurst, Clements	31,940
27th Jan	4	H	West Bromwich Alb.	0-0		53,509
30th Jan	4 Replay	A	West Bromwich Alb.	0-1		27,556
1974/75	**(WINNERS - WEST HAM UNITED)**					
4th Jan	3	H	Altrincham	1-1	Clements (pen)	34,519
7th Jan	3 Replay	A	Altrincham (Played at Old Trafford)	2-0	Latchford, Lyons	35,530

THE FA CUP RESULTS

Date	Round	Venue	Opponents	Score	Scorers	Attendance
1974/75	**(WINNERS - WEST HAM UNITED)**					
25th Jan	4	A	Plymouth Argyle	3-1	Pearson, Lyons 2	38,000
15th Feb	5	H	Fulham	1-2	Kenyon	45,233
1975/76	**(WINNERS - SOUTHAMPTON)**					
3rd Jan	3	A	Derby County	1-2	G. Jones	31,647
1976/77	**(WINNERS - MANCHESTER UNITED)**					
8th Jan	3	H	Stoke City	2-0	Lyons, McKenzie (pen)	32,981
29th Jan	4	A	Swindon Town	2-2	McKenzie, Latchford	24,347
1st Feb	4 Replay	H	Swindon Town	2-1	Dobson, Jones	38,063
26th Feb	5	A	Cardiff City	2-1	Latchford, McKenzie	35,582
19th Mar	6	H	Derby County	2-0	Latchford, Pearson	42,409
23rd Apr	SF	N	Liverpool	2-2	McKenzie, Rioch	52,637
27th Apr	SF Replay	N	Liverpool	0-3		52,579
1977/78	**(WINNERS - IPSWICH TOWN)**					
7th Jan	3	H	Aston Villa	4-1	King, Ross (pen), McKenzie, Latchford	46,320
28th Jan	4	A	Middlesbrough	2-3	Telfer, Lyons	33,652
1978/79	**(WINNERS - ARSENAL)**					
10th Jan	3	A	Sunderland	1-2	Dobson	28,602
1979/80	**(WINNERS - WEST HAM UNITED)**					
5th Jan	3	H	Aldershot	4-1	Latchford, Hartford, King, Kidd	23,700
26th Jan	4	H	Wigan Athletic	3-0	McBride, Latchford, Kidd	51,853
16th Feb	5	H	Wrexham	5-2	Megson, Eastoe 2, Ross (pen), Latchford	44,830
8th Mar	6	H	Ipswich Town	2-1	Latchford, Kidd	45,104
12th Apr	SF	N	West Ham United	1-1	Kidd (pen)	47,685
16th Apr	SF Replay	N	West Ham United	1-2 aet	Latchford	40,720
1980/81	**(WINNERS - TOTTENHAM HOTSPUR)**					
3rd Jan	3	H	Arsenal	2-0	Sansom o.g., Lyons	34,236
24th Jan	4	H	Liverpool	2-1	Eastoe, Varadi	53,804
14th Feb	5	A	Southampton	0-0		24,152
17th Feb	5 Replay	H	Southampton	1-0 aet	O'Keefe	49,192
7th Mar	6	H	Manchester City	2-2	Eastoe, Ross (pen)	52,791
11th Mar	6 Replay	A	Manchester City	1-3	Eastoe	52,532
1981/82	**(WINNERS - TOTTENHAM HOTSPUR)**					
2nd Jan	3	A	West Ham United	1-2	Eastoe	24,431
1982/83	**(WINNERS - MANCHESTER UNITED)**					
8th Jan	3	A	Newport County	1-1	Sheedy	9,527
11th Jan	3 Replay	H	Newport County	2-1	Sharp, King	18,565
30th Jan	4	H	Shrewsbury Town	2-1	Sheedy, Heath	35,188
19th Feb	5	H	Tottenham Hotspur	2-0	King, Sharp	42,995
12th Mar	6	A	Manchester United	0-1		58,198

THE FA CUP RESULTS

Date	Round	Venue	Opponents	Score	Scorers	Attendance
1983/84	**(WINNERS - EVERTON)**					
6th Jan	3	A	Stoke City	2-0	Gray, Irvine	16,462
28th Jan	4	H	Gillingham	0-0		22,380
31st Jan	4 Replay 1	A	Gillingham	0-0		15,339
6th Feb	4 Replay 2	A	Gillingham	3-0	Sheedy 2, Heath	17,817
18th Feb	5	H	Shrewsbury Town	3-0	Irvine, Reid, Griffin o.g.	27,106
10th Mar	6	A	Notts County	2-1	Richardson, Gray	19,534
14th Apr	SF	N	Southampton	1-0 aet	Heath	46,587
19th May	F	N	Watford	2-0	Sharp, Gray	100,000
1984/85	**(WINNERS - MANCHESTER UNITED)**					
5th Jan	3	A	Leeds United	2-0	Sharp (pen), Sheedy	21,211
26th Jan	4	H	Doncaster Rovers	2-0	Steven, Stevens	37,535
16th Feb	5	H	Telford United	3-0	Reid, Sheedy (pen), Steven	47,402
9th Mar	6	H	Ipswich Town	2-2	Sheedy, Mountfield	36,468
13th Mar	6 Replay	A	Ipswich Town	1-0	Sharp (pen)	27,737
13th Apr	SF	N	Luton Town	2-1 aet	Sheedy, Mountfield	45,289
18th May	F	N	Manchester United	0-1		100,000
1985/86	**(WINNERS - LIVERPOOL)**					
5th Jan	3	H	Exeter City	1-0	Stevens	22,726
25th Jan	4	H	Blackburn Rovers	3-1	Van den Hauwe, Lineker 2	41,831
4th Mar	5	A	Tottenham Hotspur	2-1	Heath, Lineker	23,338
8th Mar	6	A	Luton Town	2-2	Donaghy o.g., Heath	15,529
12th Mar	6 Replay	H	Luton Town	1-0	Lineker	44,264
5th Apr	SF	N	Sheffield Wednesday	2-1 aet	Harper, Sharp	47,711
10th May	F	N	Liverpool	1-3	Lineker	98,000
1986/87	**(WINNERS - COVENTRY CITY)**					
10th Jan	3	H	Southampton	2-1	Sharp 2	32,320
31st Jan	4	A	Bradford City	1-0	Snodin	15,519
22nd Feb	5	A	Wimbledon	1-3	Wilkinson	9,924
1987/88	**(WINNERS - WIMBLEDON)**					
9th Jan	3	A	Sheffield Wednesday	1-1	Reid	33,304
13th Jan	3 Replay 1	H	Sheffield Wednesday	1-1 aet	Sharp	32,935
25th Jan	3 Replay 2	H	Sheffield Wednesday	1-1 aet	Steven	37,414
27th Jan	3 Replay 3	A	Sheffield Wednesday	5-0	Sharp 3, Heath, Snodin	38,953
30th Jan	4	H	Middlesbrough	1-1	Sharp	36,564
3rd Feb	4 Replay 1	A	Middlesbrough	2-2 aet	Watson, Steven	25,235
9th Feb	4 Replay 2	H	Middlesbrough	2-1	Sharp, Mowbray o.g.	32,222
21st Feb	5	H	Liverpool	0-1		48,270
1988/89	**(WINNERS - LIVERPOOL)**					
7th Jan	3	A	West Bromwich Alb.	1-1	Sheedy (pen)	31,186
11th Jan	3 Replay	H	West Bromwich Alb.	1-0	Sheedy	31,697
28th Jan	4	A	Plymouth Argyle	1-1	Sheedy (pen)	27,566
31st Jan	4 Replay	H	Plymouth Argyle	4-0	Nevin, Sharp 2, Sheedy	28,542
18th Feb	5	A	Barnsley	1-0	Sharp	32,551
19th Mar	6	H	Wimbledon	1-0	McCall	24,562
15th Apr	SF	N	Norwich City	1-0	Nevin	46,553
20th May	F	N	Liverpool	2-3 aet	McCall 2	82,800

THE FA CUP RESULTS

Date	Round	Venue	Opponents	Score	Scorers	Attendance
1989/90	**(WINNERS - MANCHESTER UNITED)**					
6th Jan	3	A	Middlesbrough	0-0		20,075
10th Jan	3 Replay 1	H	Middlesbrough	1-1 aet	Sheedy	24,352
17th Jan	3 Replay 2	H	Middlesbrough	1-0	Whiteside	23,866
28th Jan	4	A	Sheffield Wednesday	2-1	Whiteside 2	31,754
17th Feb	5	A	Oldham Athletic	2-2	Sharp, Cottee	19,320
21st Feb	5 Replay 1	H	Oldham Athletic	1-1 aet	Sheedy (pen)	36,663
10th Mar	5 Replay 2	A	Oldham Athletic	1-2 aet	Cottee	19,346
1990/91	**(WINNERS - TOTTENHAM HOTSPUR)**					
5th Jan	3	A	Charlton Athletic	2-1	Ebbrell 2	12,234
27th Jan	4	A	Woking	1-0	Sheedy	34,724
			(Played at Goodison Park)			
17th Feb	5	A	Liverpool	0-0		38,323
20th Feb	5 Replay 1	H	Liverpool	4-4 aet	Sharp 2, Cottee 2	37,766
27th Feb	5 Replay 2	H	Liverpool	1-0	Watson	40,201
11th Mar	6	A	West Ham United	1-2	Watson	28,162
1991/92	**(WINNERS - LIVERPOOL)**					
4th Jan	3	H	Southend United	1-0	Beardsley	22,606
26th Jan	4	A	Chelsea	0-1		21,152
1992/93	**(WINNERS - ARSENAL)**					
2nd Jan	3	A	Wimbledon	0-0		7,818
12th Jan	3 Replay	H	Wimbledon	1-2	Watson	15,293
1993/94	**(WINNERS - MANCHESTER UNITED)**					
8th Jan	3	A	Bolton Wanderers	1-1	Rideout	21,702
19th Jan	3 Replay	H	Bolton Wanderers	2-3 aet	Barlow 2	34,642
1994/95	**(WINNERS - EVERTON)**					
7th Jan	3	H	Derby County	1-0	Hinchcliffe	29,406
29th Jan	4	A	Bristol City	1-0	Jackson	19,816
18th Feb	5	H	Norwich City	5-0	Limpar, Parkinson, Rideout, Ferguson, Stuart	31,616
12th Mar	6	H	Newcastle United	1-0	Watson	35,203
9th Apr	SF	N	Tottenham Hotspur	4-1	Jackson, Stuart, Amokachi 2	38,226
20th May	F	N	Manchester United	1-0	Rideout	79,592
1995/96	**(WINNERS - MANCHESTER UNITED)**					
7th Jan	3	H	Stockport County	2-2	Ablett, Stuart	28,921
17th Jan	3 Replay	A	Stockport County	3-2	Ferguson, Stuart, Ebbrell	11,283
27th Jan	4	H	Port Vale	2-2	Amokachi, Ferguson	33,168
14th Feb	4 Replay	A	Port Vale	1-2	Stuart	19,197
1996/97	**(WINNERS - CHELSEA)**					
5th Jan	3	H	Swindon Town	3-0	Kanchelskis (pen), Barmby, Ferguson	20,411
25th Jan	4	H	Bradford City	2-3	O'Brien o.g., Speed	30,007
1997/98	**(WINNERS - ARSENAL)**					
4th Jan	3	H	Newcastle United	0-1		20,885

THE FA CUP RESULTS

Date	Round	Venue	Opponents	Score	Scorers	Attendance
1998/99	**(WINNERS - MANCHESTER UNITED)**					
2nd Jan	3	A	Bristol City	2-0	Bakayoko 2	19,608
23rd Jan	4	H	Ipswich Town	1-0	Barmby	28,854
13th Feb	5	H	Coventry City	2-1	Jeffers, Oster	33,907
7th Mar	6	A	Newcastle United	1-4	Unsworth	36,504
1999/2000	**(WINNERS - CHELSEA)**					
11th Dec	3	A	Exeter City	0-0		6,045
21st Dec	3 Replay	H	Exeter City	1-0	Barmby	16,869
8th Jan	4	H	Birmingham City	2-0	Unsworth 2 (2 pens)	25,405
29th Jan	5	H	Preston North End	2-0	Unsworth, Moore	37,486
20th Feb	6	H	Aston Villa	1-2	Moore	35,331
2000/01	**(WINNERS - LIVERPOOL)**					
6th Jan	3	A	Watford	2-1	Hughes, Watson	15,635
27th Jan	4	H	Tranmere Rovers	0-3		39,207
2001/02	**(WINNERS - ARSENAL)**					
5th Jan	3	A	Stoke City	1-0	Stubbs	28,218
26th Jan	4	H	Leyton Orient	4-1	McGhee o.g., Ferguson, Campbell	35,851
17th Feb	5	H	Crewe Alexandra	0-0		29,939
26th Feb	5 Replay	A	Crewe Alexandra	2-1	Radzinski, Campbell	10,073
10th Mar	6	A	Middlesbrough	0-3		26,950
2002/03	**(WINNERS - ARSENAL)**					
4th Jan	3	A	Shrewsbury Town	1-2	Alexandersson	7,800
2003/04	**(WINNERS - MANCHESTER UNITED)**					
3rd Jan	3	H	Norwich City	3-1	Kilbane, Ferguson 2 (2 pens)	29,955
25th Jan	4	H	Fulham	1-1	Jeffers	27,862
4th Feb	4 Replay	A	Fulham	1-2 aet	Jeffers	11,551
2004/05	**(WINNERS - ARSENAL)**					
8th Jan	3	A	Plymouth Argyle	3-1	Osman, McFadden, Chadwick	20,112
29th Jan	4	H	Sunderland	3-0	Beattie, McFadden, Cahill	33,186
19th Feb	5	H	Manchester United	0-2		38,664
2005/06	**(WINNERS - LIVERPOOL)**					
7th Jan	3	A	Millwall	1-1	Osman	16,440
18th Jan	3 Replay	H	Millwall	1-0	Cahill	25,800
28th Jan	4	H	Chelsea	1-1	McFadden	29,742
8th Feb	4 Replay	A	Chelsea	1-4	Arteta (pen)	39,301
2006/07	**(WINNERS - CHELSEA)**					
7th Jan	3	H	Blackburn Rovers	1-4	Johnson (pen)	24,426
2007/08	**(WINNERS - PORTSMOUTH)**					
5th Jan	3	H	Oldham Athletic	0-1		33,086

EVERTON FA CUP RECORDS

HIGHEST HOME ATTENDANCES

DATE	OPPONENTS	SCORE	SCORERS	ATTENDANCE
14th Feb 1953	Manchester United	2-1	Eglington, Hickson	77,920
29th Jan 1958	Blackburn Rovers	1-2	Harris, J.	75,818

BIGGEST VICTORIES

DATE	OPPONENTS	SCORE	SCORERS	ATTENDANCE
18th Jan 1890	Derby County	11-2	Brady 3, Geary 3, Milward 3, Doyle, Kirkwood	10,000
28th Feb 1931	Southport	9-1	Dean 4, Dunn 2, Critchley 2, Johnson	45,647
21st Jan 1939	Doncaster Rovers	8-0	Boyes 2, Lawton 4, Stevenson, Gillick	41,115

BIGGEST DEFEATS

DATE	OPPONENTS	SCORE	ATTENDANCE
7th Jan 1922	Crystal Palace	0-6	41,000
25th Feb 1911	Derby County	0-5	22,892

EVERTON SENDINGS-OFF

DATE	OPPONENTS	SCORE	PLAYER	MINUTE
9th Jan 1915	Barnsley	3-0	George Harrison	32
9th Jan 1915	Barnsley	3-0	Bobby Parker	53
20th Feb 1915	Queens Park Rangers	2-1	Jimmy Gault	44
17th Jan 1923	Bradford Park Avenue	0-1	Hunter Hart	30
30th Jan 1974	West Bromwich Albion	0-1	Archie Styles	75
4th Jan 1975	Altrincham	1-1	Gary Jones	40
26th Jan 1980	Wigan Athletic	3-0	Brian Kidd	81
12th Apr 1980	West Ham United	1-1	Brian Kidd	63
7th Mar 1981	Manchester City	2-2	Kevin Ratcliffe	85
21st Feb 1990	Oldham Athletic	1-1 aet	Norman Whiteside	50
8th Jan 1994	Bolton Wanderers	1-1	Barry Horne	56
23rd Jan 1999	Ipswich Town	2-1	Marco Materazzi	48
6th Jan 2001	Watford	2-1	Joe-Max Moore	85

OPPONENTS' SENDINGS-OFF

DATE	CLUB	SCORE	PLAYER	MINUTE
9th Jan 1915	Barnsley	3-0	Fred Barson	32
8th Jan 1958	Sunderland	3-1	Ambrose Fogarty	92
24th Jan 1959	Charlton Athletic	2-2	Will Duff	89
15th Jan 1972	Crystal Palace	2-2	John Hughes	53
30th Jan 1974	West Bromwich Albion	0-1	Willie Johnston	75
7th Jan 1978	Aston Villa	4-1	Leighton Phillips	87
9th Mar 1985	Ipswich Town	2-2	Steve McCall	72
18th May 1985	Manchester United	0-1 aet	Kevin Moran	78
18th Feb 1995	Norwich City	5-0	Jon Newsome	56
5th Jan 1997	Swindon Town	3-0	Ian Culverhouse	1
5th Jan 1997	Swindon Town	3-0	Gary Elkins	75
20th Feb 2000	Aston Villa	1-2	Benito Carbone	90
6th Jan 2001	Watford	2-1	Robert Page	82

EVERTON FA CUP TRIVIA

- Our first three final victories at Wembley – in 1906, 1933 and 1966 – came after seasons in which we had finished 11th in the league. In our next victory – in 1984 – it was the turn of opponents Watford to finish 11th. In 1984 there was an Everton double, with our namesakes in Chile lifting their country's cup.
- In winning the FA Cup in 1966, 1984 and 1995, Everton played a total of 22 matches and kept an astonishing 19 clean sheets – conceding only to Sheffield Wednesday (1966), Notts County (1984) and Tottenham Hotspur (1995 – a penalty).
- Only one father and son combination have scored against Everton in the FA Cup – Frank Lampard Snr netted a crucial semi-final goal for West Ham in 1980, and 26 years later Lampard Jnr scored in both matches for Chelsea in the fourth round.

MOST EVERTON GOALS BY ROUND

ROUND	PLAYER	YEAR OF 1ST & LAST GOAL	TOTAL
3rd	Dave Hickson	(1952–59)	9
4th	Dixie Dean	(1926–37)	10
5th	Jimmy Settle	(1900–08)	7
6th	Dixie Dean	(1926–37)	5
	Jimmy Husband	(1967–72)	5
Semi-final	Edgar Chadwick	(1890–99)	3
	Jack Sharp	(1900–10)	3
Final	Mike Trebilcock	(1966)	2
	Stuart McCall	(1989)	2

- Everton have only lost one of their last 18 away matches in the third round – to Shrewsbury Town in 2003.
- The last time Everton played an FA Cup tie at a neutral venue – aside from a semi-final or final – was in 1975 when the fourth-round replay against Altrincham was moved to Old Trafford, with Everton triumphing 2-0 with goals by Bob Latchford and Mick Lyons.
- The quickest sending-off in Cup history was Ian Culverhouse's 55-second red card at Goodison for Swindon Town in January 1997. The subsequent penalty by Andrei Kanchelskis inside two minutes is the fastest from the start of any Everton match.
- The last Everton player to make his club debut in an FA Cup tie was Victor Anichebe, against Chelsea in the fourth round in 2006.
- There have been only two first-minute goals by Everton players in FA Cup matches – Dixie Dean at Anfield (30 seconds) on 19th January 1932 and Peter Scott (37 seconds) at Goodison against Crystal Palace almost 40 years to the day later.
- Steve Bruce is the only player to appear against Everton in two of our FA Cup-winning runs – he was in the Gillingham side beaten at the third attempt in the fourth round in 1984 and 11 years later he was Manchester United's captain in the final.
- The youngest player to appear for Everton in the FA Cup is Wayne Rooney, who was 17 years 72 days at Shrewsbury in 2003. The youngest goalscorer is the great Tommy Lawton, who netted in the 4-3 defeat at Tottenham Hotspur in February 1937 at 17 years 139 days.
- History was made on 27th January 1974 when for the first time Everton played a Sunday fixture – a goalless draw against West Bromwich Albion in front of a crowd of more than 53,000.
- Between the third round in January 1964 and the fifth round in March 1965, Fred Pickering netted a club-record seven successive FA Cup matches.
- Everton's 2-2 draw at Hillsborough in the third round in January 1965 was the first ever FA Cup tie broadcast on *Match of the Day*.

THE LEAGUE CUP RESULTS

Note Everton did not compete between 1961/62 and 1966/67 inclusive, and 1970/71 due to European commitments

Date	Round	Venue	Opponents	Score	Scorers	Attendance
1960/61	**(WINNERS - ASTON VILLA)**					
12th Oct	1	H	Accrington Stanley	3-1	Wignall 2, J. Harris	18,246
31st Oct	2	H	Walsall	3-1	Webber, Vernon, Collins	14,137
23rd Nov	3	H	Bury	3-1	Wignall 2, J. Harris	20,724
21st Dec	4	A	Tranmere Rovers	4-0	Wignall 3, Bingham	14,967
15th Feb	5	A	Shrewsbury Town	1-2	Young	15,399
1967/68	**(WINNERS - LEEDS UNITED)**					
13th Sep	2	A	Bristol City	5-0	Kendall 2, Royle, Hurst, Brown	22,054
11th Oct	3	H	Sunderland	2-3	Young 2	39,914
1968/69	**(WINNERS - SWINDON TOWN)**					
3rd Sep	2	H	Tranmere Rovers	4-0	Royle, Whittle 2, Ball	35,477
24th Sep	3	H	Luton Town	5-1	Husband, Royle 2 (1 pen), Ball, Morrissey	30,405
16th Oct	4	H	Derby County	0-0		44,705
23rd Oct	4 Replay	A	Derby County	0-1		34,370
1969/70	**(WINNERS - MANCHESTER CITY)**					
3rd Sep	2	A	Darlington	1-0	Ball	18,000
24th Sep	3	A	Arsenal	0-0		36,102
1st Oct	3 Replay	H	Arsenal	1-0	Kendall	41,140
15th Oct	4	A	Manchester City	0-2		45,643
1971/72	**(WINNERS - STOKE CITY)**					
7th Sep	2	A	Southampton	1-2	Johnson	17,833
1972/73	**(WINNERS - TOTTENHAM HOTSPUR)**					
5th Sep	2	A	Arsenal	0-1		35,230
1973/74	**(WINNERS - WOLVERHAMPTON WANDERERS)**					
8th Oct	2	H	Reading	1-0	Buckley	15,772
30th Oct	3	H	Norwich City	0-1		22,046
1974/75	**(WINNERS - ASTON VILLA)**					
11th Sep	2	A	Aston Villa	1-1	Latchford	29,640
18th Sep	2 Replay	H	Aston Villa	0-3		24,595
1975/76	**(WINNERS - MANCHESTER CITY)**					
9th Sep	2	H	Arsenal	2-2	Smallman, Lyons	17,174
23rd Sep	2 Replay	A	Arsenal	1-0	Kenyon	21,813
8th Oct	3	H	Carlisle United	2-0	Latchford, Dobson	20,010
11th Nov	4	H	Notts County	2-2	G Jones, Irving	19,169
25th Nov	4 Replay	A	Notts County	0-2		23,404
1976/77	**(WINNERS - ASTON VILLA)**					
30th Aug	2	H	Cambridge United	3-0	Latchford, Dobson, King	10,898
20th Sep	3	A	Stockport County	1-0	Latchford	15,031
26th Oct	4	H	Coventry City	3-0	King 2, Lyons	21,572
1st Dec	5	A	Manchester United	3-0	King 2, Dobson	57,738
18th Jan	SF Leg 1	H	Bolton Wanderers	1-1	McKenzie	54,032

THE LEAGUE CUP RESULTS

Date	Round	Venue	Opponents	Score	Scorers	Attendance
1976/77	**(WINNERS - ASTON VILLA)**					
15th Feb	SF Leg 2	A	Bolton Wanderers	1-0	Latchford	50,413
12th Mar	F	N	Aston Villa	0-0		96,223
16th Mar	F Replay 1	N	Aston Villa	1-1 aet	Latchford	54,840
13th Apr	F Replay 2	N	Aston Villa	2-3 aet	Latchford, Lyons	54,749
1977/78	**(WINNERS - NOTTINGHAM FOREST)**					
30th Aug	2	A	Sheffield United	3-0	Latchford, McKenzie, King	18,571
25th Oct	3	H	Middlesbrough	2-2	King, Telfer	32,766
31st Oct	3 Replay	A	Middlesbrough	2-1	Lyons, Pearson	28,409
29th Nov	4	A	Sheffield Wednesday	3-1	Lyons, Dobson, Pearson	36,079
18th Jan	5	A	Leeds United	1-4	Thomas	35,020
1978/79	**(WINNERS - NOTTINGHAM FOREST)**					
29th Aug	2	H	Wimbledon	8-0	Latchford 5 (1 pen), Dobson 3	23,137
3rd Oct	3	H	Darlington	1-0	Dobson	23,682
7th Nov	4	H	Nottingham Forest	2-3	Burns o.g., Latchford	48,503
1979/80	**(WINNERS - WOLVERHAMPTON WANDERERS)**					
28th Aug	2 Leg 1	H	Cardiff City	2-0	Kidd 2	18,061
5th Sep	2 Leg 2	A	Cardiff City	0-1		9,698
25th Sep	3	A	Aston Villa	0-0		22,635
9th Oct	3 Replay	H	Aston Villa	4-1	Kidd, Latchford 2, Rimmer o.g.	22,088
30th Oct	4	A	Grimsby Town	1-2	Kidd	22,043
1980/81	**(WINNERS - LIVERPOOL)**					
26th Aug	2 Leg 1	H	Blackpool	3-0	Eastoe, Latchford, McBride	20,156
3rd Sep	2 Leg 2	A	Blackpool	2-2	Latchford 2	10,579
24th Sep	3	H	WBA	1-2	Gidman	23,546
1981/82	**(WINNERS - LIVERPOOL)**					
6th Oct	2 Leg 1	H	Coventry City	1-1	Ferguson	17,228
27th Oct	2 Leg 2	A	Coventry City	1-0	Ferguson	13,770
11th Nov	3	H	Oxford United	1-0	O'Keefe	14,910
15th Dec	4	H	Ipswich Town	2-3	McMahon 2	15,759
1982/83	**(WINNERS - LIVERPOOL)**					
5th Oct	2 Leg 1	A	Newport County	2-0	McMahon, King	8,293
27th Oct	2 Leg 2	H	Newport County	2-2	King, Johnson	8,941
9th Nov	3	H	Arsenal	1-1	Stevens	13,089
23rd Nov	3 Replay	A	Arsenal	0-3		19,547
1983/84	**(WINNERS - LIVERPOOL)**					
4th Oct	2 Leg 1	A	Chesterfield	1-0	Sharp	10,713
26th Oct	2 Leg 2	H	Chesterfield	2-2	Heath,Steven	8,067
9th Nov	3	H	Coventry City	2-1	Heath, Sharp	9,080
30th Nov	4	A	West Ham United	2-2	Reid, Sheedy	19,702
6th Dec	4 Replay	H	West Ham United	2-0	King, Sheedy	21,609
18th Jan	5	A	Oxford United	1-1	Heath	14,333
24th Jan	5 Replay	H	Oxford United	4-1	Richardson, Sheedy, Heath, Sharp	31,011
15th Feb	SF Leg 1	H	Aston Villa	2-0	Sheedy, Richardson	40,006
22nd Feb	SF Leg 2	A	Aston Villa	0-1		42,426
25th Mar	F	N	Liverpool	0-0 aet		100,000
28th Mar	F Replay	N	Liverpool	0-1		52,089

THE LEAGUE CUP RESULTS

Date	Round	Venue	Opponents	Score	Scorers	Attendance
1984/85	**(WINNERS - NORWICH CITY)**					
26th Sep	2 Leg 1	A	Sheffield United	2-2	Mountfield, Sharp	16,345
10th Oct	2 Leg 2	H	Sheffield United	4-0	Mountfield, Bracewell, Sharp, Heath	18,742
30th Oct	3	A	Manchester Utd	2-1	Sharp (pen), Gidman o.g.	50,918
20th Nov	4	H	Grimsby Town	0-1		26,298
1985/86	**(WINNERS - OXFORD UNITED)**					
25th Sep	2 Leg 1	H	Bournemouth	3-2	Lineker, Marshall, Hefferman o.g.	13,930
8th Oct	2 Leg 2	A	Bournemouth	2-0	Lineker, Richardson	8,081
29th Oct	3	A	Shrewsbury Town	4-1	Sharp, Hughes o.g., Sheedy, Heath	10,246
26th Nov	4	A	Chelsea	2-2	Sheedy, Bracewell	27,544
10th Dec	4 Replay	H	Chelsea	1-2	Lineker	26,373
1986/87	**(WINNERS - ARSENAL)**					
24th Sep	2 Leg 1	H	Newport County	4-0	Langley, Heath, Wilkinson 2	11,957
7th Oct	2 Leg 2	A	Newport County	5-1	Wilkinson 3, Sharp, Mullen o.g.	7,172
28th Oct	3	H	Sheffield Wed.	4-0	Wilkinson 2, Heath, Mountfield	24,638
19th Nov	4	A	Norwich City	4-1	Steven, Sharp, Steven (pen), Heath	17,988
21st Jan	5	H	Liverpool	0-1		53,323
1987/88	**(WINNERS - LUTON TOWN)**					
22nd Sep	2 Leg 1	H	Rotherham Utd	3-2	Snodin, Wilson, Clarke (pen)	15,369
6th Oct	2 Leg 2	A	Rotherham Utd	0-0		12,995
28th Oct	3	A	Liverpool	1-0	Stevens	44,071
17th Nov	4	H	Oldham Athletic	2-1	Watson, Adams	23,315
20th Jan	5	H	Manchester City	2-0	Heath, Sharp	40,014
7th Feb	SF Leg 1	H	Arsenal	0-1		25,476
24th Feb	SF Leg 2	A	Arsenal	1-3	Heath	51,148
1988/89	**(WINNERS - NOTTINGHAM FOREST)**					
27th Sep	2 Leg 1	H	Bury	3-0	Sharp, McDonald (pen), McCall	11,071
11th Oct	2 Leg 2	A	Bury	2-2	Steven (pen), Sharp	4,592
8th Nov	3	H	Oldham Athletic	1-1	Steven (pen)	17,230
29th Nov	3 Replay	A	Oldham Athletic	2-0	Cottee 2	14,573
14th Dec	4	A	Bradford City	1-3	Watson	15,055
1989/90	**(WINNERS - NOTTINGHAM FOREST)**					
19th Sep	2 Leg 1	A	Leyton Orient	2-0	Newell, Sheedy	8,214
3rd Oct	2 Leg 2	H	Leyton Orient	2-2	Whiteside, Sheedy	10,128
24th Oct	3	H	Luton Town	3-0	Newell 2, Nevin	18,428
22nd Nov	4	A	Nottingham Forest	0-1		21,324
1990/91	**(WINNERS - SHEFFIELD WEDNESDAY)**					
25th Sep	2 Leg 1	A	Wrexham	5-0	Cottee 3, McDonald, Nevin	9,072
9th Oct	2 Leg 2	H	Wrexham	6-0	Sharp 3, Cottee, Ebbrell, McDonald	7,415
30th Oct	3	A	Sheffield United	1-2	Pemberton o.g.	15,045

Everton in the League Cup, 1980s - Coventry are defeated at Goodison, 1983 (top) while Howard Kendall reflects on what might have been, following the 1984 League Cup final at Wembley

THE LEAGUE CUP RESULTS

Date	Round	Venue	Opponents	Score	Scorers	Attendance
1991/92	**(WINNERS - MANCHESTER UNITED)**					
24th Sep	2 Leg 1	H	Watford	1-0	Beardsley	8,264
8th Oct	2 Leg 2	A	Watford	2-1	Newell, Beardsley	11,561
30th Oct	3	H	Wolverhampton W.	4-1	Beagrie 2, Cottee, Beardsley	19,065
4th Dec	4	H	Leeds United	1-4	Atteveld	25,467
1992/93	**(WINNERS - ARSENAL)**					
23rd Sep	2 Leg 1	A	Rotherham United	0-1		7,736
7th Oct	2 Leg 2	H	Rotherham United	3-0	Rideout 2, Cottee	10,302
28th Oct	3	H	Wimbledon	0-0		9,541
10th Nov	3 Replay	A	Wimbledon	1-0	Beardsley	3,686
2nd Dec	4	H	Chelsea	2-2	Barlow, Beardsley	14,457
16th Dec	4 Replay	A	Chelsea	0-1		19,496
1993/94	**(WINNERS - ASTON VILLA)**					
21st Sep	2 Leg 1	A	Lincoln City	4-3	Rideout 3, Cottee	9,153
6th Oct	2 Leg 2	H	Lincoln City	4-2	Rideout, Snodin, Cottee 2	8,375
26th Oct	3	H	Crystal Palace	2-2	Beagrie, Watson	11,547
10th Nov	3 Replay	A	Crystal Palace	4-1	Watson 2, Ward (pen), Young o.g.	14,662
30th Nov	4	H	Manchester United	0-2		34,052
1994/95	**(WINNERS - LIVERPOOL)**					
20th Sep	2 Leg 1	H	Portsmouth	2-3	Samways, Stuart (pen)	14,043
5th Oct	2 Leg 2	A	Portsmouth	1-1	Watson	13,605
1995/96	**(WINNERS - ASTON VILLA)**					
20th Sep	2 Leg 1	A	Millwall	0-0		12,053
4th Oct	2 Leg 2	H	Millwall	2-4 aet	Hinchcliffe (pen), Stuart	14,891
1996/97	**(WINNERS - LEICESTER CITY)**					
18th Sep	2 Leg 1	H	York City	1-1	Kanchelskis	11,527
24th Sep	2 Leg 2	A	York City	2-3	Rideout, Speed	7,854
1997/98	**(WINNERS - CHELSEA)**					
16th Sep	2 Leg 1	A	Scunthorpe United	1-0	Farrelly	7,145
1st Oct	2 Leg 2	H	Scunthorpe United	5-0	Stuart, Oster , Barmby 2, Cadamarteri	11,562
15th Oct	3	A	Coventry City	1-4	Barmby	10,087
1998/99	**(WINNERS - TOTTENHAM HOTSPUR)**					
15th Sep	2 Leg 1	A	Huddersfield Town	1-1	Watson	15,395
23rd Sep	2 Leg 2	H	Huddersfield Town	2-1	Dacourt, Materazzi	18,718
28th Oct	3	A	Middlesbrough	3-2	Ferguson, Bakayoko, Hutchison	20,748
11th Nov	4	H	Sunderland	1-1 aet	Collins	28,132
			(Sunderland won 5-4 on penalties)			
1999/2000	**(WINNERS - LEICESTER CITY)**					
14th Sep	2 Leg 1	A	Oxford United	1-1	Cadamarteri	7,345
22nd Sep	2 Leg 2	H	Oxford United	0-1		10,006

THE LEAGUE CUP RESULTS

Date	Round	Venue	Opponents	Score	Scorers	Attendance
2000/01	**(WINNERS - LIVERPOOL)**					
20th Sep	2 Leg 1	H	Bristol Rovers	1-1	Campbell	25,564
27th Sep	2 Leg 2	A	Bristol Rovers	1-1 aet	Jeffers	11,045
			(Bristol Rovers won 4-2 on penalties)			
2001/02	**(WINNERS - BLACKBURN ROVERS)**					
12th Sep	2	H	Crystal Palace	1-1 aet	Ferguson (pen)	21,128
			(Crystal Palace won 5-4 penalties)			
2002/03	**(WINNERS - LIVERPOOL)**					
1st Oct	2	A	Wrexham	3-0	Campbell, Rooney 2	10,073
6th Nov	3	A	Newcastle United	3-3 aet	Campbell, Watson, Unsworth (pen)	26,950
			(Everton won 3-2 on penalties)			
4th Dec	4	A	Chelsea	1-4	Naysmith	32,322
2003/04	**(WINNERS - MIDDLESBROUGH)**					
24th Sep	2	H	Stockport County	3-0	Ferguson 2 (1 pen), Chadwick	19,807
29th Oct	3	H	Charlton Athletic	1-0	Linderoth	24,863
3rd Dec	4	A	Middlesbrough	0-0 aet		18,568
			(Middlesbrough won 5-4 on penalties)			
2004/05	**(WINNERS - CHELSEA)**					
22nd Sep	2	A	Bristol City	2-2 aet	Ferguson (pen), Chadwick	15,264
			(Everton won 4-3 on penalties)			
27th Oct	3	H	Preston North End	2-0	Carsley, Bent	33,922
11th Nov	4	A	Arsenal	1-3	Gravesen	27,791
2005/06	**(WINNERS - MANCHESTER UNITED)**					
26th Oct	3	H	Middlesbrough	0-1		25,844
2006/07	**(WINNERS - CHELSEA)**					
19th Sep	2	A	Peterborough	2-1	Stirling o.g., Cahill	10,756
24th Oct	3	H	Luton Town	4-0	Cahill, Keane o.g., McFadden, Anichebe	27,149
8th Nov	4	H	Arsenal	0-1		31,045
2007/08	**(WINNERS - TOTTENHAM HOTSPUR)**					
26th Sep	3	A	Sheffield Wednesday	3-0	McFadden 2, Yakubu	16,463
31st Oct	4	A	Luton Town	1-0 aet	Cahill	8,944
12th Dec	5	A	West Ham United	2-1	Osman, Yakubu	28,777
8th Jan	SF Leg 1	A	Chelsea	1-2	Yakubu	41,178
23rd Jan	SF Leg 2	H	Chelsea	0-1		37,086

EVERTON LEAGUE CUP RECORDS

HIGHEST HOME ATTENDANCES

DATE	OPPONENTS	SCORE	SCORERS	ATTENDANCE
18th Jan 1977	Bolton Wanderers	1-1	McKenzie	54,032
21st Jan 1987	Liverpool	0-1		53,323
7th Nov 1978	Nottingham Forest	2-3	Burns o.g., Latchford	48,503
16th Oct 1968	Derby County	0-0		44,705
1st Oct 1969	Arsenal	1-0	Kendall	41,140
20th Jan 1988	Manchester City	2-0	Heath, Sharp	40,014
15th Feb 1984	Aston Villa	2-0	Sheedy, Richardson	40,006

BIGGEST VICTORIES

DATE	OPPONENTS	SCORE	SCORERS	ATTENDANCE
29th Aug1978	Wimbledon	8-0	Latchford 5 (1 pen), Dobson 3	23,137
9th Oct 1990	Wrexham	6-0	Sharp 3, Cottee, Ebbrell, McDonald	7,415
13th Sept 1967	Bristol City	5-0	Kendall 2, Royle, Hurst, Brown	22,054
25th Sept 1990	Wrexham	5-0	Cottee 3, McDonald, Nevin	9,072
1st Oct 1997	Scunthorpe United	5-0	Stuart, Oster, Barmby 2, Cadamarteri	11,562

BIGGEST DEFEATS

DATE	OPPONENTS	SCORE	SCORER	ATTENDANCE
18th Jan 1978	Leeds United	1-4	Thomas	35,020
4th Dec 1991	Leeds United	1-4	Atteveld	25,467
15th Oct 1997	Coventry City	1-4	Barmby	10,087
4th Dec 2002	Chelsea	1-4	Naysmith	21,128

EVERTON SENDINGS-OFF

DATE	OPPONENTS	SCORE	PLAYER	MINUTE
18th Jan 1978	Leeds United	1-4	Mark Higgins	45
26th Nov 1985	Chelsea	2-2	Kevin Sheedy	28
30th Oct 1990	Sheffield United	1-2	Dave Watson	60
23rd Sept 1998	Huddersfield Town	2-1	Marco Materazzi	70
27th Oct 2004	Preston North End	2-0	Lee Carsley	72
8th Nov 2006	Arsenal	0-1	James McFadden	19

OPPONENTS' SENDINGS-OFF

DATE	CLUB	SCORE	PLAYER	MINUTE
28th Oct 1986	Sheffield Wednesday	4-0	Lawrie Madden	60
7th Oct 1992	Rotherham United	3-0	Billy Mercer	31
16th Dec 1992	Chelsea	0-1	Gareth Hall	64
6th Nov 2002	Newcastle United	3-3 aet	Stephen Caldwell	110
8th Jan 2008	Chelsea	1-2	John Mikel Obi	55

EVERTON LEAGUE CUP TRIVIA

- Everton have reached the final on two occasions, in 1977 and 1984, with midfielder Andy King being the only player to appear in both finals.
- Peter Reid and Kevin Richardson, with Bolton Wanderers and Arsenal respectively, have played both for and against Everton in the semi-finals.
- Three players have scored their only goal for Everton in this competition – Tobias Linderoth (2003), David Irving (1975) and Keith Webber (1960).
- The only player to make the only start of his Everton career in this competition is midfielder Kevin McLeod, against Crystal Palace in September 2001.
- Everton's 8-0 win over Wimbledon in August 1978 featured hat-ticks by Bob Latchford and Martin Dobson, the only time this has happened in a post-war Everton match.
- Arsenal are the most common opponents in the competition, with the sides meeting on 10 occasions.
- Both teams scored in the opening two minutes of the tie at Chelsea in October 1985, and then again in our next away match in the competition at Newport County 12 months later.
- Duncan Ferguson was in the Everton side that lined up against Huddersfield Town at Goodison Park in September 1998, which was the Yorkshire side's first visit to the ground since December 27th 1971 - the date the big Scot was born.
- Our failure to defeat York City in either leg of our 1995 tie means that they remain the only side, out of the 103 domestic clubs we have faced, that Everton have never beaten.
- Donal Murphy, who played for Coventry City in our 3-0 League Cup win in October 1976, also appeared for UC Dublin against the Toffees in the Cup Winners' Cup eight years later – making him the first player to appear against us in both domestic and European competition.

Martin Dobson, hat-trick hero in 1978

THE OTHER COMPETITION RESULTS

Date	Round	Venue	Opponents	Score	Scorers	Attendance
1928/29	**FA CHARITY SHIELD**					
24th Oct	-	Old Trafford	Blackburn Rovers	2-1	Dean 2	4,000
1932/33	**FA CHARITY SHIELD**					
12th Oct	-	A	Newcastle United	5-3	Dean 4, Johnson	10,000
1933/34	**FA CHARITY SHIELD**					
18th Oct	-	H	Arsenal	0-3		18,000
1963/64	**FA CHARITY SHIELD**					
17th Aug	-	H	Manchester United	4-0	Gabriel, Stevens, Temple, Vernon	54,844
1963/64	**BRITISH CHAMPIONSHIP**					
27th Nov	Leg 1	A	Rangers	3-1	Scott, Temple, Young	64,006
2nd Dec	Leg 2	H	Rangers	1-1	Young	42,202
1966/67	**FA CHARITY SHIELD**					
13th Aug	-	H	Liverpool	0-1		63,329
1970/71	**FA CHARITY SHIELD**					
8th Aug	-	A	Chelsea	2-1	Kendall, Whittle	43,547
1970/71	**FA CUP 3RD/4TH PLACE PLAY-OFF**					
7th May	-	Selhurst P.	Stoke City	2-3	Whittle, Ball	5,031
1973/74	**TEXACO CUP**					
18th Sep	1 Leg 1	H	Hearts	0-1		12,536
3rd Oct	1 Leg 2	A	Hearts	0-0		24,903
1984/85	**FA CHARITY SHIELD**					
18th Aug	-	N	Liverpool	1-0	Grobbelaar o.g.	100,000
1985/86	**FA CHARITY SHIELD**					
10th Aug	-	N	Manchester United	2-0	Steven, Heath	82,000
1985/86 & 1986/87	**SCREEN SPORT SUPER CUP**					
18th Sep	Group	A	Manchester United	4-2	Lineker, Sharp, Sheedy 2	33,859
2nd Oct	Group	H	Norwich City	1-0	Lineker	10,329
23rd Oct	Group	A	Norwich City	0-1		12,196
4th Dec	Group	H	Manchester United	1-0	Stapleton o.g.	20,542
5th Feb	SF Leg 1	A	Tottenham Hotspur	0-0		7,548
19th Mar	SF Leg 2	H	Tottenham Hotspur	3-1	Mountfield, Heath, Sharp	12,008
16th Sep	F Leg 1	A	Liverpool	1-3	Sheedy	20,660
30th Sep	F Leg 2	H	Liverpool	1-4	Sharp (pen)	26,068
1986/87	**FA CHARITY SHIELD**					
16th Aug	-	N	Liverpool	1-1	Heath	88,231

THE OTHER COMPETITION RESULTS

Date	Round	Venue	Opponents	Score	Scorers	Attendance
1986/87	**FULL MEMBERS CUP**					
3rd Dec	3	H	Newcastle United	5-2	Sharp 3, Heath, Sheedy	7,530
3rd Mar	4	H	Charlton Athletic	2-2	Steven, Wilkinson	7,914
			(Charlton Athletic won 6-5 on penalties)			
1987/88	**FA CHARITY SHIELD**					
1st Aug	-	N	Coventry City	1-0	Clarke	88,000
1987/88	**MERCANTILE CREDIT FOOTBALL LEAGUE CENTENARY CHALLENGE**					
25th Nov		H	Bayern Munich	3-1	Sharp 2, Heath	13,083
1987/88	**DUBAI CHAMPIONS CUP**					
8th Dec		N	Rangers	2-2	Watson, Sheedy	8,000
			(Rangers won 8-7 on penalties)			
1987/88	**SIMOD CUP**					
16th Feb	3	H	Luton Town	1-2	Power	5,207
1988/89	**MERCANTILE CREDIT FOOTBALL LEAGUE CENTENARY TROPHY**					
29th Aug	1	A	Manchester United	0-1		16,439
1988/89	**SIMOD CUP**					
20th Dec	3	H	Millwall	2-0	Cottee, Hurlock o.g.	3,703
18th Jan	4	A	Wimbledon	2-1	Clarke 2	2,477
28th Feb	SF	H	QPR	1-0	Nevin	7,072
30th Apr	F	N	Nottingham Forest	3-4 aet	Sharp, Cottee 2	46,604
1990/91	**ZENITH DATA SYSTEMS CUP**					
18th Dec	2	A	Blackburn Rovers	4-1	Newell, Cottee, Watson 2	5,410
22nd Jan	3	H	Sunderland	4-1	Cottee 4	4,609
13th Mar	SF (Nrth)	A	Barnsley	1-0	Cottee	10,287
19th Mar	F Leg 1 (N)	A	Leeds United	3-3	Beagrie, Warzycha, Milligan	13,387
21st Mar	F Leg 2 (N)	H	Leeds United	3-1	Cottee 2, Ebbrell	12,603
7th Apr	F	N	Crystal Palace	1-4 aet	Warzycha	52,460
1991/92	**ZENITH DATA SYSTEMS CUP**					
1st Oct	2	H	Oldham Athletic	3-2	Watson, Newell, Cottee	4,588
27th Nov	3	A	Leicester City	1-2	Beardsley	13,242
1995/96	**FA CHARITY SHIELD**					
13th Aug	-	N	Blackburn Rovers	1-0	Samways	40,149

MOST CUP APPEARANCES

Not surprisingly, a certain Welsh goalkeeper holds the record for most cup appearances by an Everton player, the former Footballer of the Year taking the field on 168 occasions – a record that will take some beating.

OVERALL EVERTON CUP APPEARANCES

PLAYER	FA CUP	LEAGUE CUP	EUROPE	OTHERS	TOTAL
Neville Southall	70	65	13	20	168
Kevin Ratcliffe	57	46	9	17	129
Graeme Sharp	54	48	8	9	119
Dave Watson	48	39	2	13	102
Kevin Sheedy	38	32	5	15	90
Gary Stevens	38	30	9	6	83
Mick Lyons	36	37	7	2	82
Trevor Steven	33	27	9	11	80
Brian Labone	45	15	19	0	79
Adrian Heath	29	35	4	8	76

(Other – Full Members Cup, Screen Sport Super Cup, Texaco Cup, Simod Cup, Zenith Data Systems Cup)

Neville Southall - Cup record holder

MOST CUP GOALS

The advent of the League Cup and European competitions – plus some others that were instantly forgettable – means that, unusually, the record for most cup goals is not held by Dixie Dean; like Southall's record for matches played, Graeme Sharp's goalscoring tally is one that perhaps will never be beaten.

OVERALL EVERTON CUP GOALS

PLAYER	FA CUP	LEAGUE CUP	EUROPE	OTHERS	TOTAL
Graeme Sharp	20	15	4	7	46
Bob Latchford	10	19	3	0	32
Kevin Sheedy	15	9	2	4	30
Dixie Dean	28	0	0	0	28
Tony Cottee	4	11	0	12	27
Adrian Heath	6	11	1	2	20
Andy King	4	11	4	0	19
Joe Royle	9	4	4	0	17
Dave Hickson	16	0	0	0	16
Alex Young	15	0	0	0	15

(Other – Full Members Cup, Screen Sport Super Cup, Texaco Cup, Simod Cup, Zenith Data Systems Cup)

Graeme Sharp nets one of his record 46 cup goals for Everton, at Leeds United in 1985

THE FA YOUTH CUP RESULTS

Date	Round	Venue	Opponents	Score	Scorers
1952/53	**(WINNERS - MANCHESTER UNITED)**				
17th Sep	1	A	South Liverpool	7-0	Gregory 5, Farrall 2
11th Oct	2	A	Liverpool	3-0	Williams 2, Rea
29th Nov	3	A	Blackpool	3-0	Scorers not known
4th Feb	4	A	Manchester United	0-1	
1953/54	**(WINNERS - MANCHESTER UNITED)**				
24th Oct	1	A	Manchester United	0-1	
1954/55	**(WINNERS - MANCHESTER UNITED)**				
28th Oct	2	H	Manchester City	1-3	Keeley (pen)
1955/56	**(WINNERS - MANCHESTER UNITED)**				
29th Oct	2	A	Bury	3-1	Scorers not known
17th Dec	3	H	Blackpool	5-2	Jones (pen), Llewellyn 3, King
1st Feb	4	A	Bolton Wanderers	0-4	
1956/57	**(WINNERS - MANCHESTER UNITED)**				
14th Nov	2	A	Bolton Wanderers	1-0	Llewellyn
8th Dec	3	A	Middlesbrough	6-1	Llewellyn 4, Temple, Ashworth
6th Feb	4	H	Manchester United	2-2	Ashworth 2
27th Feb	4 R	A	Manchester United	2-5	Llewellyn, Temple
1957/58	**(WINNERS - WOLVERHAMPTON WANDERERS)**				
12th Oct	1	H	Liverpool	4-1	Blain 2, Folksman, Barton
9th Nov	2	H	Bury	7-2	Blain 2, Barton, Ashworth 2, Todd, Folksman
7th Dec	3	H	Bolton Wanderers	1-1	Ashworth
16th Dec	3 R	A	Bolton Wanderers	0-1	
1958/59	**(WINNERS - BLACKBURN ROVERS)**				
15th Oct	1	H	Leeds United	3-0	Jones 3
17th Nov	2	A	Manchester United	2-2	Peat, Boner
26th Nov	2 R	H	Manchester United	1-2	Penman
1959/60	**(WINNERS - CHELSEA)**				
30th Sep	Prel	H	Rhyl	5-2	Bentley 3, Tyrer, Boner
13th Oct	1	A	Blackburn Rovers	2-2	Morton, Tyrer
21st Oct	2	H	Blackburn Rovers	1-0	Bentley
18th Nov	3	A	Manchester City	0-2	
1960/61	**(WINNERS - CHELSEA)**				
19th Sep	Prel	A	Tranmere Rovers	9-0	Webber 4, Chester 3, Morton 2
3rd Oct	1	H	Burnley	7-2	Edwards, Webber 4, Tyrer, Morton
9th Nov	2	H	Blackpool	3-1	Webber, Sharples, Morton
19th Dec	3	H	Bolton Wanderers	4-1	Morton, Webber 2, Tyrer
25th Jan	4	A	Middlesbrough	2-1	Edwards, Jarvis
6th Mar	5	A	Sheffield Wednesday	0-0	
14th Mar	5	H	Sheffield Wednesday	5-0	Sharples, Edwards, Tyrer 3
29th Mar	SF (1)	A	Stoke City	2-1	Webber, Maddocks
19th Apr	SF (2)	H	Stoke City	3-1	Edwards, Sharples, Morton
22nd Apr	Final (1)	A	Chelsea	1-4	Edwards
29th Apr	Final (2)	H	Chelsea	2-1	Edwards, Webber

THE FA YOUTH CUP RESULTS

Date	Round	Venue	Opponents	Score	Scorers
1961/62	**(WINNERS - NEWCASTLE UNITED)**				
13th Sep	2	A	Manchester United	2-3	Bennett, Shaw
1962/63	**(WINNERS - WEST HAM UNITED)**				
4th Dec	2	H	Huddersfield Town	6-0	Glover 3, Wright 2, Harvey
22nd Dec	3	H	Sheffield United	0-2	
1963/64	**(WINNERS - MANCHESTER UNITED)**				
17th Dec	2	H	Liverpool	1-0	Hurst
14th Jan	3	H	Wigan Athletic	12-1	Maher 2, Humphreys 3, Hurst 4, Husband 3
12th Feb	4	H	Leeds United	1-2	Maher
1964/65	**(WINNERS - EVERTON)**				
8th Dec	2	H	Manchester United	5-0	Husband 2, McLoughlin 2, Wallace
6th Jan	3	A	Blackburn Rovers	3-0	Husband, McLoughlin, Maher
16th Feb	4	H	Burnley	4-0	McLoughlin 3, Maher
2nd Mar	5	H	Stoke City	1-0	McLoughlin
24th Mar	SF (1)	H	Sunderland	4-0	McLoughlin, Husband 2, Maher
17th Apr	SF (1)	A	Sunderland	1-0	Maher
28th Apr	Final (1)	A	Arsenal	0-1	
3rd May	Final (2)	H	Arsenal	3-1	McLoughlin, Hurst (pen), Maher
1965/66	**(WINNERS - ARSENAL)**				
23rd Dec	2	A	Wrexham	0-1	
1966/67	**(WINNERS - SUNDERLAND)**				
6th Dec	2	H	Manchester United	0-0	
13th Dec	2 R	A	Manchester United	2-3	Brindle, Royle
1967/68	**(WINNERS - BURNLEY)**				
27th Nov	2	A	Tranmere Rovers	3-2	Owen, Johnson, Whittle
3rd Jan	3	H	Bury	3-0	Whittle, Owen, Thornton
29th Jan	4	A	Stoke City	3-1	Owen, Whittle, Johnson
12th Mar	5	H	Sunderland	1-0	Whittle
26th Mar	SF (1)	H	Burnley	0-0	
2nd Apr	SF (2)	A	Burnley	2-3	Darracott, Whittle (pen)
1968/69	**(WINNERS - SUNDERLAND)**				
26th Nov	2	H	Manchester City	1-0	Johnson
30th Dec	3	H	Preston North End	4-0	Kenny, G. Jones 2, Lyons
28th Jan	4	A	Huddersfield Town	1-1	Lyons
31st Jan	4 R	H	Huddersfield Town	3-2	G. Jones 2, Johnson
3rd Mar	5	A	Manchester United	0-0	
12th Mar	5 R	H	Manchester United	1-3	Johnson
1969/70	**(WINNERS - TOTTENHAM HOTSPUR)**				
2nd Dec	2	A	Blackburn Rovers	3-3	Johnson 2, Kenny
9th Dec	2 R	H	Blackburn Rovers	5-0	Wilson 2, Kenny (pen), Lyons 2
30th Dec	3	H	Manchester United	1-2	Johnson
1970/71	**(WINNERS - ARSENAL)**				
1st Dec	2	H	Manchester City	2-2	Buckley, Goodlass
8th Dec	2 R	A	Manchester City	0-1	

THE FA YOUTH CUP RESULTS

Date	Round	Venue	Opponents	Score	Scorers
1971/72	**(WINNERS - ASTON VILLA)**				
1st Dec	2	A	Manchester United	1-1	Goodlass
7th Dec	2 R	H	Manchester United	2-1	Bacon, Telfer
22nd Dec	3	H	Sheffield Wednesday	3-2	Bacon, Telfer, Peters o.g
24th Jan	4	A	Liverpool	2-3	Marshall, Goodlass
1972/73	**(WINNERS - IPSWICH TOWN)**				
29th Nov	2	A	Tranmere Rovers	3-2	Threlfall, Marshall, Telfer
9th Jan	3	A	Hull City	2-0	Marshall 2
29th Jan	4	H	Bristol City	0-1	
1973/74	**(WINNERS - TOTTENHAM HOTSPUR)**				
3rd Dec	2	H	Shrewsbury Town	4-0	Esser 2, Marshall, Williams
1st Jan	3	H	Sheffield Wednesday	0-1	
1974/75	**(WINNERS - IPSWICH TOWN)**				
10th Dec	2	A	Preston North End	3-1	Esser, Mowat, O'Halloran
14th Jan	3	A	Blackpool	0-0	
4th Feb	3 R	H	Blackpool	1-0	O'Halloran
11th Feb	4	A	Manchester United	1-0	Sharp
11th Mar	5	H	Huddersfield Town	1-2	Esser
1975/76	**(WINNERS - WEST BROMWICH ALBION)**				
17th Nov	2	H	Blackpool	2-0	Jack, Kelly
16th Dec	3	H	Oldham Athletic	1-2	Coffey
1976/77	**(WINNERS - CRYSTAL PALACE)**				
6th Dec	2	A	Tranmere Rovers	6-1	Monaghan 2, Jack 2, McBride, Murray
11th Jan	3	H	Nottingham Forest	3-1	Monaghan 2, Jack
8th Feb	4	A	Oldham Athletic	4-3	Monaghan 2, Jack, Murray
8th Mar	5	H	Middlesbrough	3-0	Jack 2, Murray
4th Apr	SF (1)	A	Derby County	2-0	Coffey, McBride
9th Apr	SF (2)	H	Derby County	1-1	Russell
5th May	Final (1)	H	Crystal Palace	0-0	
13th May	Final (2)	A	Crystal Palace	0-1	
1977/78	**(WINNERS - CRYSTAL PALACE)**				
21st Dec	2	A	Liverpool	0-1	
1978/79	**(WINNERS - MILLWALL)**				
5th Dec	2	H	Liverpool	2-0	Kelly, Dobie
10th Jan	3	A	Hereford United	3-0	S. McMahon 2, Dobie
8th Mar	4	A	Bristol Rovers	2-2	S. McMahon 2, McBride
12th Mar	4 R	H	Bristol Rovers	1-1	McBride
15th Mar	4 (R2)	A	Bristol Rovers	4-1	Borrows, S. McMahon 2, Kelly
4th Apr	5	A	Coventry City	6-1	S. McMahon 2, Taylor 2, Ratcliffe, Kelly
11th Apr	SF (1)	H	Millwall	0-0	
23rd Apr	SF (2)	A	Millwall	0-2	
1979/80	**(WINNERS - ASTON VILLA)**				
4th Dec	2	A	Liverpool	2-0	Stevens, R. Ash
8th Jan	3	H	Manchester United	0-1	

THE FA YOUTH CUP RESULTS

Date	Round	Venue	Opponents	Score	Scorers
1980/81	**(WINNERS - WEST HAM UNITED)**				
1st Dec	2	H	Nottingham Forest	1-0	J. McMahon
19th Jan	3	A	Stoke City	3-1	Stevens, Richardson, Ward
2nd Feb	4	H	Watford	3-1	J. McMahon, Tierney 2
24th Feb	5	H	Manchester United	1-3	Goulding
1981/82	**(WINNERS - WATFORD)**				
2nd Dec	2	A	Manchester City	1-0	Evans
2nd Jan	3	H	Aston Villa	0-2	
1982/83	**(WINNERS - NORWICH CITY)**				
27th Nov	2	H	Stoke City	3-1	Wakenshaw, Farrington, S. Rimmer
19th Jan	3	H	Port Vale	0-0	
24th Jan	3 R	A	Port Vale	1-0	Wakenshaw
10th Feb	4	H	Tottenham Hotspur	5-0	S. Rimmer 3, Morrissey, Farrington (pen)
5th Feb	5	H	Barnsley	2-0	S. Rimmer, Farrington
17th Mar	SF (1)	A	Sheffield Wednesday	2-0	S. Rimmer, Marshall
7th Apr	SF (2)	H	Sheffield Wednesday	7-0	Farrington 4 (1 pen), S. Rimmer 2, Wakenshaw
25th Apr	Final (1)	A	Norwich City	2-3	Farrington 2
5th May	Final (2)	H	Norwich City	3-2	Marshall, Farrington 2 (1 pen)
9th May	Final R	H	Norwich City	0-1	
1983/84	**(WINNERS - EVERTON)**				
2nd Dec	2	H	Huddersfield Town	1-1	Wakenshaw
12th Dec	2 R	A	Huddersfield Town	1-0	Marshall (pen)
5th Jan	3	H	Blackpool	2-0	O'Brien, Fielding
30th Jan	4	A	Millwall	3-2	Wakenshaw 2, McKenzie
23rd Feb	5	H	Newcastle United	2-1	Wakenshaw 2
27th Mar	SF (1)	H	Barnsley	1-0	N. Rimmer
6th Apr	SF (2)	A	Barnsley	1-1	Hood
26th Apr	Final (1)	H	Stoke City	2-2	Wakenshaw, Rimmer
8th May	Final (2)	A	Stoke City	2-0	Hughes, Wakenshaw
1984/85	**(WINNERS - NEWCASTLE UNITED)**				
10th Dec	2	A	Newcastle United	0-6	
1985/86	**(WINNERS - MANCHESTER CITY)**				
2nd Dec	2	A	Sheffield United	2-5	Walsh 2
1986/87	**(WINNERS - COVENTRY CITY)**				
15th Nov	2	H	Billington Town	5-0	Powell 3, Carberry, Dodd
9th Dec	3	A	Hull City	3-3	Powell 2, Elliott
15th Dec	3 R	H	Hull City	1-3	Elliott
1987/88	**(WINNERS - ARSENAL)**				
2nd Nov	2	H	Huddersfield Town	5-0	Quinlan 3, Youds, Carberry
7th Dec	3	H	Barnsley	2-0	Youds, Carberry
4th Jan	4	H	Newcastle United	4-2	Quinlan 3, Elliott
8th Feb	5	A	Nottingham Forest	1-1	Wright
23rd Feb	5 R	H	Nottingham Forest	3-3	Jones 2 (1 pen), Carberry
29th Feb	5 R2	A	Nottingham Forest	1-2	Elliott

THE FA YOUTH CUP RESULTS

Date	Round	Venue	Opponents	Score	Scorers
1988/89	**(WINNERS - WATFORD)**				
5th Dec	2	A	Doncaster Rovers	1-1	Quinlan
12th Dec	2 R	H	Doncaster Rovers	4-1	Ebdon 2 (1 pen), Quinlan, Conlan
16th Jan	3	H	Leicester City	0-0	
19th Jan	3 R	A	Leicester City	1-4	Cowlishaw
1989/90	**(WINNERS - TOTTENHAM HOTSPUR)**				
9th Dec	2	H	Doncaster Rovers	0-2	
1990/91	**(WINNERS - MILLWALL)**				
3rd Dec	2	H	Scunthorpe United	1-0	McDonough (pen)
3rd Jan	3	A	Manchester United	1-1	McDonough
10th Jan	3 R	H	Manchester United	1-2	McDonough
1991/92	**(WINNERS - MANCHESTER UNITED)**				
25th Nov	2	A	Barnsley	2-1	Norris, Grant
11th Jan	3	H	Sheffield United	1-1	Jones
15th Jan	3 R	A	Sheffield United	3-2	Grant, Norris, Jones
28th Jan	4	A	Arsenal	2-1	Kenny, Unsworth
26th Feb	5	A	Tottenham Hotspur	0-4	
1992/93	**(WINNERS - LEEDS UNITED)**				
8th Dec	2	A	Preston North End	2-3	Jones 2
1993/94	**(WINNERS - ARSENAL)**				
6th Dec	2	H	Grimsby Town	0-2	
1994/95	**(WINNERS - MANCHESTER UNITED)**				
2nd Nov	1	A	Newcastle United	2-0	Woods (pen), Townsend
22nd Nov	2	A	Peterborough United	1-0	Branch,
10th Jan	3	H	Blackpool	6-5	Allen 3, Woods (pen), Weathers, Townsend
30th Jan	4	H	Sheffield United	1-3	Tynan
1995/96	**(WINNERS - LIVERPOOL)**				
11th Nov	1	H	Notts County	1-0	Hills
6th Dec	2	H	Tranmere Rovers	1-3	Hills
1996/97	**(WINNERS - LEEDS UNITED)**				
19th Nov	1	H	Nuneaton Borough	3-0	Dunne, Branch, Jevons
10th Dec	2	A	West Bromwich Alb.	2-1	Cadamarteri, Quayle
13th Jan	3	A	Bolton Wanderers	2-1	Milligan, Evans
27th Jan	4	A	Norwich City	1-1	Branch
10th Feb	4 R	H	Norwich City	0-2	
1997/98	**(WINNERS - EVERTON)**				
9th Dec	2	A	Blackpool	1-0	Milligan
22nd Jan	3	H	Stoke City	1-0	Jeffers
3rd Feb	4	A	Watford	3-2	Jevons, Osman, O'Brien
19th Mar	5	H	Ipswich Town	3-2	White o.g, Jevons, Cadamarteri
1st Apr	SF (1)	A	Leeds United	1-0	O'Brien
7th Apr	SF (2)	H	Leeds United	2-1	Regan, Jevons
1st May	Final (1)	A	Blackburn Rovers	3-1	Jevons, Cadamarteri, Osman
7th May	Final (2)	H	Blackburn Rovers	2-2	Jeffers, Eaton

THE FA YOUTH CUP RESULTS

Date	Round	Venue	Opponents	Score	Scorers
1998/99	**(WINNERS - WEST HAM UNITED)**				
19th Dec	3	A	Manchester United	2-2	Jeffers, Hibbert
6th Jan	3 R	H	Manchester United	4-0	Jeffers 2, McAlpine, Osman
26th Jan	4	H	Swindon Town	1-1	Howarth
2nd Feb	4 R	A	Swindon Town	5-1	Jeffers 3 (1 pen), Howarth, McAlpine
16th Feb	5	A	Sheffield Wednesday	1-1	Chadwick
1st Mar	5 R	H	Sheffield Wednesday	3-1	Southern, McLeod, Osman
23rd Mar	6	H	Aston Villa	1-0	Jeffers
20th Apr	SF (1)	A	West Ham United	0-3	
27th Apr	SF (2)	H	West Ham United	1-0	Symes
1999/2000	**(WINNERS - ARSENAL)**				
1st Dec	3	A	Norwich City	1-0	Merrick o.g
19th Jan	4	H	Brighton & Hove Alb.	1-0	Clarke (pen)
2nd Feb	5	H	Crewe Alexandra	0-1	
2000/01	**(WINNERS - ARSENAL)**				
28th Nov	3	H	Nottingham Forest	1-1	Chadwick
15th Dec	4	A	Nottingham Forest	2-3	Chadwick, Brown
2001/02	**(WINNERS - ASTON VILLA)**				
27th Nov	3	A	West Ham United	2-1	Symes 2
28th Jan	4	H	West Bromwich Alb.	2-0	Rooney 2
6th Feb	5	H	Manchester City	4-2	Rooney 2, Egerton o.g, Beck
12th Mar	6	H	Nottingham Forest	2-1	Rooney, Carney
27th Mar	SF (1)	H	Tottenham Hotspur	2-1	Carney, Symes
3rd Apr	SF (2)	A	Tottenham Hotspur	2-1	Rooney 2
14th May	Final (1)	H	Aston Villa	1-4	Rooney
18th May	Final (2)	A	Aston Villa	1-0	Brown
2002/03	**(WINNERS - MANCHESTER UNITED)**				
27th Nov	3	H	Port Vale	0-1	
2003/04	**(WINNERS - MIDDLESBROUGH)**				
3rd Dec	3	A	Coventry City	0-1	
2004/05	**(WINNERS - IPSWICH TOWN)**				
13th Dec	3	H	Charlton Athletic	1-0	Seargeant
19th Jan	4	A	Yeovil Town	6-0	Hopkins 2, Anichebe, Vidarsson, Vaughan
16th Feb	5	A	Tottenham Hotspur	1-2	Hopkins
2005/06	**(WINNERS - LIVERPOOL)**				
14th Dec	3	A	Reading	2-3	Kissock, Phelan (pen)
2000/01	**(WINNERS - LIVERPOOL)**				
5th Jan	3	A	Macclesfield Town	3-0	Connor, Morrison 2 (1 pen)
17th Jan	4	H	Millwall	0-1	
2007/08	**(WINNERS - MANCHESTER CITY)**				
11th Dec	3	H	Bristol City	0-2	

ARSENAL

2007/08 DETAILS

Final position: 3rd, Premier League
Best cup runs: SF, League Cup, QF, Ch. Lge
Player of season: Cesc Fabregas
Top scorer (all): 30, Emmanuel Adebayor

LEAGUE RECORD

	PL	W	D	L
Home:	87	38	23	26
Away:	87	16	13	58
Overall:	174	54	36	84

LAST 2 LEAGUE MEETINGS

04/05/2008

Arsenal	1-0	Everton
Bendtner 77		

29/12/2007

Everton	1-4	Arsenal
Cahill 19		Eduardo 47, 58
		Adebayor 78,
		Rosicky 90

CLUB DETAILS

Nickname: The Gunners
Ground: Emirates Stadium, capacity 60,432 (away allocation 3,000)
Manager: Arsene Wenger (app. 01/10/96)
Ex Evertonian: Francis Jeffers
Year formed: 1886

USEFUL INFORMATION

Website: www.arsenal.com
Address: Emirates Stadium, Highbury House, 75 Drayton Park N5 1BU
Switchboard: 0207 704 4000

TRAVEL INFORMATION

By Tube: The nearest station is Arsenal (Piccadilly Line), around three minutes' walk from the ground. Finsbury Park and Highbury & Islington are also within a ten-minute walking distance.
By Bus: Main bus stops are located on Holloway Road, Nag's Head, Seven Sisters Road, Blackstock Road and Highbury Corner. Regular services will take you to within 10 minutes' walk of the ground.

ASTON VILLA

FINAL STANDINGS 07/08

Final position: 6th, Premier League
Best cup runs: R3, League Cup, FA Cup
Player of season: Ashley Young
Top scorer (all): 13, John Carew

LEAGUE RECORD

	PL	W	D	L
Home:	93	45	24	24
Away:	93	25	22	46
Overall:	186	70	46	70

LAST 2 LEAGUE MEETINGS

27/04/2008

Everton	2-2	Aston Villa
Neville 56, Yobo 84		Agbonlahor 80,
		Carew 86

23/09/2007

Aston Villa	2-0	Everton
Carew 14, Agbonlahor 60		

CLUB DETAILS

Nickname: The Villans
Ground: Villa Park, capacity 42,573 (away allocation 3,000)
Manager: Martin O'Neill (app. 04/08/06)
Ex Evertonians: David Ginola, Steve Watson
Year formed: 1874

USEFUL INFORMATION

Website: www.avfc.co.uk
Address: Villa Park, Trinity Road, Birmingham B6 6HE
Switchboard: 0871 423 8100

TRAVEL INFORMATION

By Train: Witton station is a five-minute walk from the ground, while Aston is 15 minutes away. From New Street Station, a taxi should take 15 minutes.
By Bus: The number 7 West Midlands Travel Bus runs from Birmingham City Centre directly to the ground (Witton). To check services, go to www.travelwm.co.uk

BLACKBURN ROVERS

2007/08 STATISTICS

Final position: 7th, Premier League
Best cup runs: QF, League Cup, R3, FA Cup
Player of season: Roque Santa Cruz
Top scorer (all): 22, Roque Santa Cruz

LEAGUE RECORD

	PL	W	D	L
Home:	70	38	15	17
Away:	70	17	16	37
Overall:	140	55	31	54

LAST 2 LEAGUE MEETINGS

02/02/2008
Blackburn Rovers 0-0   Everton

25/08/2007
Everton   1-1   Blackburn Rovers
McFadden 78   Santa Cruz 15

CLUB DETAILS

Nickname: Rovers
Ground: Ewood Park, capacity 31,367
(away allocation 4,000)
Manager: Paul Ince (app. 24/06/08)
Ex Evertonian: Craig Short
Year formed: 1875

USEFUL INFORMATION

Website: www.rovers.co.uk
Address: Ewood Park, Bolton Road,
Blackburn, Lancashire BB2 4JF
Switchboard: 08701 113232

TRAVEL INFORMATION

By Train: Blackburn station is a mile and a half away, while Mill Hill is one mile from the stadium. Direct trains run from Manchester Victoria, Salford Crescent and Preston.
By Bus: The central bus station is next to the railway station. Services 3, 3A, 3B, 46, and 346 all go from Blackburn to Darwen. Ewood Park is a mile and a half along the journey.

BOLTON WANDERERS

2007/08 DETAILS

Final position: 16th, Premier League
Best cup runs: L16, UEFA Cup, R4, League Cup
Player of season: Kevin Davies
Top scorer (all): 11, Nicolas Anelka

LEAGUE RECORD

	PL	W	D	L
Home:	64	38	17	9
Away:	64	26	13	25
Overall:	128	64	30	34

LAST 2 LEAGUE MEETINGS

26/12/2007
Everton   2-0   Bolton Wanderers
Neville 51, Cahill 70

01/09/2007
Bolton Wanderers 1-2   Everton
Anelka 55   Yakubu 11, Lescott 90

CLUB DETAILS

Nickname: The Trotters
Ground: Reebok Stadium, capacity
28,000 (away allocation 3-5,000)
Manager: Gary Megson (app. 26/10/07)
Ex Evertonian: Gavin McCann
Year formed: 1874

USEFUL INFORMATION

Website: www.bwfc.co.uk
Address: Reebok Stadium, Burnden Way,
Lostock, Bolton BL6 6JW
Switchboard: 01204 673673

TRAVEL INFORMATION

By Train: Horwich Parkway station is 100 yards from the stadium, which is on the Manchester Airport to Preston and Blackpool North/Blackpool North and Preston to Manchester Airport line.
By Bus: The club operate regular buses to and from Bolton town centre.

CHELSEA

2007/08 DETAILS

Final position: 2nd, Premier League
Best cup runs: RU, Ch. League, League Cup
Player of season: Ricardo Carvalho
Top scorer (all): 20, Frank Lampard

LEAGUE RECORD

	PL	W	D	L
Home:	69	33	21	15
Away:	69	12	22	35
Overall:	138	45	43	50

LAST 2 LEAGUE MEETINGS

17/04/2008

Everton	0-1	Chelsea
		Essien 41

11/11/2007

Chelsea	1-1	Everton
Drogba 70		Cahill 90

CLUB DETAILS

Nickname: The Blues
Ground: Stamford Bridge, capacity 42,360 (away allocation 3,000)
Manager: Luiz Felipe Scolari (app. 01/07/08)
Ex Evertonians: Terry Phelan, John Spencer
Year formed: 1905

USEFUL INFORMATION

Website: www.chelseafc.com
Address: Stamford Bridge, Fulham Road, London SW6 1HS
Switchboard: 0870 300 2322

TRAVEL INFORMATION

By Tube: Fulham Broadway is on the District Line, around five minutes' walk. Take a train to Earl's Court and change for Wimbledon-bound trains. West Brompton is a new railway station accessible from Clapham Junction.
By Bus: Numbers 14, 211 and 414 go along Fulham Road from central London via West Brompton train station.

FULHAM

2007/08 DETAILS

Final position: 17th, Premier League
Best cup runs: R3, League Cup, FA Cup
Player of season: Simon Davies
Top scorers (all): 6, Clint Dempsey, David Healy, Diomansy Kamara, Danny Murphy

LEAGUE RECORD

	PL	W	D	L
Home:	20	16	4	0
Away:	20	3	4	13
Overall:	40	19	8	13

LAST 2 LEAGUE MEETINGS

16/03/2008

Fulham	1-0	Everton
McBride 67		

08/12/2007

Everton	3-0	Fulham
Yakubu 51, 61, 79		

CLUB DETAILS

Nickname: Cottagers
Ground: Craven Cottage, capacity 22,000 (away allocation 3,000)
Manager: Roy Hodgson (app. 30/12/07)
Ex Evertonians: Simon Davies, Andy Johnson
Year formed: 1879

USEFUL INFORMATION

Website: www.fulhamfc.com
Address: Craven Cottage, Stevenage Road, Fulham, London SW6 6HH
Switchboard: 0870 442 1222

TRAVEL INFORMATION

By Tube: Alight at Putney Bridge (District line) from Central London. Turn left out of station and right down Ranleigh Gardens. At the end of the road (before the Eight Bells pub) turn left into Willow Bank and right through the underpass into Bishops Park. Walk along river to ground (note park is closed after evening games).
By Bus: The numbers 74 and 220 both run along Fulham Palace Road.

HULL CITY

Final position: 3rd, Championship
Best cup runs: R3, League Cup, FA Cup
Player of season: Michael Turner
Top scorers (all): 15, Fraizer Campbell,
Dean Windass

LEAGUE RECORD

	PL	W	D	L
Home:	3	2	0	1
Away:	3	1	0	2
Overall:	6	3	0	3

LAST 2 LEAGUE MEETINGS

02/09/1953

Everton	2-0	Hull City

Fielding 22,
Buckle 86

24/08/1953

Hull City	1-3	Everton

Jenson 51 (pen)   Parker 5, Hickson 10,
                   Fielding 31

CLUB DETAILS

Nickname: The Tigers
Ground: The KC Stadium, capacity 25,404
(away allocation 4,000)
Manager: Phil Brown (app. 04/12/06)
Ex Evertonian: Nick Barmby
Year formed: 1904

USEFUL INFORMATION

Website: www.hullcityafc.premiumtv.co.uk
Address: The Circle, Walton Street,
Hull HU3 6HU
Switchboard: 08708 370 003

TRAVEL INFORMATION

By Train: Leave Hull Paragon and turn right onto Anlaby Road. Stadium is 15 minutes away.
By Road: Leave M62 at junction 38 and join the A63, towards Hull. Stay on A63 and the stadium is signposted (KC Stadium). One mile from the centre of Hull, leave A63 (signposted Hull Royal Infirmary) and take the 2nd exit at the roundabout. Turn left at the lights and then over the flyover, right at the next lights and the ground is down on the right.

LIVERPOOL

Final position: 4th, Premier League
Best cup runs: SF, Ch. League, QF, League Cup
Player of season: Fernando Torres
Top scorer (all): 33, Fernando Torres

LEAGUE RECORD

	PL	W	D	L
Home:	89	33	27	29
Away:	89	23	28	38
Overall:	178	56	55	67

LAST 2 LEAGUE MEETINGS

30/03/2008

Liverpool	1-0	Everton

Torres 7

20/10/2007

Everton	1-2	Liverpool

Hyypia 38 (o.g.)   Kuyt 54, 90 (2 pens)

CLUB DETAILS

Nickname: Reds/Pool
Ground: Anfield, capacity 45,522
(away allocation 2,000)
Manager: Rafael Benitez (app. 16/06/04)
Ex Evertonian: Gary Ablett
Year formed: 1892

USEFUL INFORMATION

Website: www.liverpoolfc.tv
Address: Anfield Road, Liverpool
L4 0TH
Switchboard: 0151 263 2361

TRAVEL INFORMATION

By Train: The nearest Merseyrail station is Kirkdale, which is accessible from Liverpool Central (take any train heading for Ormskirk or Kirkby) - from there it is a 20-25 minute walk. Alternatively, take a taxi or bus from Liverpool Lime Street Station (2 miles away).
By Bus: Numbers 26 or 27 from Paradise Street Interchange, or a 17 or 217 from Queen Square bus station run directly to the ground.

MANCHESTER CITY

2007/08 DETAILS

Final position: 9th, Premier League
Best cup runs: QF, League Cup, R4 FA Cup
Player of season: Joe Hart
Top scorer (all): 10, Elano

LEAGUE RECORD

	PL	W	D	L
Home:	75	38	22	15
Away:	75	16	17	42
Overall:	150	54	39	57

LAST 2 LEAGUE MEETINGS

25/02/2008
Manchester City 0-2 Everton
Yakubu 30, Lescott 38

12/01/2008
Everton 1-0 Manchester City
Lescott 31

CLUB DETAILS

Nickname: Blues/The Citizens
Ground: City of Manchester Stadium, capacity 48,000 (away allocation 4,800)
Manager: Mark Hughes (app. 05/06/08)
Ex Evertonians: Michael Ball, Richard Dunne
Year formed: 1887

USEFUL INFORMATION

Website: www.mcfc.co.uk
Address: City of Manchester Stadium, SportCity, Rowsley Street, Manchester M11 3FF
Switchboard: 0870 062 1894

TRAVEL INFORMATION

By Train: The nearest station is Ashburys (a ten-minute walk), which is a five-minute train ride from Manchester Piccadilly (which itself is a 20 to 25-minute walk).
By Bus: Numbers 216 and 217 are the main services from the city centre, but 53, 54, 185, 186, 230, 231, 232, 233, 234, 235, 236, 237, X36 and X37 also run to Sport City.

MANCHESTER UNITED

2007/08 DETAILS

Final position: 1st, Premier League
Best cup runs: W, Ch. League, QF, FA Cup
Player of season: Cristiano Ronaldo
Top scorer (all): 42, Cristiano Ronaldo

LEAGUE RECORD

	PL	W	D	L
Home:	79	37	17	25
Away:	79	15	20	44
Overall:	158	52	37	69

LAST 2 LEAGUE MEETINGS

23/12/2007
Manchester Utd 2-1 Everton
Ronaldo 22, 88 (p) Cahill 27

15/12/2007
Everton 0-1 Manchester Utd
Vidic 83

CLUB DETAILS

Nickname: Red Devils
Ground: Old Trafford, capacity 76,312 (away allocation 3,000)
Manager: Sir Alex Ferguson (app. 06/11/86)
Ex Evertonian: Wayne Rooney
Year formed: 1878

USEFUL INFORMATION

Website: www.manutd.com
Address: Sir Matt Busby Way, Old Trafford, Manchester M16 0RA
Switchboard: 0870 442 1994

TRAVEL INFORMATION

By Train: Special services run from Manchester Piccadilly to the clubs own railway station. There is also a Metrolink service, with the station located next to Lancashire County Cricket Club on Warwick Road, which leads up to Sir Matt Busby Way.
By Bus: Numbers 114, 230, 252 and 253 all run from the city centre to the ground.

MIDDLESBROUGH

2007/08 DETAILS

Final position: 13th, Premier League
Best cup runs: QF, FA Cup, R3, League Cup
Player of season: David Wheater
Top scorer (all): 10, Stuart Downing

LEAGUE RECORD

	PL	W	D	L
Home:	55	38	12	5
Away:	55	15	15	25
Overall:	110	53	27	30

LAST 2 LEAGUE MEETINGS

01/01/2008

Middlesbrough	0-2	Everton
		Johnson 67,
		McFadden 72

30/09/2007

Everton	2-0	Middlesbrough
Lescott 7, Pienaar 58		

CLUB DETAILS

Nickname: Boro
Ground: Riverside Stadium, capacity 35,100 (away allocation 4,000)
Manager: Gareth Southgate (app. 07/06/06)
Ex Evertonian: Abel Xavier
Year formed: 1876

USEFUL INFORMATION

Website: www.mfc.co.uk
Address: Riverside Stadium, Middlesbrough, Cleveland TS3 6RS
Switchboard: 0844 499 6789

TRAVEL INFORMATION

By Train: Middlesbrough station is about 15 minutes walk from the stadium, served by trains from Darlington. Take the back exit from the station, turn right, then after a couple of minutes turn right again into Wynward Way for the ground.
By Bus: Numbers 36, 37 and 38 go from the town centre close to the ground.

NEWCASTLE UNITED

2007/08 DETAILS

Final position: 12th, Premier League
Best cup runs: R4, FA Cup, R3, League Cup
Player of season: Habib Beye
Top scorer (all): 13,

LEAGUE RECORD

	PL	W	D	L
Home:	74	41	14	19
Away:	74	16	17	41
Overall:	148	57	31	60

LAST 2 LEAGUE MEETINGS

11/05/2008

Everton	3-1	Newcastle
Yakubu 28, 82 (p)		Owen 47 (p)
Lescott 70		

07/10/2007

Newcastle	3-2	Everton
Butt 42, Emre 86,		Johnson 53,
Owen 90		Given 90 (o.g.)

CLUB DETAILS

Nickname: Magpies
Ground: St James' Park, capacity 52,387 (away allocation 3,000)
Manager: TBA
Ex Evertonians: Peter Beardsley, Steve Watson
Year formed: 1881

USEFUL INFORMATION

Website: www.nufc.co.uk
Address: St. James' Park, Newcastle-upon-Tyne NE1 4ST
Switchboard: 0191 201 8400

TRAVEL INFORMATION

By Train: St James' Park is a ten-minute walk from Newcastle Central Station. The stadium is also served by its own Metro station (St James' Metro).
By Bus: Any bus from the town centre heading towards Gallowgate takes you past the stadium.

PORTSMOUTH

2007/08 DETAILS

Final position: 8th, Premier League
Best cup runs: W, FA Cup, R4, League Cup
Player of season: David James
Top scorer (all): 12, Benjani

LEAGUE RECORD

	PL	W	D	L
Home:	27	14	5	8
Away:	27	9	4	14
Overall:	54	23	9	22

LAST 2 LEAGUE MEETINGS

02/03/2008

Everton	3-1	Portsmouth
Yakubu 1, 81,		Defoe 38
Cahill 73		

01/12/2007

Portsmouth	0-0	Everton

CLUB DETAILS

Nickname: Pompey
Ground: Fratton Park, capacity 20,200
(away allocation 2,000)
Manager: Harry Redknapp (app. 07/12/05)
Ex Evertonian: David Unsworth
Year formed: 1898

USEFUL INFORMATION

Website: www.pompeyfc.co.uk
Address: Fratton Park,
Frogmore Road,
Portsmouth,
Hants PO4 8RA
Switchboard: 0239 273 1204

TRAVEL INFORMATION

By Train: Fratton Bridge Station is a ten-minute walk from the ground - on arrival by train you pass the ground on your left. Portsmouth mainline station is at least a 25-minute walk.
By Bus: 13, 17 and 18 run to the ground, while other services that stop nearby are the 3, 16, 16A, 24, 27 (all Fratton Bridge); 4, 4A, 6 (all Milton Road).

STOKE CITY

2007/08 DETAILS

Final position: 2nd, Championship
Best cup runs: R3, FA Cup, R1, League Cup
Player of season: Liam Lawrence
Top scorers (all): 15, Ricardo Fuller,
Liam Lawrence

LEAGUE RECORD

	PL	W	D	L
Home:	52	34	11	7
Away:	52	16	16	20
Overall:	104	50	27	27

LAST 2 LEAGUE MEETINGS

20/04/1985

Stoke City	0-2	Everton
		Sharp 22, Sheedy 47

17/11/1984

Everton	4-0	Stoke City
Heath 29, 34,		
Reid 70, Steven 74		

CLUB DETAILS

Nickname: The Potters
Ground: Britannia Stadium, capacity
28,384 (away allocation 4,800)
Manager: Tony Pulis (app. 13/06/06)
Ex Evertonian: Steve Simonsen
Year formed: 1863

USEFUL INFORMATION

Website: www.stokecityfc.premiumtv.co.uk
Address: Stanley Matthews Way,
Stoke-on-Trent
ST4 4EG
Switchboard: 01782 592 222

TRAVEL INFORMATION

By Train: Stoke-on-Trent station is two minutes from Glebe Street, where buses to the stadium run. Turn right out of the station and then next right. Follow the road to the end then turn left, down a bank into Glebe Street. Buses depart on the left by the church.
By Bus: From Hanley Bus Station, take the 23 to Glebe Street where shuttle bus services to the stadium depart. Service is at 15-minute intervals until 15 minutes before kick-off.

SUNDERLAND

2007/08 DETAILS

Final position: 15th, Premier League
Best cup runs: R3, FA Cup, R2, League Cup
Player of season: Kenwyne Jones
Top scorer (all): 7, Kenwyne Jones

LEAGUE RECORD

	PL	W	D	L
Home:	73	45	11	17
Away:	73	18	11	44
Overall:	146	63	22	61

LAST 2 LEAGUE MEETINGS

09/03/2008

Sunderland	0-1	Everton
		Johnson 55

24/11/2007

Everton	7-1	Sunderland
Yakubu 12, 73,		Yorke 45
Cahill 17, 62,		
Pienaar 43,		
Johnson 80, Osman 85		

CLUB DETAILS

Nickname: The Black Cats
Ground: Stadium of Light, capacity 49,000 (away allocation 3,600)
Manager: Roy Keane (app. 28/08/06)
Ex Evertonians: John Oster, Alan Stubbs
Year formed: 1879

USEFUL INFORMATION

Website: www.safc.com
Address: The Sunderland Stadium of Light, Sunderland SR5 1SU
Switchboard: 0191 551 5000

TRAVEL INFORMATION

By Train: Sunderland mainline station is a ten to 15-minute walk. The Metro service also runs from here, with St. Peter's or the Stadium of Light stations nearest the stadium.
By Bus: Numbers 2, 3, 4, 12, 13, 15 and 16 all stop within a few minutes walk of the ground. All routes connect to the central bus station, Park Lane Interchange.

TOTTENHAM HOTSPUR

2007/08 DETAILS

Final position: 11th, Premier League
Best cup runs: W, League Cup, L16, UEFA Cup
Player of season: Robbie Keane
Top scorers (all): 23, Dimitar Berbatov, Robbie Keane

LEAGUE RECORD

	PL	W	D	L
Home:	71	30	24	17
Away:	71	15	20	36
Overall:	142	45	44	53

LAST 2 LEAGUE MEETINGS

30/01/2008

Everton	0-0	Tottenham H.

14/08/2007

Tottenham H.	1-3	Everton
Gardner 26		Lescott 3, Osman 37,
		Stubbs 45

CLUB DETAILS

Nickname: Spurs
Ground: White Hart Lane, capacity 36,240 (away allocation 3,500)
Manager: Juande Ramos (app. 27/10/07)
Ex Evertonian: Vinny Samways
Year formed: 1882

USEFUL INFORMATION

Website: www.spurs.co.uk
Address: Bill Nicholson Way, 748 High Road, Tottenham, London N17 0AP
Switchboard: 0208 365 5000

TRAVEL INFORMATION

By Tube: The nearest tube station is Seven Sisters (Victoria line - a 25-minute walk), with trains running to Liverpool Street. The nearest mainline station is White Hart Lane, approx five minutes' walk, on the Liverpool Street-Enfield Town line.
By Bus: A regular service runs from Seven Sisters past the stadium entrance (numbers 259, 279, 149).

WEST BROMWICH ALBION

2007/08 DETAILS

Final position: 1st, Championship
Best cup runs: SF, FA Cup, R3, League Cup
Player of season: Kevin Phillips
Top scorer (all): 24, Kevin Phillips

LEAGUE RECORD

	PL	W	D	L
Home:	69	40	15	14
Away:	69	15	17	37
Overall:	138	55	32	51

LAST 2 LEAGUE MEETINGS

07/05/2006

Everton	2-2	West Brom
Anichebe 84,		Gera 14, Martinez 47
Ferguson 90		

19/11/2005

West Brom	4-0	Everton
Ellington 45 (p), 69		
Clement 51, Earnshaw 90		

CLUB DETAILS

Nickname: Baggies/Albion
Ground: The Hawthorns, capacity 27,877 (away allocation 3,000)
Manager: Tony Mowbray (app. 13/10/06)
Ex Evertonian: Kevin Campbell
Year formed: 1878

USEFUL INFORMATION

Website: www.wba.premiumtv.co.uk
Address: Halfords Lane, West Bromwich, West Midlands B71 4LF
Switchboard: 08700 668 888

TRAVEL INFORMATION

By Train: The Hawthorns Metro stop is ten minutes away from the ground, served by a service from Birmingham Snow Hill station. Smethwick Rolf Street is 15 minutes away, served by local trains from Birmingham New Street.
By Bus: 74 (between Birmingham and Dudley), 79 (Birmingham and Wolverhampton) and 450 (Bearwood and West Bromwich) all stop at Birmingham Road.

WEST HAM UNITED

2007/08 DETAILS

Final position: 10th, Premier League
Best cup runs: QF, League Cup, R3, FA Cup
Player of season: Robert Green
Top scorer (all): 11, Dean Ashton

LEAGUE RECORD

	PL	W	D	L
Home:	53	34	9	10
Away:	53	18	13	22
Overall:	106	52	22	32

LAST 2 LEAGUE MEETINGS

22/03/2008

Everton	1-1	West Ham
Yakubu 8		Ashton 68

15/12/2007

West Ham	0-2	Everton
		Yakubu 45,
		Johnson 90

CLUB DETAILS

Nickname: The Hammers
Ground: Upton Park, capacity 35,647 (away allocation 2,000)
Manager: TBA
Ex Evertonian: Richard Wright
Year formed: 1895

USEFUL INFORMATION

Website: www.whufc.com
Address: Boleyn Ground, Green Street, Upton Park, London E13 9AZ
Switchboard: 0208 548 2748

TRAVEL INFORMATION

By Tube: Upton Park is the closest Tube station, around 45 minutes from Central London on the District (and also Hammersmith & City) line. When you exit the station, turn right - the stadium is then a two-minute walk away. East Ham and Plaistow stations, which are further away, may also be worth using to avoid congestion after the match.
By Bus: Routes 5, 15, 58, 104, 115, 147, 330 and 376 all serve the Boleyn Ground.

WIGAN ATHLETIC

2007/08 DETAILS

Final position: 14th, Premier League
Best cup runs: R4, FA Cup, R2, League Cup
Player of season: Paul Scharner
Top scorer (all): 7, Marcus Bent

LEAGUE RECORD

	PL	W	D	L
Home:	3	1	1	1
Away:	3	2	1	0
Overall:	6	3	2	1

LAST 2 LEAGUE MEETINGS

20/01/2008

Wigan	1-2	Everton
Jagielka 53 (o.g.)		Johnson 39, Lescott 42

11/08/2007

Everton	2-1	Wigan
Osman 26,		Sibierski 80
Anichebe 75		

CLUB DETAILS

Nickname: The Latics
Ground: JJB Stadium,
capacity 25,023
(away allocation 5,000+)
Manager: Steve Bruce (app. 26/11/07)
Ex Evertonians: Marcus Bent, Kevin Kilbane
Year formed: 1932

USEFUL INFORMATION

Website: www.wiganlatics.co.uk
Address: JJB Stadium, Robin Park,
Newtown, Wigan WN5 0UZ
Switchboard: 01942 774000

TRAVEL INFORMATION

By Train: Wigan Wallgate and Wigan North Western are a 15-minute walk from the stadium. From either station, head under the railway bridge and keep to the right - following the road (A49) for ten minutes. The complex should soon be visible.
By Bus: No particular route, as the venue is within easy distance of the station.

Everton's UEFA Cup first round opponents, Standard Liege, receive a warm welcome from their fans ahead of their UEFA Champions League third qualifying round home tie, August 2008

Don't forget lads, one Evertonian is worth twenty Liverpudlians

Brian Labone 1940-2006

THE LEGEND DIXIE D FORGOTTEN

OWN WORDS LEGENDARY DIXIE DEAN FORGOTTEN TAPES - brought to life on CD

EvertonWay.com
Everton Academy Online

Everton Football Club

TICKET INFORMATION

Address

The Fan Centre,
Goodison Park,
Goodison Road,
Liverpool
L4 4EL

Telephone Number

0870 442 1878

Email

customer.contactcentre@evertonfc.com

Box Office Hours

Monday-Friday 8am-6pm
Saturday (non-matchdays) 10am to 4pm
Sunday closed
Matchdays (Saturday) 9am to kick-off and after the game
Matchdays (Sunday) 9am to kick-off and after the game
Matchdays (midweek) 8am to kick-off and after the game

Ticket prices 2008/09

Top Balcony		Lower Bullens	
Adult	£33	Adult	£30
Under 16	£17	Under 16	£17
Main Stand		OAPs (over 65)	£21
Adult	£35	**Paddock**	
Under 16	£19	Adult	£33
OAPs (over 65)	£23	Under 16	£17
Upper Gwladys		**Park End**	
Adult	£33	Adult	£36
Under 16	£17	Under 16	£19
Lower Gwladys		**Family Enclosure**	
Adult	£30	Adult	£33
Under 16	£17	Under 16	£15
OAPs (over 65)	£21		
Upper Bullens			
Adult	£35		
Under 16	£19		

Please note that an additional £4 will be charged for adult prices for the Liverpool and Manchester United Premier League fixtures

Everton E-Ticketing

NO BOOKING FEES APPLICABLE
Before you register to order your tickets at **evertonfc.com**, please note that you must have a valid email address.

Charter of Complaint

The club endeavour to act on any feedback or complaints within seven working days - and to resolve issues within 28 working days.
Please note - Everton FC accept feedback in any written form.

EXECUTIVE LOUNGE MEMBERSHIP

About
Hospitality packages are usually sold for the season, although a limited range of options may also be available on a match-by-match basis.
With food created by top chefs and top-quality service together with the well-stocked bars, luxurious surroundings and some of the best seating at Goodison Park, the lounges are the perfect environment for fans who want something unique from their visit, offering something for everyone.

Executive Boxes
Private box offering the finest food and drink for up to 10 people with access to a private balcony offering the best views in the stadium.

Dixie Dean Platinum Suite
Named after one of the Blues' finest players, this lounge offers food, wines and liqueurs, the best service and directors' box seating.

Blues 100
Great hospitality and directors' box seating make this one of the most popular boxes.

Brian Labone Suite
Located in the Main Stand and named after a true legend, top-class facilities and directors' box seating are available here.

1878 Suite
Main Stand seating is available in this area, as well as a visit from the Man of the Match.

Alex Young Suite
Directors' box seating and a three-course meal with wine are standard features in the 'Alex'.

Joe Mercer Suite
Bar-lounge for fans in the directors' box.

The People's Club
Pre-match buffet, top seats and private bar access are amongst the attractions.

The Captains' Table
Pre-match carvery, cash-bar and Park End seating all available.

The Marquee
Pre-match meal, complementary bar and top Main Stand seats available through the season.

Blues 100 and (below) The Marquee

Sponsorship
A range of matchday packages are available, offering a unique promotion opportunity through programme and perimeter board advertising, PA announcements and scoreboard messages.

What Packages?
Match sponsor
Matchball sponsor
Programme sponsor
Mascot sponsor

More info
First-class hospitality and entertainment also come with sponsorship packages.
For more information call 0151 530 5300.

GETTING TO GOODISON

How to get there - by car
From the North and South:
Take the M6 exit at junction 26 onto the M58 and continue until the end.
At the gyratory, go left to join the M57 Junction 7. Exit the M57 at Junction 4 to turn right into East Lancashire Road (A580). Follow the road, across Queen's Drive, into Walton Lane. Goodison Road is less than a mile along, on the right.
From the East:
From the M62, exit Junction 6 onto the M57, go to the end of the motorway and then left onto the A59 Ormskirk Road. Then follow the same route for north.
From the West:
From the M53, continue to Wallasey and follow Liverpool via the Kingsway Mersey Tunnel. Turn left at the end into Scotland Road, taking the right fork to the A58 Kirkdale Road. Follow the road round for two miles and Goodison will appear in front of you.

How to get there - by train
Kirkdale Station is the closest to Goodison on the Northern Line (about a mile away), although Sandhills Station, the stop before from the city centre, has the benefit of a bus service to the ground (Soccerbus). Both stations can be reached by first getting a train from Liverpool Lime Street (which is more than three miles from the ground) to Liverpool Central (Merseyrail Northern Line), and then changing there for trains to Sandhills (two stops away) or Kirkdale (three stops). Note: only trains to Ormskirk or Kirkby go to Kirkdale station. A taxi from Liverpool Lime Street should cost between £5 and £7.

How to get there - Soccerbus
There are frequent shuttle buses from Sandhills Station to Goodison Park for all Everton home Premiership and Cup matches. Soccerbus will run for two hours before each match (the last bus from Sandhills Station is approximately 15 minutes before kick-off) and for 50 minutes after the final whistle (subject to availability). You can pay as you board the bus. Soccerbus is FREE for those who hold a valid TRIO, SOLO or SAVEAWAY ticket or Merseytravel Free Travel Pass.

How to get there - by bus
Take the 102 (daytime only) or 130 (evenings/Sunday) from Paradise Street Bus Station or the 19/19A, 20, 21, 130 (evenings/Sunday), 311, 345 or 350/351 from Queen Square bus station directly to the ground.
Other services which serve Goodison Park (not from the city centre) include the 68/168 (Bootle-Aigburth Vale) and 62/162 (Crosby/Bootle-Penny Lane).

How to get there - by air
Liverpool John Lennon Airport is around 11 miles from the ground, and taxis should be easily obtainable. Alternatively, you can catch the 80A or 86A bus to Liverpool South Parkway Station, and take a Northern Line train to Sandhills to connect for the Soccerbus service.

To check bus and train times
Traveline Merseyside	0871 200 22 33
	(7am-8pm Mon-Fri, 8am-8pm Sat, Sun, Bank Holidays)
	merseytravel.gov.uk
Soccerbus	0151 330 1066

EVERTON STADIUM TOUR

About   Have you ever wondered what goes on behind the scenes at Goodison Park? Would you like to experience the special atmosphere of the players' dressing rooms before walking down the tunnel and up the steps to the pitch to the famous Z-Cars tune?
Of course you would!

Booking   A warm welcome awaits all our visitors to Goodison Park and advance booking is advised. All tours are non-smoking and last approximately one hour 25 minutes. Small parties or large groups can be accommodated.
Tours operate Monday, Wednesday, Friday and Sunday 11am and 1pm.
(Please note that tours do not operate on match days or the afternoon before a first-team home fixture.)
Please call 0151 330 2212 or email **stadiumtours@evertonfc.com**

Guides   All tours are taken by experienced tour guides and Everton legend Dave Hickson appears on special occasions.

Prices   Adults   - £8.50
Children & Senior Citizens   - £5.00
Family Ticket   - £20.00 (2 Adults and 2 U16s)
Under 5s   - Free
* Concessions available for large bookings.

Everton legends Joe Royle and Dave Hickson, pictured at Goodison

EVERTON TV

![evertontv logo]

About

The club's official online subscription TV service, evertonTV continues to provide the full Everton experience to supporters. Offering exclusive access to the manager and first-team stars, there are a wide variety of features on offer.

Features

Extended highlights of every first-team games from 2006 onwards.
Archived interviews with Blues legends.
Fresh content every day.
A dedicated fan channel.
High quality video available on demand.
Regular live games, including pre-season and European matches.
Live commentary on every first-team game.
evertonTVod provides classic games to Windows Vista users.

New

evertonTV will also soon be offered as an off-the-shelf product, giving fans the chance to buy the product from retailers.

Subscriptions cost £4.99 per month or just £40 for the whole year.
For more details, visit evertonfc.com

EVERTON MOBILE

About

Look out for the new WAP site (wap.evertonfc.com), which will make more features available to fans. You'll be able to get the latest club news, ticket information, downloads and much more.

To visit the official WAP portal on your phone, text EVERTON to 61718*

Features

Text alerts - Not at the match? But never far away...Get the latest news, scores and match updates straight to your mobile. NEW for 2008/09 - Text Alert Season Ticket.
Wallpapers - Choose from match action pictures, customised shirts, Everton legends, stadium shots, official club crests and first-team player images.
Ringtones - Get your mobile bouncing with Evertonian chants, real tones, polyphonics and more.
Games - Everton-branded games (including Football Manager) plus all the top mobile games including Pro Evolution Soccer 2008.
Animations - Get 3D shirts, player animations, crests and more straight to your mobile.
Videos - Match action, including every 2008/09 goal, classic goals, highlights and top fives. Plus interviews with players past and present.
Ask Sharpy - The club's own text question service. Any questions answered!
Reverse Auction - Everton Reverse Auction is our fantastic competition, where the LOWEST UNIQUE BID wins, not the highest. Bid by text or on our website for the chance to win incredible prizes for pennies!

***Your mobile must be WAP enabled. Standard network charges apply**

EVERTON WEBSITE

About

Re-launched in 2008, the club's award-winning official website offers a whole host of facilities for fans to enjoy. Register your details to receive regular email newsletters and access a whole host of interactive options, including YourEverton, podcasts, quizzes, eCards, wallpapers, Davey's Newsdesk, screensavers, kids zone, Ask Sharpy and live webchats!

New

The new YourEverton social network is just one of the new features now available. In terms of innovation, **evertonfc.com** continues to develop apace. Recent developments saw Everton become the first Premier League club to have a Facebook application, and site options also include:

The Blue Room   The popular chat forum where fans can go to discuss the current issues at the Club.

Email   Everton webmail options now available, giving supporters the chance to register an Everton email address and make use of 5gb of online storage.

Megastore   Full range of merchandise available to buy online, including kits, training range, ladies and children's leisure wear, souvenirs - and much more.

DVD Shop   Order a range of Everton releases, including season reviews, classic matches and goal compilation collections.

Everton Stats   Compiled by our statistician Gavin Buckland, up-to-date and unrivalled information on players and matches can be found here. Everton are the only club to provide full details on their website of every game played in their history.

Academy   Everything related to the club's future first-team prospects.

Interactive   We give fans the option of posting a comment in reply to any news article. A user can also click a 'thumbs up' button if they liked the story.

eAuction   Signed shirts, photos and balls can be bid for online (and via SMS), as well as unique items that will never be made available ever again, such as match-worn jerseys and boots.

Lotteries   You can find information on Toffee Lotto - the Everton FC lottery game – and the matchday game - Grab-A-Grand.

Latest news on the homepage, August 2008

EVERTONIA

evertonia

evertonia

About

The Official Members' Club for Evertonians of all ages, everywhere.
Membership fees remain at £19.99 for adults and £9.99 for juniors - providing great value for fans.

Three ways to join

- Call 0871 663 1878.
- Visit the Goodison Park Box Office.
- Online at **evertonfc.com**

Adult benefits for Evertonia (£19.99)

- A three-day ticket priority period to ensure you are first in line to purchase home Barclays Premier League tickets.
- Free entry to Everton Reserves and Ladies home fixtures.
- Free membership to the Away Travel Club (worth £5).
- Two £5-off vouchers for use on selected home Barclays Premier League fixtures.
- Regular Evertonia email updates (email address required).
- Exclusive invitation to an open training day.
- £5 off an Everton Tigers full Season Ticket.
- £1 off an Everton Tigers home match ticket.
- Free wallpaper from Everton mobile (mobile telephone number required - note phone must be WAP enabled; small data charge may apply).

Junior benefits for Evertonia (£9.99)

- A three-day ticket priority period to ensure you are first in line to purchase home Barclays Premier League tickets.
- The chance to be selected as an Everton, Toffee Lady or Everton Tigers mascot.
- Free entry to Everton Reserves and Ladies home fixtures.
- Free membership to Away Travel Club (worth £5) – please note you must be accompanied by an adult.
- Two x £5-off vouchers for selected Barclays Premier League fixtures.
- 10% off exclusive Soccer Schools.
- The chance to attend our Christmas Party to meet the players and much more.
- Exclusive invitation to an open training day to watch the players put through their paces.
- £5 off an Everton Tigers full Season Ticket.
- £1 off an Everton Tigers home match ticket.
- Free wallpaper from Everton mobile (mobile telephone number required - note phone must be WAP enabled. Small data charge may apply).

EVERTONWAY

About

One of the club's biggest off-field developments in the last 12 months, evertonway.com is the Blues' online coaching Academy geared towards players and coaches. Everton are the first professional club to reveal their Academy programme, which has developed players such as Rooney, Dunne, Ball, McCann, Osman, Hibbert, Vaughan and Anichebe, with more to follow this season.

Site content includes

- Video clips, diagrams, audio commentary and supporting notes guide players and coaches through the programme.
- All age ranges in the Academy are covered, but are broken down into age specific sections to ensure relevant practices for the specific groups: 5-11, 12-15 and 16-18.
- The site replicates every Academy department with detailed information on technical coaching, sports science, education and welfare, recruitment and physiotherapy.
- The site is updated regularly with new material of footage from the Academy.
- Additional features include a coaches forum and live chat time with Academy coaches.

Successes

- Due to evertonway.com, the club has had fantastic success in growing relationships with Youth football organisations around the globe.
- In the USA, the Blues are using this tool, along with visits from Academy coaches, to work with many youth organisations including Illinois Youth Soccer Association which has 85,000 players under its control.
- In Canada, Everton is using this tool to deepen ties with Ontario Soccer Association and several other clubs to help maximise player development opportunities in the region.
- In India, the club has an agreement with the Indian Football Association (West Bengal) with the aim of improving grass roots through to elite level football in the area where evertonway.com will help enhance coaching standards.
- The club has agreed to play a major role in the establishment of the Kuwait Premier Academy - which will follow the Everton Way programme to give Kuwaiti youngsters a chance to develop further.
- In July 2008, Everton held its first International Youth Football Tournament in Pennsylvania, USA. The 'Everton Cup USA' featured more than 60 youth teams and our Under-10 Academy team triumphed in the inaugural event to highlight the value of 'The Everton Way'.
- Further relationships with youth football have been established in Norway and Cyprus, and this program is helping to take us to a whole new audience of potential Evertonians!

A 12-month subscription costs £49.99 - to apply, go to academy.evertonfc.com

EVERTON RETAIL

New for 2008/09

As well as three new kit launches and the new training kit range, the successful pink charity shirts are planned to be released in late 2008. The 1,000 limited-edition shirts sold out within a day in spring 2008, and the new batch will incorporate the new kit design, whilst also benefiting our nominated charities.

Shop online

You can also order the new catalogue, use the web or call us.

shop.evertonfc.com

0871 641 2292 (Customer Services)
0870 005 2300 (Telephone Ordering)

There are 320 JJB Stores in the UK that stock Everton products. Check **jjbsports.com** for store details near you. If you cannot buy Everton merchandise in your JJB Store, order online or call our order hotline.

Where we are

Everton FC Official Club Store
Goodison Road, Liverpool, L4 4EL
United Kingdom
Opening times: Mon-Fri 9am-5.30pm
Saturdays 9am-6pm, Sundays 11am-3pm
Longer opening times on match days/nights

Birkenhead Official Club Store
Unit 30, Pyramids Centre, Birkenhead
United Kingdom
Opening times: Mon-Sat 9am-5.30pm
Closed Sunday

Licensing and Brand Protection Programme

To be granted permission to use the official Everton crest, you must contact Gary Wilton:

gary.wilton@evertonfc.com

Please be aware that trading standards and local police monitor the use of the club's crest.

Ayegbeni Yakubu sporting the new home shirt for 2008/09

EVERTON PUBLICATIONS

EFC

One of the Premier League's top matchday programmes, EFC continues to improve with fresh content, features and coverage included for 2008/09. Published for every home fixture, exclusive interviews with players, managers and coaching staff, as well as in-depth club information, will remain as standard.

How to subscribe

Phone: 0845 143 0001 (Monday-Friday 9am-5pm)

Website: **merseyshop.com**

The Evertonian

Published on a monthly basis, the new-look magazine offers a more in-depth look at Everton. The publication has been made more fan-orientated and contains a number of fresh features while also including articles on players past and present, managers and coaching staff, and superb colour posters.

How to subscribe

Phone: 0845 143 0001 (Monday-Friday 9am-5pm)

Website: **merseyshop.com**

BLUES

The official Everton bi-monthly magazine for youngsters, which includes features for the junior generation such as cartoons, quizzes and competitions, along with large, pull-out posters.

How to order

Phone: 0845 143 0001 (Monday-Friday 9am-5pm)

Website: **merseyshop.com**

THE EVERTON COLLECTION CHARITABLE TRUST

About

The David France Collection is recognised as one of the most sought-after in the world, and in a bid to secure the collection for the club the Everton Collection Charitable Trust was registered. Consisting of more than 10,000 items related to the birth and development of Everton Football Club, the £800,000 needed to attain the collection was raised in autumn 2007.

The money raised came from Everton Football Club, Lord Grantchester, proceeds from the Heritage Week events held in March 2007, plus a sizeable sum from the Heritage Lottery Fund.

Dr David France

An avid Evertonian, Dr France spent decades - and no small fortune - amassing his incredible collection of memorabilia. Its scope is staggering, tracing the family tree and bloodlines of Everton. It took 20 years or so to compile these items from his homes in North America, using a network of UK memorabilia dealers. Dr France, who travelled more than two million miles following Everton, said:

"My obsession was not compiling the collection but finding a suitable home for it, a home where it will be looked after and made available for public viewing. That took six years. I was only the guardian of our heritage and was committed to transferring it to an independent body representative of a cross-section of Evertonians. I was both pleased and relieved by the conclusion of events."

In the Collection

Medals awarded for just about every triumph since 1890;
Programmes from 1886, including every home issue from the inaugural League season 1888/89;
Season tickets from the club's days in Stanley Park, Priory Road and Anfield;
Tenders for the construction of the Anfield ground;
Team photographs from 1881;
Club correspondence dating back to 1888;
The Everton Scriptures - hand-written record books documenting the decisions made at the board meetings held between 1886 and 1965 which shaped one of the great institutions of football.

Blue Heritage

Dr France's collection has been acknowledged by experts as the finest in the world. All sorts of dealers wanted to get their hands on the priceless items. Also, because Everton and Liverpool shared the same matchday programme for 30 years since 1904, he had amassed inadvertently the greatest collection of Liverpool items. This attracted investment syndicates worldwide. Dr France added:

"Some three years ago I received formal offers for £1,250,000 from the Middle East and Far East but I was content with the £800,000, about half of its current market value, from the Everton Collection Charitable Trust. Also I promised Brian Labone and Alan Ball that our heritage would never fall into unfriendly hands or be broken up and dispersed. There was no way that I would ever let down men like Labby and Bally – they never ever let Everton down."

Future Plans

Lord Grantchester, chairman of the Everton Collection Charitable Trust, said:

"Future generations of Evertonians will be indebted to the single-minded dedication, indefatigable patience and uncommon generosity of David France. His legacy is simply amazing. I'm sure that every football club wished that they had their very own David France."

THE EVERTON COLLECTION CHARITABLE TRUST

Conditions for the Collection

- Every single item to be catalogued and secured to ensure that none go missing;
- No items will be disposed of;
- All items to be preserved by experts;
- The collection to be built on with quality additions;
- A physical display of the items in Liverpool for public access;
- A dedicated website involving the digitisation of the printed materials for worldwide access;
- That the collection promotes the history of Everton and Merseyside football, and educates the next generations of fans;

Final Words

Dr France is adamant that most Evertonians would have done the same. He said:

"I was fortunate in that I had the opportunity to compile these treasures. It's just a part of doing my bit for the Everton family. People talk of my legacy - the Everton Former Players' Foundation, the Everton books, the Gwladys Street Hall of Fame, but none of these would have been successful without the Everton fans."

As of January 1, 2008 the memorabilia is known as **The Everton Collection**.

In Words and Pictures

The amazing story of the finest collection of football memorabilia in the world, and the man who made it possible, is now available. First released as a limited-edition publication to raise funds for the Trust, a significantly expanded version of the book entitled **Dr Everton's Magnificent Obsession** has been published by Trinity Mirror Sport Media (ISBN 9781905266791).

Dr France has teamed up with David Prentice to produce a lovingly crafted book celebrating Everton's DNA. The 312-page hardcover publication contains illustrations of 200 priceless artefacts - a remarkable piece of memorabilia in itself.

Cover of Dr France's Magnificent Obsession (left), and handing over the keys to the collection

EVERTON TIGERS

About

Everton Tigers formed in June 2007 after Everton Football Club and Everton in the Community teamed up with the Toxteth Tigers basketball programme. The Toxteth Tigers have enjoyed success from grassroots level right up to international standard, having been formed in 1968.

The Tigers continue to enjoy a strong community presence, with youth development being one of the main goals of the club. They are the biggest provider of basketball opportunities in Liverpool. The long-term ambition of the Tigers is for them to compete regularly at the Echo Arena, having made their debut there in March 2008 against Cheshire Jets in front of a 6,000-strong crowd - the biggest for a British basketball match in nearly a decade.

Season 2007/08

First game: Manchester Magic (a), 29/09/07 - 76-71.
First comp. game: Plymouth Raiders (a), 06/10/07 - 73-82.
BBL Ch'ship: 7th
BBL Play-offs: QF
BBL Cup: R1
BBL Trophy: Group Phase
Record Win: 123-90 v Worcester Wolves
Top points scorer: 531, David Aliu

Information
Greenbank Sports Academy (Capacity 950)
Sefton Park, Greenbank Lane
Liverpool
L17 1AG
Telephone: 0151 280 7757
Fax: 0151 280 2267
Ticket Prices
Adult: £10
Junior/Student: £5

How to get there

By Road: From the end of the M62 (Junction 4) take the extreme left-hand lane (before the flyover) that joins the A5058 (Queens Drive). Continue straight on at the lights to a roundabout. Take the 3rd exit and continue to a set of lights – straight on. Move to the right-hand lane (marked Queens Drive and City Centre) before another roundabout and travel straight on (2nd lane from the left) through the lights (road marked Queens Drive). Continue through a set of pedestrian lights, under a railway bridge to another set of lights. Turn right into Mossley Hill Road (North), which becomes Greenbank Road. Continue straight on, passing Penny Lane to the right. Greenbank Lane follows shortly on the left hand side. The entrance to Greenbank Sports Academy is situated 400m further on the left.

Season 2008/09

Coach: Tony Garbelotto
The GB assistant was installed in April 2008, replacing Henry Mooney, who has taken up a position as head of basketball development. Beginning his coaching career with London Towers in 1992, Garbelotto has been England assistant coach, head of England U23s and enjoyed coaching spells at Newcastle Eagles, Birmingham Bullets and London United - as well as a spell in Iceland.

Chairman: Gary Townsend
2008/09 Squad: Delme Herriman (GBR), John Simpson (GBR), Chris Haslam (GBR), Stephen Bradley (GBR), Richard Midgley (GBR), Caleb Butler (GBR), Chiz Onuora (GBR), Mohamed Niang (Senegal).
Assistant-coach: Henry Mooney
08/09 Incoming: Tony Dorsey (Guildford Heat), James Jones (Guildford Heat), Andre Smith (Niigata Albirex), Marcus Bailey (TSV Troester Breitenguessbach), Josh Gross (Austin Toros).
08/09 Outgoing: Calvin Davis (Cheshire Jets), Tony Robertson, Tony Miller, David Aliu, Adam Nowell.

EVERTON TIGERS FIXTURES 2008/09

OCTOBER

03	Sheffield Sharks	(A)
10	London Capitals	(H)
11	Leicester Riders	(A)
17	Plymouth Raiders	(H)
19	Scottish Rocks	(A) - BBL Cup, 5pm
24	Worcester Wolves	(H)
31	MK Lions/S. Rocks	(A) - BBL Cup

NOVEMBER

07	Guildford Heat	(H)
14	Worthing Thunder	(H)
21	Leicester Riders	(H)
23	Guildford Heat	(A) - 3pm
30	Cheshire Jets	(A) - 5.30pm

DECEMBER

05	Newcastle Eagles	(H)
13	London Capitals	(A)
17	Worcester Wolves	(A) - 7pm
19	Sheffield Sharks	(H)
28	Plymouth Raiders	(A) - 4pm

JANUARY

04	Cheshire Jets	(A) - BBL Trophy, 5.30pm
09	Leicester Riders	(H) - BBL Trophy
16	Newcastle Eagles	(H)
18	BBL CUP FINAL	- Birmingham

JANUARY

23	Cheshire Jets	(H) - BBL Trophy
24	Leicester Riders	(A) - BBL Trophy
30	MK Lions	(A)

FEBRUARY

06	Sheffield Sharks	(H)
08	Guildford Heat	(A) - 3pm
13	Scottish Rocks	(H)
14	Worthing Thunder	(A) - 7pm
20	Newcastle Eagles	(A)

MARCH

06	London Capitals	(H)
08	Scottish Rocks	(A) - 5pm
13	Plymouth Raiders	(H)
14	Leicester Riders	(A)
15	BBL TROPHY FINAL	- Guildford
20	MK Lions	(H)
22	Cheshire Jets	(A) - 5.30pm

APRIL

03	Worthing Thunder	(H)
04	Worcester Wolves	(A) - 7pm
10	MK Lions	(A)
17	Cheshire Jets	(H)
19	Scottish Rocks	(A) - 5pm

All fixtures 7.30pm unless stated, subject to change.

Action from Everton Tigers' clash with London Capitals during the 2007/08 campaign

EVERTON IN THE COMMUNITY (EITC)

About

From June 2004 Everton Football in the Community (EFITC) has operated as a financially independent, registered charitable company (No. 1099366).

The charity is completely financially independent of Everton Football Club, which is the main sponsor and provides substantial non-financial support.

The charity is governed by a board of trustees that is made up of a balance between Everton Football Club officials and local, independent non-Everton staff.

A devoted Everton in the Community website is also set to be launched, with a more individual look than the official club website, emphasising its charity status. It will include blogs, podcasts, video clips, news, 'how to get involved' and messageboards.

Notable EITC projects, successes and statistics:

- Voted runners-up in the 2007/08 Community Club of the Year awards.
- Employ 50 full-time and part-time staff.
- Sizeable disability presence in UK football and football teams.
- Run programmes on social inclusion (kids at risk from various aspects of society – drugs; gun and knife crime).
- Successful women and girls' programmes – including Everton Ladies support.
- Biggest mental health programme in football - Everton were the first club to employ a specialist mental health expert, and they work with agencies across the North West.
- Creators of the healthy schools bus: two buses have seven people working on the project. A partnership with Liverpool City Council means that EITC is involved in every Liverpool school, as part of the Liverpool School Sport Partnership.
- Soccer camps – 28 a year both locally and internationally.
- Volunteer programme has more than 150 people involved, some of whom offer more than 100 hours a month.
- Everton Tigers being welcomed into the Everton fold – the aim is for EITC to attract other sports, which fits in with the EITC mission "to motivate, educate and inspire by harnessing the power of football and sport". Thus the decision to drop the initial moniker "Football in the Community".
- Plan for general expansion of current projects, and the introduction of new initiatives across Merseyside and beyond.
- Everton were one of the first Premier League clubs to enter the Chinese market, helping to develop grassroots disability football. Two permanent staff are based in Shanghai, working with B&Q (China) and Tesco (China).

Everton Tigers Initiatives:

- Primary School programme known as 'Hoops 4 Health' due to visit 70 schools during the 2008/09 season. Using basketball to spread the message of healthy eating, exercise and no smoking.
- Social inclusion programme 'Hoops 4 Housing' has an anti-street crime message emphasising the need for respect in the community.
- Junior teams include a boys' Under 13 and U14 team, and a girls' U13 side - all of which compete regionally.
- A wheelchair team now compete in a national competition.

If you would like to contact us, you can call:

0151 330 2307 or email: **community@evertonfc.com**

EVERTON CHARITIES

2008/09 Support

Everton will again offer support to two major charities during the 2008/09 season - the NSPCC and Everton in the Community (see page 199 for details), while also continuing to support the Everton Former Players' Foundation. The club commented:

"We are extremely proud of the charitable work we have undertaken at Everton in recent years and many worthy causes have raised many thousands of pounds.
"Everybody connected with Everton will be working very hard to ensure that the partnership with Everton in the Community and the NSPCC is successful and will see much-needed funds raised for these fantastic charitable organisations."

2007/08 Beneficiaries

Alder Hey Children's Hospital and Claire House were amongst last season's charities, with thousands of pounds raised by the club through a range of fund-raising initiatives.

Requests

Graeme Sharp remains the figurehead of all charitable requests. He accepts hundreds every week via email, telephone and letter, be it requests for signed shirts, or to arrange special visits. Player appearances are also linked in – they are very aware of their responsibilities in the community.
The Creating Chances charity is also supported by Everton. An ongoing Premier League initiative, it showcases the off-field work of players.

To send in a request, call 0151 530 5314 or email: **charity@evertonfc.com**

NSPCC

The NSPCC's Merseyside campaign - the Safe Place Appeal – is based at the Hargreaves Centre in Everton.
The NSPCC is the UK's leading charity in child protection and the prevention of cruelty to children, and money will be raised to help change the lives of the region's most vulnerable youngsters.

To donate to the NSPCC or find out more, please visit:

nspcc.org.uk

The Everton players also choose a charity of their choice, which they will visit throughout the season and help to raise awareness about.

A group of children from Chernobyl enjoy their visit to Finch Farm, June 2008

EVERTON FORMER PLAYERS' FOUNDATION

About

The charitable organisation, which raises money to help provide financial and medical assistance to former players, continues to go from strength to strength.

Funds continue to be raised from various functions and golf days, plus the auction of Everton memorabilia, while recent donations included a generous sum from Lee Carsley, a parting gift following his departure in the summer of 2008.

Players from all eras continue to benefit, many who bear the physical scars of their on-field efforts for the club. Recent names to benefit include:

Sandy Brown
Tommy Clinton
Iain Jenkins
Mick Buckley
Dave Hickson
Jimmy Tansey

The people behind the Everton Former Players' Foundation

Bill Kenwright - Patron
Barry Horne - Patron
Duncan McKenzie - Patron
Graeme Sharp - Patron
Alan Stubbs - Patron
Alex Young - Patron
Laurence Lee - Trustee and Chairman
Patrick Gaul - Trustee
Darren Griffiths - Trustee
Tony Jones - Trustee
Barry Joseph - Trustee
Richard Lewis - Trustee
Gerry Moore - Trustee
Rev. Harry Ross - Trustee
Pat Labone - Secretary

Website: evertonfc.com/club/everton-former-players-foundation.html

Contact the Everton Former Players' Foundation at:

PO Box 354
Liverpool
L69 4QS
United Kingdom

The Foundation is a registered charity (#1080101), accountable to the Charities Commission.

Every penny is gratefully received and put to very good use.

EVERTON DISABLED SUPPORTERS' ASSOCIATION

About
The inaugural EDSA meeting was held in July 1995, and official charitable status was secured in April 2003. The main objective of the association is to negotiate with the club on behalf of all disabled Evertonians.

Membership
All disabled fans can join, as well as able-bodied supporters who have empathy with the EDSA objectives. The average membership is around 250 people per season worldwide.
The yearly membership fee is £10 for adults and £5 for juniors.

Tickets
EDSA oversee the issue of match tickets in disabled areas of Goodison Park on a rota system to ensure that all non-season ticket members are able to attend an equal number of games. The disabled car parking allocation is also allocated by EDSA on the same rota system.
We also hold social events during the year.

Committee
Chairman: Steve Henneghan
Vice-chairman: Bruce Rogers
Secretary: Pat Rooney
Treasurer: Sharon Norbury
Committee: Tony Kirkham Snr, Tony Kirkham Jnr, Bill Sanders, Reg Fletcher, Paul Thomas.
Everton FC EDSA representative: Natasha Hayes.
Meetings are held every month, with the committee elected at the annual AGM.

Contacts
Prospective members, or anybody interested in EDSA, should contact:

Steve Henneghan, 22 Sandon Street, Waterloo, Liverpool L22 5NW.
Email: **stevehen@blueyonder.co.uk**
or
Bruce Rogers, Brooksmead, Bronygarth Road, Weston Rhyn, Oswestry SY10 7RQ.
Email: **bruce.rogers@talk21.com**

Website: evertonfc.com/club/edsa.html

Joleon Lescott - Voted EDSA's Player of the Year in 2007/08

EVERTON AGAINST RACISM

2007/08 Events

Everton were once again prominent in backing anti-racism events.

The **Kick It Out** Week of Action is one of the most high-profile anti-racism and community engagement initiatives in England and Wales, and the Merseyside derby at Goodison was one of 1,000 events taking place between October 18–30.

The Week of Action is part of the ongoing bid to promote greater inclusion in football and celebrates the contribution made to football by black, Asian and other ethnic minorities, whilst continuing the call to challenge racism.

Throughout the season, Everton again united with communities of all races, cultures and religious beliefs to back the message 'One Game, One Community'.

Everton also played host to an event supporting **Show Racism the Red Card**.

The anti-racism event for local young people was attended by Ayegbeni Yakubu and featured a question and answer session on racism. Ged Grebby, SRTRC Project Coordinator, said:

"Show Racism the Red Card has been extremely pleased to continue our programme of educational events around England, and Everton have hosted many of them over the years, and it is brilliant that they give their full support to the campaign.

"Show Racism the Red Card has been in existence for 11 years. The organisation aims to harness the high profile of professional footballers to combat racism in society. We use footballers as anti-racist role models in our educational resources, which have been acclaimed throughout Europe."

EXTRA TIME STUDY CENTRE

About

Having been established in 2001, the Extra Time Study Centre has helped to raise the achievement of children and young people in Liverpool through literacy, numeracy and ICT. Based at Goodison Park, the centre works with the club and Everton in the Community to offer educational programmes in sports broadcasting, animation, enhanced podcasting, digital photography and film-making.

2008 Programmes and Events

Up to 300 local school children have benefitted from courses on offer at the centre since July 2007, with the various sports broadcasting courses proving popular. Sports broadcasts are analysed, before the children are asked to produce their own scripts for broadcast. They are then required to programme the autocue and film the broadcast, complete with music and jingles. Various Everton Tigers players have also helped by giving their time.

April 2008 saw the launch of the National Year of Reading in the city, which took place at Goodison Park. Author Anthony Horowitz entertained more than 1,000 young people and adults in the Park End stand with a speech and special question and answer session.

Future Programmes and Events

There will be continued involvement with the Year of Reading, which includes initiatives such as storytelling; involvement of children from schools throughout the Merseyside area; after-school sessions throughout the school term; matchday projects for pupils involving Everton first-team players; and links with Everton Tigers, including trips to watch the team in action.

Contacts

Telephone:	0151 284 0625/0151 330 2320
Fax:	0151 330 0544

General Enquiry Email: extratime@evertonfc.com

Author Anthony Horowitz performs at Goodison as part of the National Year of Reading

2009	Jan	Feb	March	April	May	Jun
Monday						1
Tuesday						2
Wednesday				1		3
Thursday	1			2		4
Friday	2			3	1	5
Saturday	3			4	2	6
Sunday	4	1	1	5	3	7
Monday	5	2	2	6	4	8
Tuesday	6	3	3	7	5	9
Wednesday	7	4	4	8	6	10
Thursday	8	5	5	9	7	11
Friday	9	6	6	10	8	12
Saturday	10	7	7	11	9	13
Sunday	11	8	8	12	10	14
Monday	12	9	9	13	11	15
Tuesday	13	10	10	14	12	16
Wednesday	14	11	11	15	13	17
Thursday	15	12	12	16	14	18
Friday	16	13	13	17	15	18
Saturday	17	14	14	18	16	20
Sunday	18	15	15	18	17	21
Monday	18	16	16	20	18	22
Tuesday	20	17	17	21	18	23
Wednesday	21	18	18	22	20	24
Thursday	22	18	18	23	21	25
Friday	23	20	20	24	22	26
Saturday	24	21	21	25	23	27
Sunday	25	22	22	26	24	28
Monday	26	23	23	27	25	29
Tuesday	27	24	24	28	26	30
Wednesday	28	25	25	29	27	
Thursday	29	26	26	30	28	
Friday	30	27	27		29	
Saturday	31	28	28		30	
Sunday			29		31	
Monday			30			
Tuesday			31			

July	Aug	Sept	Oct	Nov	Dec	
						Monday
		1			1	Tuesday
		2			2	Wednesday
		3	1		3	Thursday
		4	2		4	Friday
1	1	5	3		5	Saturday
2	2	6	4	1	6	Sunday
3	3	7	5	2	7	Monday
4	4	8	6	3	8	Tuesday
5	5	9	7	4	9	Wednesday
6	6	10	8	5	10	Thursday
7	7	11	9	6	11	Friday
8	8	12	10	7	12	Saturday
9	9	13	11	8	13	Sunday
10	10	14	12	9	14	Monday
11	11	15	13	10	15	Tuesday
12	12	16	14	11	16	Wednesday
13	13	17	15	12	17	Thursday
14	14	18	16	13	18	Friday
15	15	18	17	14	18	Saturday
16	16	20	18	15	20	Sunday
17	17	21	18	16	21	Monday
18	18	22	20	17	22	Tuesday
18	18	23	21	18	23	Wednesday
20	20	24	22	18	24	Thursday
21	21	25	23	20	25	Friday
22	22	26	24	21	26	Saturday
23	23	27	25	22	27	Sunday
24	24	28	26	23	28	Monday
25	25	29	27	24	29	Tuesday
26	26	30	28	25	30	Wednesday
27			29	26	31	Thursday
28			30	27		Friday
29			31	28		Saturday
30				29		Sunday
31				30		Monday

OTHER USEFUL CONTACTS

The Premier League
30 Gloucester Place,
London W1U 8PL
Phone: 0207 864 9000
Email: **info@premierleague.com**

The Football Association
25 Soho Square,
London W1D 4FA
Phone: 0207 745 4545

The Football League
Edward VII Quay, Navigation Way,
Preston PR2 2YF
Email: **fl@football-league.co.uk**

Professional Footballers' Association
2 Oxford Court,
Bishopsgate,
Off Lower Mosley Street,
Manchester M2 3WQ
Phone: 0161 236 0575
Email: **info@thepfa.co.uk**

Everton Former Players' Foundation
PO Box 354,
Liverpool L69 4QS
Donations can be made by cheque, made
payable to Everton Former Players' Association

Published in Great Britain in 2008 by: Trinity Mirror Sport Media, PO Box 48, Old Hall Street, Liverpool L69 3EB

ISBN: 1 9052 6666 1

Printed and finished by Scotprint, Haddington, Scotland